Text and Canon

John H. Sailhamer

Text and Canon

Essays in Honor of John H. Sailhamer

EDITED BY
Robert L. Cole
AND
Paul J. Kissling

☙PICKWICK *Publications* • Eugene, Oregon

TEXT AND CANON
Essays in Honor of John H. Sailhamer

Copyright © 2017 Wipf and Stock Publishers. All rights reserved. Except for brief quotations in critical publications or reviews, no part of this book may be reproduced in any manner without prior written permission from the publisher. Write: Permissions, Wipf and Stock Publishers, 199 W. 8th Ave., Suite 3, Eugene, OR 97401.

Pickwick Publications
An Imprint of Wipf and Stock Publishers
199 W. 8th Ave., Suite 3
Eugene, OR 97401

www.wipfandstock.com

PAPERBACK ISBN: 978-1-61097-623-7
HARDCOVER ISBN: 978-1-4982-8534-6
EBOOK ISBN: 978-1-5326-3213-6

Cataloguing-in-Publication data:

Names: Cole, Robert L., editor | Paul J. Kissling, editor.

Title: Text and canon : essays in honor of John H. Sailhamer / edited by Robert L. Cole and Paul J. Kissling.

Description: Eugene, OR: Pickwick Publications, 2017 | Includes bibliographical references.

Identifiers: ISBN 978-1-61097-623-7 (paperback) | ISBN 978-1-4982-8534-6 (hardcover) | ISBN 978-1-5326-3213-6 (ebook)

Subjects: LCSH: Bible. O.T.—Criticism, interpretation, etc. | Sailhamer, John.

Classification: BS1188 T41 2017 (print) | BS1188 (ebook)

Manufactured in the U.S.A.   08/29/17

Contents

Preface / Robert L. Cole / vii

Biography of John H. Sailhamer / Patty Sailhamer / xi

List of Abbreviations / xvii

1 The Testament of Jacob and the Blessing of Moses:
   A Narrative Approach / 1
   —*Paul J. Kissling* (Lincoln Christian Seminary)

2 Abram as Israel, Israel as Abram: Literary Analogy
   as Macro-Structural Strategy in the Torah / 16
   —*Seth D. Postell* (Israel College of the Bible)

3 Wisdom is Worth a Thousand Laws: Legal Insufficiency
   and Exception as Intentional Compositional Strategy in
   the Pentateuch / 37
   —*Kevin Chen* (Union University)

4 What's in a Name: Shear Yashub and the Sign of Immanuel / 60
   —*Jan Verbruggen* (Western Seminary)

5 Persuasion and Allusion: The Rhetoric of Text-Referencing
   in Ezekiel / 76
   —*Michael Lyons* (Simpson University)

6 Edom's Desolation and Adam's Multiplication:
   Parallelism in Ezekiel 35:1—36:15 / 90
   —*Tracy McKenzie* (Southeastern Baptist Theological Seminary)

7   The New Exodus in the Composition of the Twelve / 120
    —*Michael B. Shepherd* (Cedarville University)

8   Psalm 3: Of Whom Does David Speak, of Himself or Another? / 137
    —*Robert L. Cole*

9   Canonical Approaches, New Trajectories, and the Book of Daniel / 149
    —*Jordan M. Scheetz*

10 Ezra, Nehemiah, and Ezra-Nehemiah: When Characters and Characterization Collide / 167
    —*Ray Lubeck* (Multnomah University)

11 Choosing the Right Words: Kings, Chronicles, and the Canon / 189
    —*Joshua Williams* (Southwestern Baptist Theological Seminary)

John H. Sailhamer: A Comprehensive Bibliography / 207
—*Prepared by Ched Spellman*

Preface

It was around thirty years ago as a seminary student that I enrolled in a summer course on OT Theology taught by John Sailhamer, a new member of the faculty at that time. Little did I know the profound effect his teaching would have on my view of the nature and message of the Bible in general and the Old Testament in particular. The same was true undoubtedly for many of his students, including those contributing to this volume, and as a small token of our appreciation we dedicate it to him.

Professor Sailhamer's influence on students and the evangelical world of scholarship in general was due largely to his pedagogical as well as literary gifts. An appealing combination of winsome teaching style, relaxed atmosphere, and humor, along with stimulating and innovative ideas drew large numbers to his classrooms. Those ideas taught so engagingly have had a lasting effect. He could take an art form like cinematography to illustrate literary and compositional features in the Bible. For instance, he would creatively use old westerns to illustrate the conjunction of narrative and poetry in the Pentateuch. Numerous students like myself were intrigued sufficiently by his teaching to continue their studies beyond seminary and now teach in schools across North America and the globe.

John's lectures and exegesis were driven by the same basic idea that the one and only locus of meaning was the biblical text. The oft-repeated phrase, "text versus event" expressed succinctly the priority of his methodology. He was not disinterested in the historical events of the past, but recognized correctly that they do not replace the text as the object of study. To interpret an event such as the exodus apart from the biblical account is to miss the author's point. He never rejected study of historical background and in fact was well versed in the subject through his training at UCLA and later research. However, he insisted on its proper role and function. This was a subject about which he was quite sensitive and so I choose my words carefully. In case of any imprecision in my description, I quote him here directly:

My treatment of evangelical theologians and biblical scholars, and their views of history and the Bible, stands at the center of the argument of this book. Simply put, real (historical) biblical events such as the exodus, though rightly accepted and studied as history, came to replace the biblical version of that history found on pages of the OT. Hans Frei calls the shift away from the historical narratives of Scripture to the "raw facts" pointed to by those narratives an "eclipse" of biblical narrative.[1]

John's dedication to the text was something he not only taught but also practiced. The modern critical edition of the Hebrew Bible, usually referred to affectionately by the acronym BHS, was his constant companion and principal text. Students attending his lectures also learned quickly the acronyms GKC and BDB. His mastery of the Hebrew text was an example for his students to follow and never once did I observe him using an English translation in the classroom. I recall once in later years he showed me a mistake caught by his keen eye in the accentuation of Isa 14:8 of earlier editions of BHS. Instead of an *athnach* at the verse's midpoint, there was a *machpakh*. John sent off a letter to the publishers and to his delight, it was corrected in later editions.

Other terms or phrases commonly heard in John's classes were: composition, texture, canon, final shape, intextuality, innertextuality, intertextuality, contextuality, syntext, Pentateuch 1.0 and 2.0, texts as paintings or windows, glosses, effective history, and certainly others that his students will recall. Several of these terms illustrate his interest in the detection of literary seams at various levels that point to the compositional purposes of its writer/composer. He was interested not only in the final canonical form but also the redactional or compositional stages immediately preceding it.

Principal among the many scholars that influenced his thinking and that were often mentioned in class included, Hans Frei, Brevard Childs, Rolf Rendtorff, and Hans-Georg Gadamer. Earlier individuals of great influence such as Coccejus or Rashi were also commonly mentioned and discussed in the classroom and in his writings.

Sitting in his classes I often felt John was a fellow learner along with the rest of us. Most questions were taken and entertained at length. He often noted how teaching drives writing and undoubtedly it was because he knew and was confident that his students' observations and questions contributed to his own understanding. There were times when a student's observation or query would cause him to pause while he processed its implications for

---

1. Sailhamer, *The Meaning of the Pentateuch: Revelation, Composition and Interpretation* (Downers Grove, IL: IVP Academic, 2009) 604.

interpretation. Such occasions would of course contribute enormously to students' self-esteem and confidence in their own abilities as interpreters.

Two other terms often heard in his classrooms were "messianic" and "eschatological." I had arrived at seminary after spending a year and a half in Israel and found much to my surprise that the method of reading the OT by modern evangelical scholars was undeniably different than what NT writers evinced. The arrival of John Sailhamer to the school thus proved for me a godsend. For the first time, I heard a sensible defense of apostolic exegesis, not by reading the New Testament back into the Old, appealing to some variety of *sensus plenior*, or to apostolic privilege, but by a close reading of the Old Testament itself. As he rightly observed, the Old Testament's reading and interpretation of itself sheds an enormous amount of light on the New Testament's reading of it. The story is told that at one point in his teaching career John informed the registrar that he intended to teach a class on the Old Testament's use of the Old Testament. The registrar was convinced that it was a mistake and responded that surely he meant the New Testament's use of the Old Testament!

The following essays have been prepared in honor of the career and teachings of John Sailhamer by his students. It is a small token of our gratitude and appreciation to him.

Robert L. Cole
Luke 2:27–32

Biography of John H. Sailhamer

JOHN SAILHAMER WAS BORN in Moline, Illinois on October 17, 1946. He lived his "Tom Sawyer" years as a boy in San Antonio, Texas, and the Deep South of Vicksburg, Mississippi. He spent his teenage years under the Southern California sun where he graduated from Lakewood High School.

College took John back to the Midwest before he was assigned by the U.S. Army to spend two years working at the Pentagon. After two years in the service John completed an undergraduate degree in journalism at California State University in Long Beach (CSULB), a Th.M. degree at Dallas Theological Seminary (DTS), and an M.A. and Ph.D. in Ancient Near East Languages from the University of California at Los Angeles (UCLA).

John was the youngest of three children born to Claude and Belva Sailhamer. Claude was a "preacher" and Belva was a school teacher. John's faith journey began one Sunday night in 1951 in response to an evangelistic message delivered by his father. He was baptized soon after at the First Baptist Church of Vicksburg along with his older brother, Paul, age 7, and his namesake, their grandfather, John Frederick Sailhamer.

The late 1950's and early 1960's were a wonderful time to be a kid in Southern California, where the family had moved in 1956. John enjoyed his friends, girlfriends, sports, surfing, a .22 caliber rifle, his motorcycle, and his 1934 Ford pick-up truck which he and his brother in law, Bill Miller, had in running shape for his 16th birthday and first driver's license. Yet John's intellectual gifts were also beginning to blossom, including a love of mathematics, a growing interest in the German language, and a developing proficiency in writing and typing.

In 1964, John graduated from Lakewood High School in Long Beach, California. The next fall John left by Greyhound bus with a buddy to start his post-high school education at Bethel College in St. Paul, Minnesota. In his junior year, he transferred to Wheaton College in Illinois. Also studying at Wheaton that semester was Patty Engdahl who would later meet John in California where they would become engaged. (They did not know one another while at Wheaton.)

During his senior year at Wheaton, John withdrew from the college, returned to Southern California, and volunteered for the draft. The war in Vietnam was in a build-up phase and John wanted to serve his country. His parents were terrified at the prospect of him fighting in Vietnam and prayed for God's hand to be upon their youngest son in a special way. Until he was drafted, John worked, read, traveled, and pursued a variety of interests that attracted his attention.

His draft notice came through after several months and John was sent to Fort Ord on the central coast of California for U.S. Army Basic Training. The weeks in training and the results of a series of tests that he took contributed to a very surprising first assignment as a soldier: John was ordered to go to Army headquarters in Fort Myer, Virginia, across the Potomac River from Washington, D.C. He spent the next two years (1968-1970) working in a small office in the Pentagon that was in charge of expediting re-assignments for U.S. Army soldiers all over the globe.

Providentially, John met a couple of solid Christians who introduced him to a Navigator group at the fort, one of whom discipled him and became a friend for life. In addition, John enjoyed a ministry opportunity at the McLean Bible Church in Fairfax County, Virginia.

Following his honorable discharge from the Army John headed back to California for the completion of his undergraduate education. He enrolled as a journalism major at California State University in Long Beach (CSULB), where his sister, Claudette, had graduated. He wrote a regular column for the "49er," a campus newspaper at CSULB, became involved with Campus Crusade, and worked with junior high students at the First Grace Brethren Church, also in Long Beach.

John used his journalism skills to publish a small magazine called The Southern California Youth Review. These were the years of the "Jesus Movement" and the magazine chronicled events of that era. The first edition had a lengthy interview with Hal Lindsey whose book, *The Late Great Planet Earth*, had just been published. It also included a photo essay and interview with "Christian rocker," Larry Norman.

During this second round of college John met and fell in love with Patty Engdahl, who had graduated from Wheaton, joined Campus Crusade staff and was assigned to CSULB. Patty was from the St. Paul area where her parents, Phyllis and Gordon Engdahl, were lay-Christian leaders. Her father worked for 3M.

Upon graduation from CSULB in 1971 with a B.A. in journalism, Patty and John were married in her hometown, where John had begun his college education. The following fall John and his new bride packed up their 1963

Volkswagen and headed for Texas, where John earned a Th.M. at Dallas Theological Seminary (DTS).

While studying at DTS John's love of the Hebrew language flourished along with the beginnings of his philosophy of how Hebrew should be taught to new students. He also kept his fingers in the journalism world working at the *Dallas Morning News* throughout his seminary years. After completing the Th.M. degree in three years, including summer school, Patty and John reloaded the Volkswagen and headed west again to California for a continuation of his studies at UCLA.

At UCLA John earned an M.A. and a Ph.D. in Ancient Near East Languages completing his classroom studies there in 1978. During this time, John and Patty welcomed their first son, David, and later their only daughter, Elizabeth, into their family. John also began his teaching career. He taught classes at LOGOS Bible Study Center in the San Fernando Valley, Western Graduate School of Theology in Long Beach, Biola College in La Mirada, and Los Angeles Baptist College in Santa Clarita.

In 1978, John and his growing family headed back to St. Paul, Minnesota, for his first full-time teaching assignment at Bethel College for a year and a half, and then at Bethel Seminary for three and a half years. It was a joy for John to now teach where he had started his college career as a student in 1964.

While at Bethel, some of John's teaching "mannerisms" began to develop: his elaborate diagrams using simple stick figures with beards, crowns, and the unforgettable Mr. Redfingers, to illustrate difficult concepts for his students. He loved to call the author of the Torah, "Cecil B. DeMoses" as he discussed the way the biblical narrative is revealed to the careful reader of the text. (His students may not have known that he attended Cecil B. DeMille Junior High School in Long Beach. The legendary film director had just released his most successful film ever, *The Ten Commandments*, when John and his brother were students at the new campus named in his honor).

John loved the written word and would often tell his students as well as his wife and children, "If you have a thought, write it down." The day that John turned in the final draft of his Ph.D. thesis to UCLA he came home and sat down at his typewriter to start his first book. John was also known for keeping his vocabulary cards with him at all times, ready to review them in an idle moment. He had cards for German, Latin, French, Greek, Aramaic, Syriac, Ugaritic, and, of course, his beloved Hebrew. At the conclusion of his time at Bethel, John's first book, a commentary on *First & Second Chronicles*, was published by Moody Press.

In the spring of 1983, John was ordained by the Evangelical Free Church. That summer, the family moved to Deerfield, Illinois, and John began a new teaching position at Trinity Evangelical Divinity School where he taught for 11 years. During this period, he honed many of the concepts that made his handling of the Scriptures trustworthy and understandable. In addition, his focus on the messianic theme of the Old Testament grew in its strength and clarity. He liked to emphasize Scriptures such as Luke 24:25-27 and especially verse 44, "all things that are written about me in the Law of Moses and the Prophets, and the Psalms must be fulfilled."

John's important years from 1993 to 1999 are difficult for some to understand. In early 1993 John was asked by the Board of Dallas Seminary and its new President-elect, Dr. Charles Swindoll, to participate in a new arrangement for leadership of the school. Swindoll knew his call was to pastor and preach, yet his heart was moved by the leadership needs of his alma mater, DTS. He conceived of an arrangement that would allow him to continue to pastor his congregation at the First Evangelical Free Church in Fullerton, California, and use his DTS presidential role to model the type of ministry approach the seminary was committed to producing in Dallas.

Swindoll then asked John to become the provost of the seminary and to be the on-site leader to implement the teaching philosophy they had been working on together. John agreed and resigned his faculty position at Trinity. He began preparing for this transition to Dallas, laying the groundwork for this new leadership arrangement at DTS.

Chuck Swindoll is the kind of ministry pioneer and creative leader who could have made such an arrangement work. However, as he began to get more involved with the plan he felt his own heart being drawn to the more conventional day to day, on-site, leadership role of a seminary president.

By the end of 1993, Swindoll had decided to move to Dallas. His hopes were that John would agree to stay on as provost and assist him for the next decade at DTS. After due consideration, John decided he would best serve by continuing to teach and he withdrew from the plan to become provost. Still, he had already resigned from Trinity and felt that chapter of his life was closed.

From 1994 to 1999 John was a bit like one of the western heroes he had enjoyed watching on television as a boy, Richard Boone as Paladin: "Have Gun Will Travel." John's calling card would have read, "Have Hebrew Text…Will Travel." During those years, he flew to Philadelphia to teach at Philadelphia College of Bible. He was scholar in residence at Northwestern College in St. Paul, while concurrently teaching at Western Seminary in Portland, Oregon. For years he continued to teach many summer sessions at their Portland and Northern California campuses.

In 1995, John moved his family back to North Oaks, Minnesota and kept things stable for his children while they finished their high school years. This meant that John spent many hours flying around the country to teach and speak at conferences. During this time he served a term as the President of the Evangelical Theological Society. John also kept up a mentoring relationship with many of his former students, something he did throughout his teaching career.

In retrospect, this was also a very productive time as the majority of his more than 15 books were published. Having already completed a commentary on Genesis in *The Expositor's Bible Commentary* series and *The Pentateuch as Narrative* (published by Zondervan), John continued to write the *NIV Compact Bible Commentary, Introduction to Old Testament Theology* and 7 volumes of the *Zondervan Quick-Reference Library*. *Genesis Unbound* was published in 1996, along with dozens of articles, reviews, essays and scholarly papers. (A complete listing can be found in this volume).

In 1999 John became professor of Hebrew and Old Testament at Southeastern Baptist Theological Seminary (SEBTS) in Wake Forest, North Carolina. The focus of his time for the next seven and a half years was spent advising Th.M. and Ph.D. students through the thesis and dissertation process. While at SEBTS, he submitted a draft of his last major manuscript, later entitled, *The Meaning of the Pentateuch*, as well as serving on Bible translation projects.

In 2006, John and Patty packed up their SUV in Wake Forest to return to Southern California after living and teaching elsewhere for almost three decades. Returning with them was their oldest son, David, who was born with Down Syndrome. As an adult, David has worked on campuses where his father has taught. Their other three adult children were finishing their education and beginning their careers.

John had been asked by Golden Gate Baptist Theological Seminary (GGBTS) to become Professor of Old Testament and teach primarily at their campus in Brea, California, while frequently traveling to its main campus to teach and mentor Old Testament Ph.D. students in Mill Valley, just north of San Francisco. John and Patty settled nearby the city of Brea in Fullerton, close to family and the First Evangelical Free Church in Fullerton where John had taught an adult fellowship class back in his UCLA days. He also went to work finishing his major book, *The Meaning of the Pentateuch*, which needed an introduction and a conclusion, editing to reduce his thousand-page manuscript to its final size of over 700 pages, and a thorough checking of hundreds of references, footnotes and bibliography.

During the process of attempting to finish the book, a new chapter of John's life opened. Two years after being back in California John began to notice signs that unusual things were happening in his body and his brain. After many tests and consultations with physicians, John was diagnosed with having Parkinson's Disease (PD). He was graciously granted by GGBTS to take the rest of the semester off and returned to the classroom for the next year and a half. With Patty's tireless assistance, he was able to finish the introduction to his new book and complete the checking of the notes and references.

In the fall of 2010, John had to take a full disability retirement from teaching. A year later, the diagnosis was elevated to Parkinson's Plus with Lewy Body disease. This meant that his form of the disease was fast moving and his symptoms more severe. His world became no longer one of study, writing, teaching, debate and mentoring. He had good days and many not so good days. However, he always managed a smile when someone mentioned how great it was that he didn't wait until retirement to write his books.

Two huge blessings during this period were the marriages of their three younger adult children and the birth of grandchildren. With great effort, John was able to attend and participate in each wedding. Within two years each couple presented John and Patty with a grandchild, a boy and two girls. This meant that David became an uncle three times over. Today, there are a total of eight grandchildren.

John passed into the presence of the Lord on January 9, 2017. A memorial service was held for him at the First Evangelical Free Church in Fullerton, CA on January 13, 2017. The service included tributes from each of his four children and from his brother Paul Sailhamer. Though unable to attend, John Piper, Chuck Swindoll, Walt Kaiser, and Wayne Grudem each prepared tributes that were read to those in attendance. The service was recorded and is available for viewing on YouTube. John's personal library, including many rare scholarly works along with his copious personal notes and papers, were donated to SEBTS and are available for use by both students and scholars.

John's youngest son, Peter, spent 15 months in Iraq with the 82nd Airborne after graduating from college. Today he is trained to fly an F-16 for the Wisconsin Air National Guard. Pete is married to Angela. They have three children: Joshua, Troy, and Evangeline. John's third born, also named John, is an engineer who lives in the Boston area with his wife, Kelly, and their two children, Ally and John (also known as Jack). John's daughter, Elizabeth (Betsy), is a pediatric surgeon now practicing and living in Manchester, NH, with her husband, Jason Soukup, and their three children Sadie, Samuel, and Simeon.

John's book, *The Meaning of the Pentateuch*, was published in 2009, by InterVarsity Press. It was to be his final book, and likewise he had taught his final course and mentored his last young student. Yet John Sailhamer's work will continue, as long as the Lord tarries, in the sermons, research, papers, lectures, courses, and lives of those who knew him, whether in the seminary class or the Sunday school class, as Dr. Sailhamer.

Patty Sailhamer

Joshua 1:8

Abbreviations

AB	Anchor Bible
BZAW	Beihefte zur Zeitschrift für die alttestamentliche Wissenschaft
FAT	Forschungen zum Alten Testament
GKC	*Gesenius' Hebrew Grammar*. Edited by E. Kautzsch. Translated by A. E. Cowley. 2nd ed. 1910
JBL	*Journal of Biblical Literature*
JPSTC	JPS Torah Commentary
JSOTSup	Journal for the Study of the Old Testament Supplement Series
JSS	*Journal of Semitic Studies*
LHBOTS	Library of Hebrew Bible/Old Testament Studies
LXX	Septuagint
MT	Masoretic text
OG	Old Greek
OTL	Old Testament Library
SBLDS	Society of Biblical Literature Dissertation Series
TOTC	Tyndale Old Testament Commentaries
VT	*Vetus Testamentum*
VTSup	Vetus Testamentum Supplements
WBC	Word Biblical Commentary
WTJ	*Westminster Theological Journal*
ZAW	Zeitschrift für die alttestamentliche Wissenschaft

1

The Testament of Jacob and the Blessing of Moses

A Narrative Approach

Paul J. Kissling

Lincoln Christian Seminary

Introduction

JOHN SAILHAMER FIRST ALERTED me to the importance of Genesis 49 and Deuteronomy 33 in the canonical redaction of the Hebrew Bible.[1] Standing on his shoulders in this essay, I will attempt to use a narrative approach to the intertextual relationship between these two important chapters that focuses on the narratorial connections to the preceding text in Genesis 1–48, the intermediate texts in Genesis 50—Deuteronomy 32, and the succeeding texts in the remainder of the Hebrew Bible which follow Deuteronomy 33.

Walter Brueggemann in his 1982 commentary has this to say about Jacob's testamentary blessing of his sons in Genesis 49:

> The poem very probably is early. But its placement here is secondary. It has no evident connection with the context and no bearing on the larger narrative . . . While it poses as an anticipation, it is surely descriptive of a situation of a later time of history, at the time of its composition. Thus, it is of primary interest for the historical data it supplies. Probably, it intends to be political propaganda to advance some tribal claims at the

---

1. For his mature understanding, see Sailhamer, *The Meaning of the Pentateuch*, 36–37, 48–49, 324–337.

expense of others ... [T]he poem of chapter 49 seems to have no important connection with its context ... Its interpretation is not likely to serve a theological expositor very richly.[2]

Although Brueggemann can perhaps be excused given the date of publication of his commentary and the virtual infancy of narrative analysis at the time, his assertions seem today to be transparently in error. Not only is the "blessing" or testament of Jacob connected in many ways to its narrative context but it serves for the rest of the Pentateuch what Laurence Turner has termed within the book of Genesis as an "announcement of plot" much as the promise to Abram in 12:1–3, the birth prophecy of Jacob and Esau in 25:23, and the dreams of Joseph in 37:1–17 do for the book of Genesis as a whole.[3] Just as in the other "announcements of plot," Genesis 49 has no simplistic narrative resolution and the differences between Jacob's testament and Moses's blessing at the end of the Pentateuch are striking. In this essay I will examine Genesis 49 (the "testament"[4] of Jacob) and Deuteronomy 33 (the "blessing of Moses") *intertextually*, asking how the intervening (Genesis 50—Deuteronomy 32) and following narratives help to explain the differences between them and asking what this implies about the nature of Jacob's words. Perhaps then the potential richness of its theological ore will be more apparent.

The Big Four: Reuben, Simeon, Levi, and Judah

The first four sons of Jacob, all through his "hated"[5] wife Leah, begin both the testament of Jacob and the blessing of Moses. Taken as a whole Jacob's testamentary statements explain why Reuben the firstborn, and Simeon and Levi, the second and third sons, are passed over as the royal and leading tribe.

Jacob's testamentary statement for Reuben recalls his earlier affair with Jacob's concubine Bilhah:

> Reuben, you are my firstborn, my might and the first fruits of my vigor, excelling in rank and excelling in power. Unstable as water, you shall no longer excel because you went up onto your

---

2. Brueggemann, *Genesis*, 365–66.
3. Turner, *Announcements of Plot in Genesis*.
4. While this text is often referred to as the "testament" of Jacob because his statements for several of the tribes hardly seem to be "blessings," the narrator regards it as a "blessing" (Gen 49:28b) unless this narratorial comment be regarded as ironic.
5. See Gen 29:31. The English versions try to soften this with such euphemisms as "unloved" (NRSV) or "not loved" (NIV).

father's bed; then you defiled it—you went up onto my couch! (Gen 49:3–4)[6]

By contrast, Moses's blessing is muted, saying more by what is not said than by what is said: "May Reuben live, and not die out, even though his numbers are few" (Deut 33:6).[7] In his "blessing" Jacob ends his long silence about Reuben's sexual liaison with Jacob's concubine[8] Bilhah, Rachel's handmaid, which he had "heard" about (Gen 35:22) in the aftermath of the death of his beloved Rachel. The excelling of Reuben in dignity and strength will be ended by or because of his moral instability (פַּחַז). Laurence Turner suggests that Jacob's "miserly" blessing of Reuben serves to characterize Jacob as much as Reuben:

> While Reuben might well be receiving his just deserts, it also reveals a somewhat vindictive side of Jacob, who waits until his deathbed (cf. 49.29) to vent his spleen on his son. In addition, Jacob's assessment is hardly evenhanded. Since this is supposedly a chapter of blessings (49.28), one might have expected some positive aspects of Reuben to be recalled. He was the one, after all, who saved Joseph's life (37.21–22, 29; cf. 42.22). While this matter might be unknown to Jacob, he had witnessed Reuben's magnanimous if somewhat impulsive gesture, when trying to persuade Jacob to send Benjamin to Egypt (42.37). One gets the impression that Reuben is being treated somewhat unfairly. One reckless act of sexual impropriety, ignored by Jacob up to this point, appears to outweigh any virtue he might possess.[9]

But this may be an ungenerous reading of Jacob. Wright suggests that the sexual liaison with Bilhah was an attempt to "prematurely la[y] claim to the patriarchal rights and responsibilities of the firstborn."[10] De Hoop suggests that "Reuben's action might be construed as an attempt to grab power by seizing his father's 'harem.'"[11] He compares the similarities in language between Reuben's actions here and Absalom's in 2 Sam 16:21. In both cases the person "went" to his "father's concubine(s)" and "Israel" would or did "hear" of it. Since Absalom is transparently starting a revolt against his

---

6. Unless otherwise noted, all translations are from the NRSV.

7. The NIV has, "Let Reuben live and not die, nor his men be few," but notes the alternative in a footnote.

8. In Gen 35:22 Bilhah is not referred to by the narrator as a (secondary) wife but specifically as a concubine (פילגש).

9. Turner, *Genesis*, 201.

10. Wright, "Reuben," 691.

11. De Hoop, *Genesis 49*, 512.

father it is possible to understand Reuben's actions in the same way. One problem with this suggestion is that Reuben only slept with one of Jacob's concubines, not his entire "harem," something he did not have, unlike Absalom's father David.

Reuben's involvement in the sexual politics of the family through providing his mother Leah the mandrakes with which she then "purchased" sex with Jacob to birth Issachar is perhaps another example of this tendency (Gen 30:14–18).

In any case Reuben fares little better in the blessing of Moses. The tribe is, or will be in danger of dying out.[12] If Jacob's "virtual curse" of Reuben can be read as being tainted by his own skewed perspective that does not account for the tepid blessing of Moses. In the intervening narratives, Reuben's descendants Dathan, Abiram (and initially On) join Korah in challenging the legitimacy of Moses's and Aaron's leadership roles in Israel. The severity of the Lord's judgment on that occasion may help explain a small decline in numbers during the wilderness period.[13] That the challenge is directed at Moses's and Aaron's leadership may help explain the less than enthusiastic blessing by Moses. But as de Hoop[14] has noted, this event hardly explains the differences between Jacob's and Moses's blessings. Korah, from the tribe of Levi, led the rebellion in which the Reubenites, Dathan, and Abiram participated and yet Korah's tribe, Levi, receives a greatly enhanced blessing by Moses.

There is another possibility. By the time of Deuteronomy 33 Reuben had become a transjordanian tribe over the initial objections and the continuing concerns (Num 32:6–15), but also the permission of, Moses (Num 32:20–42). Reuben is thus separated geographically, economically, politically, and religiously from the rest of Israel and surrounded by potentially (or actually) hostile neighbors without ready access to their support in times of trouble. It is hard to ignore the fact that in the ensuing centuries Reuben fades away as a tribe and its territory seems to be taken over by Gad and

---

12. Christenson, *Deuteronomy 21:10–34:12*, 840, 843, 848, following Dahood and O'Connor, re-points מִסְפָּר to מִסְפָּר "from counting" i.e. "beyond counting." This may be the Hebrew *Vorlage* behind the LXX καὶ ἔστω πολὺς ἐν ἀριθμῷ. He argues that the disjunctive accent under מְתָיו מִסְפָּר in this case separates it from other examples of the phrase מְתֵי מִסְפָּר which have a conjunctive accent (Gen 34:30; Deut 4:27; Jer 44:28; Ps 105:12) and mean "few in number" and is more like Ps 40:6. This does make it clearer that Moses' words are a blessing on Reuben.

13. Num 1:21—46,500 in the first census; 43,730 in the second census—Num 26:7. If the word understood as "thousands" instead be taken to mean "clan" and only the hundreds and tens are to be read as actual numbers there was an increase from 500 to 730 during the wilderness period.

14. De Hoop, *Genesis 49*, 512.

Moab.[15] The later conquests by the Syrians (2 Kgs 10:22–23) and Assyrians (1 Chron 5:16) show its vulnerability.[16] With Moab to the south, Ammon to the northeast, the Dead Sea to the west and the King's highway bringing trade, but also troops running right through the middle of it, Reuben was in a tenuous position. Both Jacob and Moses[17] agree that Reuben will never see the fruits of his birthright as firstborn son.

The second and third sons of Jacob, like Reuben born of hated Leah, are treated as a pair in Jacob's testament. Only Levi is mentioned in Moses's blessing, the total absence of Simeon speaking volumes about the fulfillment of Jacob's curse. Jacob addresses his second and third sons with the words:

> Simeon and Levi are brothers; weapons of violence are their swords. May I never come into their council; may I not be joined to their company—for in their anger they killed men, and at their whim they hamstrung oxen [שׁוֹר].[18] Cursed be their anger, for it is fierce, and their wrath, for it is cruel! I will divide them in Jacob, and scatter them in Israel. (Gen 49:5–7)

Simeon and Levi are condemned in Gen 49:5–7 for their anger and violence, apparently for using the rite of circumcision as a ruse for mercilessly murdering the men of Shechem in defense of their full-sister Dinah. While the other sons participated in the plundering of the city, it was only Simeon and Levi who actually murdered the vulnerable Shechemite men (Gen 34:25–29). While Jacob rebuked them at that time on pragmatic grounds, here he rebukes them for their acted-out anger on principle.[19] The consequence of that anger is to be divided and scattered as tribal groups within

---

15. Wright, "Reuben," 692: "David's census—and hence royal Israelite control—included the region of Reuben, even though 2 Samuel 24:5 does not mention that tribe by name. Some believe that by this time Reuben had already been absorbed into the tribe of Gad . . . The annexation of lands held by Reuben by the Moabite king Mesha is known from both 2 Kgs 1:1; 3:4–5 and the Moabite Stone (mid-ninth century BC); the latter mentions Gad, the land of Medeba and cities within Reuben's inheritance (e.g., Dibon, Baal-meron, Nebo and Bezer) but not the tribe of Reuben."

16. Ibid.

17. Cf. 1 Chr 5:1b-2: "He [Reuben] was the firstborn, but because he defiled his father's bed his birthright was given to the sons of Joseph son of Israel, so that he is not enrolled in the genealogy according to the birthright; though Judah became prominent among his brothers and a ruler came from him, yet the birthright belonged to Joseph."

18. The Hebrew is singular, contrary to the translations. De Hoop suggests this is a metaphor for Shechem the prince.

19. Turner, Genesis, 201: "Jacob's attitude to their violence seems to have changed, however. At the time his only concern was fear for his life (34.30). He did not bring forward any moral objections to the act itself. Yet here, he condemns their violence and anger apparently as a matter of principle."

the nation. While Simeon still exists as a tribe in Moses's mind, taking their place on mount Gerizim to announce blessings over Israel, the scattering of the tribe in fulfillment of the testament of Jacob has already begun.[20] Of all the tribes Simeon had by far the largest population decline during the wilderness period dropping an astonishing 37,100 from 59,300 to 22,200 which begs for a narrative explanation! Two pieces of evidence are suggestive. While not specifically mentioned by Jacob in Genesis 49 Simeon had a child through a Canaanite woman (Gen 46:10; Exod 6:15) although apparently he did not marry her. Numbers 25:14 informs us that the man who had sexual relations with a Midianite woman while the congregation was dealing with the aftermath of the Baal of Peor incident was a Simeonite. In any case Moses's silence about them implies that they should not expect a blessed future. The fact that Simeon ends up being largely absorbed by the tribe of Judah (Josh 19:1–9), shows that the curse of Jacob and the absence of Simeon from Moses's blessing have their effects on subsequent history as the Old Testament narrates it.

Jacob's testamentary words for Simeon are also addressed to Levi. But rather than Moses passing over Levi as he did with Simeon, Levi receives a fulsome blessing:

> And of Levi he said: Give to Levi your Thummim, and your Urim to your loyal one, whom you tested at Massah, with whom you contended at the waters of Meribah; who said of his father and mother, "I regard them not"; he ignored his kin, and did not acknowledge his children. For they observed your word, and kept your covenant. They teach Jacob your ordinances, and Israel your law; they place incense before you, and whole burnt offerings on your altar. Bless, O LORD, his substance, and accept the work of his hands; crush the loins of his adversaries, of those that hate him, so that they do not rise again. Deut 33:8–10

While Levi receives the same curse from Jacob for the same reasons as Simeon, the results are very different. In Levi's case the contrast between

---

20. The scattering of Simeon is a long and complicated one. In 2 Chr 15:9 deserters from Ephraim, Manasseh, and Simeon resided as aliens with Judah and Benjamin in the time of Joash. Simeon exists as a tribe in the time of Josiah, 2 Chr 34:5-7: "He [Josiah] also burned the bones of the priests on their altars, and purged Judah and Jerusalem. In the towns of Manasseh, Ephraim, and Simeon, and as far as Naphtali, in their ruins all around, he broke down the altars, beat the sacred poles and the images into powder, and demolished all the incense altars throughout all the land of Israel. Then he returned to Jerusalem." Simeon is given a portion in the new temple/new Israel described by Ezekiel to the south of the temple district (Ezek 48:24–25) and a gate named after him as one of the tribes on the south side of the city (48:33). Interestingly Simeon reappears among the 12 tribes of Israel sealed in Rev 7:4–8.

the testament of Jacob and the blessing of Moses could hardly be greater. Levi is cursed for using circumcision as a ruse to kill the Shechemites and Moses asks the LORD to crush *the loins* of his enemies (v. 11). The basis of this blessing is clear, although the reference to Massah and Meribah is somewhat perplexing. The words do not refer to specific places but are used when Israel tests the LORD's patience and quarrels with Moses over the LORD's provision of water. Here the LORD is said to have tested Levi at Massah and Meribah. Psalm 81:7 makes it clear that the testing process was reciprocal. Israel tested the LORD's patience with their grumbling but the LORD also tested Israel and Levi as a part of Israel. The specific event that Moses seems to allude to is the golden calf episode when the Levites rally to him and Moses commands them to "kill your brother, your friend, and your neighbor" (Exod 32:27). He then informs the Levites that they have ordained themselves[21] for [the service of] the LORD because each of the Levites who stood with Moses did so against his son or his brother (v. 29). The blessing which Levi received because of this risky act of faithfulness is the priesthood. Clearly according to Moses, Levi has been given the responsibilities of the priesthood including the Thummim and Urim, the responsibility of offering incense and burnt offerings at the Tabernacle altars and the task of teaching the law to Israel. Although relatively few in number at the first census[22] Levi formally and publicly replaces the firstborn of the other tribes as priests (Num 3). The faithfulness of Levi at a crucial juncture in the nation's history effectively, albeit partially, reverses the curse of Jacob and turns the anticipated scattering from a curse into a blessing. While Simeon who received the identical curse ended up playing out their destiny, Levi, by their faithfulness, turned that destiny on its head. Ironically or perhaps significantly, a similar sort of zeal against sexual impropriety appears in both the Dinah and golden calf incidents.

With his three older brothers disqualified by Jacob, what appears to be the most positive message is left for Judah who will take over the leadership role in the family's heritage which his older brothers had forfeited.

---

21. Reading with the LXX and Vulgate a perfect, not the MT's imperative.

22. Perhaps the small numbers of Levites in the first census (22,000) may reflect the fact that many Levites died in the golden calf incident?

Judah, your brothers shall praise you; your hand shall be on the neck of your enemies; your father's sons shall bow down before you. Judah is a lion's whelp; from the prey, my son, you have gone up. He crouches down, he stretches out like a lion, like a lioness—who dares rouse him up? The scepter shall not depart from Judah, nor the ruler's staff from between his feet, until tribute[שילה]²³ comes to him; and the obedience of the peoples is his. Binding his foal to the vine and his donkey's colt to the choice vine, he washes his garments in wine and his robe in the blood of grapes; his eyes are darker than wine, and his teeth whiter than milk.

Gen 49:8–12

And this he said of Judah: O LORD, give heed to Judah, and bring him to his people; strengthen his hands for him, and be a help against his adversaries.

Deut 33:7

Jacob has effectively cursed his three oldest sons, Reuben, Simeon, and Levi, although we have seen that in the latter's case it is a reversible curse. Judah, the fourth son, is now given the preeminent position. Jacob blesses Judah with words remarkably like the blessing which he had earlier stolen from Isaac.²⁴ Isaac had unwittingly blessed Jacob with the words, "Be LORD over your brothers, and may your mother's sons bow down to you" (Gen 27:29b). Here Jacob had echoed those words to Judah, "your father's sons shall bow down before you" (Gen 49:8b). Turner notes the connection between this passage and Joseph's dreams:

> Joseph's dreams had predicted, in part, subservience of his brothers, and this has been fulfilled more than once. But now Jacob predicts that Judah's brothers, a grouping which necessarily includes Joseph, will bow before Judah. In addition, images of royal authority more appropriate to Joseph's status in Egypt (49.10), are applied to Judah. It reads like an attempt to reverse Joseph's dreams. What will have precedence, boyhood dream or deathbed blessing?²⁵

---

23. NRSV suggests four possibilities for this difficult word שילה: "until he comes to whom it belongs" following the Syriac; "until tribute comes to him"; "until Shiloh comes" a personal name; and "until he comes to Shiloh" a location. The Qere has שילו.

24. Turner, *Genesis*, 202.

25. Ibid., 202.

Jacob had never bowed down to Joseph[26] and his mother had died giving birth to Benjamin, making it impossible for her literally to bow down to him. The second dream is never fulfilled in the way one might expect. But the first dream does find fulfillment. Here Jacob suggests that in the future even the first dream will be undone. Judah is to have the ruling role until some future person comes to claim it who has the right to the obedience of the nations. Again the reader must ask how much of this blessing is divine revelation and how much is Jacob's own personal agenda.

Judah receives unqualified praise and this seems slightly odd given that Judah was responsible for sending Joseph into slavery. Further Judah's role in the Tamar episode which "interrupts" the Joseph narrative serves to contrast Judah negatively with Joseph. While Judah does show compassion for his father and offers his own enslavement rather than rob Jacob of his beloved Benjamin (Gen 44:18–34) Jacob is hardly even-handed with his four oldest sons.

Such a detail merely highlights the nagging question that a reader might legitimately ask about the efficacy of these blessings (Gen 49:26a notwithstanding). Isaac's prediction concerning the subservience of Esau to Jacob was reversed in Gen 33:3–15. And Jacob himself has never bowed down to Joseph, as his dreams had predicted, at least as Jacob quite naturally understood them (see Gen 42:8; 43:26–28), but again the prediction was reversed (Gen 48:12).

Compounding such reservations is Jacob's remarkably one-sided appraisal of Judah. He receives unqualified praise, yet the narrative has more than once dwelt on his failings. When the brothers had plotted Joseph's fate it is true that Judah had counseled against killing him, but not in order to release him, rather to enslave him (Gen 37:26–28). His assignation with Tamar had forced from him the confession that, "She is more in the right than I" (Gen 38:26). While it could be argued that Jacob did not know about the former incident, the latter public display and subsequent birth of children (Gen 38:27–30) could hardly have been kept from him. While Judah is not presented as an unqualified villain (cf. Gen 44:18–34), Jacob's blessing brackets out all censure. The LORD's inscrutable attachment to Jacob is replicated in Jacob's treatment of Judah.

Moses's blessing of Judah, by contrast, is quite brief and though not negative lacks any explicit reference to leadership over the other tribes. This is often seen to reflect the post-exilic situation in which the defunct dynasty of David is replaced by the priestly tribe of Levi, the leaders in the second

---

26. I find de Hoop's, *Genesis 49 in Its Literary and Historical Context*, 328–32, attempt to translate "upon the top of his bed (staff)" as "to the head of the tribe" unconvincing.

temple. Be that as it may, the difference in the blessings of Jacob and Moses calls for some sort of narrative explanation.

One possibility is to reflect on what Judah as a tribe did not do. Though given the leading role by Jacob in Genesis 49, the tribe, unlike Levi, does not stand with Moses and the Lord during the golden calf episode. Another possibility is to reflect on the law of kingship in Deut 17:14-20. It may be that given the failure of the monarchy and Moses's strong reservations about kingship as it was typically defined ("a king like the nations") would lead a canonical readership to understand Moses's rather tepid blessing of Judah as reflecting those reservations. Being the royal tribe in Israel is not an unmitigated blessing

Still another possibility is to recognize that Judah's royal status has been transferred to God or perhaps Moses according to the Blessing of Moses (Deut 33:5) since the (narrative) time when Judah was promised royal authority in Jacob's blessing.

The Sons of the Concubines

As sons of the concubines and not those of his proper wives, the brevity of Jacob's "blessings" on them shows his relative lack of concern for them. The blessings also display ambiguity.[27] Does Dan's blessing (Gen 49:17) refer to military defeat of his foes or is it an allusion to the crushing of the serpent's head (Gen 3:14-15)? Is Asher's rich food (Gen 49:20) a blessing or a sign of excess? Is the most hopeful future for Gad a draw (Gen 49:19) with his enemies? Is Gen 49:18, "I wait for your salvation, O Lord," a plea for the blessing that so far has been beyond Jacob's reach or a sign of faith that Yahweh would in fact save the tribe of Dan?

Dan, the full brother of Naphtali, is born fifth of Jacob's sons by Rachel's handmaiden Bilhah.[28] He is the first son mentioned after the six sons of Leah. In both testaments Dan is depicted as a crafty animal who clandestinely attacks his prey. The Dan of Deuteronomy 33 is the stronger animal. His northern location is presumed ("leaps forth from Bashan," a transjordanian location that extends to the north of the sea of Chinnereth and next to the city of Laish, which Dan conquered when it moved from the south), even though the tribe is given an original allotment in the south to the west of Benjamin and the northwest of Judah. The word "Laish" (ליש) used four

---

27. For what follows see Turner, *Genesis*, 203.

28. Wright, "Naphtali," 587: "Bilhah's two sons were born 'on Rachel's knees' (Gen 30:3), a phrase signifying Jacob's formal recognition of their sonship through Rachel. Significantly, this phrase does not appear in connection with the birth of Zilpah's sons."

times in Judges 18 in relation to Dan's territory is the same as the word for "old lion" (ליש) in Isaiah, Job, and Proverbs, and while Deuteronomy 33:22 does not use the same word (אריה), there may still be an echo. In either case, Dan's migration to the north sometime after the conquest is anticipated/reflected in Moses's testament.[29]

The ambiguity of Jacob's "blessing" of Naphtali (Gen 49:21) is obvious. Is the animal analogy one which is naturally wild and being let loose is a sign of healthy freedom ("doe") or is it a vulnerable animal such as a sheep? In Deuteronomy Moses commands Naphtali to possess the sea (west?) and the south. The sea would seem to be either Chinnereth or a call to expand toward the Mediterranean. If we translate less literally, it is merely a call to possess those portions of the land of Canaan to its south and west or perhaps the west and south edges of Chinnereth. The expansion of territory is an encouragement for Naphtali to fully possess their allotted land.

The Testament of Jacob's commentary on Gad (Gen 49:19) seems to echo the curse on the serpent in some ways. But here he is merely nipping at the heels of those who raid him. There is a perplexing turnaround for Gad in the Blessing of Moses (Deut 33:20–21) which begs for a narratological explanation. Certainly Gad declines significantly in numbers during the wilderness period (45,650 to 40,500, a loss of 5,150) so it is difficult to see the enlargement of Gad numerically. Perhaps the fact that Gad along with Reuben choose land in the transjordan allows them to have more land than they would have had had they settled in cisjordan. But that choice is ambiguous at best. Notice that Moses at first regards it as a repetition of the rebellion and un-faith of the 12 spies (Num 32:14, 15). The choosing of "the best for himself" may allude to the selfishness of the choice of Reuben and Gad (Deut 33:21). The coming at the "head of his people" (Deut 33:21) may allude to the "hurrying" or "vanguard" which Reuben and Gad promise to be for the armies of Israel in the cisjordanian conquest (Num 32:17). Is Moses predicting that Gad will perform this function, or is he implicitly warning them that they must do so?

Asher is to be the provider of rich food for the royal court according to Jacob, taking the role of an exalted servant (Gen 49:20).[30] Moses's blessing of Asher is effusive, confusingly so in light of the relatively insignificant place of the tribe in later Israelite history. For Moses he is to be the most blessed of

---

29. The fact that Dan does not appear among the tribal list of the 144,000 sealed in Rev 7:4–8 (Manasseh takes his place even though Joseph is already included) may be another instance, in terms of Christian biblical theology, of a conditional element in whether a tribe has a future.

30. Following the MT's "from Asher." NRSV follows LXX, Syriac, and the Vulgate in translating, "Asher's food shall be rich."

the sons and the favorite of his brothers, enjoying the luxury of using olive oil to sooth his feet. Asher will maintain his steely strength as long as the tribe endures (Deut 33:24).

The Latter Sons of Leah: Issachar and Zebulun

The two tribes are paired together because they were born in a deal between Leah and Rachel, Rachel getting the aphrodisiac mandrakes of Leah, and Leah getting the right to sleep with Jacob in return. They are late in life sons of Leah (along with Leah's daughter Dinah). While Issachar is the firstborn of the latter sons of Leah, he is mentioned after Zebulun in both the testament of Jacob and the blessing of Moses. The reversal of what might be the expected roles of older and younger is also clear from the wordings of their respective blessings. In both versions, Issachar is the more passive, lying down and finding a resting place even at the cost of servitude (or is it merely hard work?[31]) in the testament and remaining in tents in the blessing. By contrast Zebulun is to rejoice in his going out and the extension of Zebulun's borders to Sidon in the testament, even if it merely reflects Jacob's hope, also implies a more active future for Zebulun. In both, Zebulun is somehow related to the sea(s), even though the tribe does not end up bordering on the sea. Asher is on the coast and Naphtali is along the west side of Chinnereth (Galilee).

In any case Issachar's "mixed blessing" from Jacob may be indicative of Jacob's attitude toward him. He was born as a result of Leah hiring[32] Jacob for the night from Rachel in return for some of Reuben's aphrodisiac mandrakes.

Zebulun, by contrast, is conceived without such coercion. Moses's blessing does not seem to carry the baggage of the unusual birth circumstances of Issachar as he and Zebulun together "call peoples to the mountain,"[33] "offer righteous sacrifices," and "suck the affluence" that comes

---

31. Sailhamer (ad loc) seems to read this more positively than most, who take the words as referring to submitting to enforced labor, perhaps being "content to perform corvée labor for the local overLORDs in return for a quiet existence" (Sarna, *Genesis*, 340).

32. Heck, "Issachar," 458: "Most critical scholars think that Gen 49:14–15 reflects a time when Issachar submitted to slave labor rather than do the hard work of subjugating the land. The oracle in Gen 49:14–15 is generally considered one of derision of the freemen who had let themselves be enticed by the fertile plain and had thereby become humiliated as beasts of burden."

33. The mountain to which the two tribes call peoples is hard to pin down. Is it mount Carmel on the Mediterranean or mount Tabor or some other?

from controlling either the sea[34] itself or the trade routes with access to it.[35] Moses's blessing amounts to a reversal of the virtual curse of Issachar by Jacob and a reaffirmation of the blessing of Zebulun.

The Sons of Rachel: Joseph and Benjamin

The chart below uses bold italics to indicate the striking intertextuality between the testament of Jacob and the blessing of Moses in regard to Joseph. He receives the longest blessing by Jacob and Moses and has a leading role among his brothers/fellow tribes in each. Moses's blessing, when read intertextually, is largely a repetition and reaffirmation of Jacob's blessing.

The differences are also interesting. In Jacob's testament the deity is referred to as: "the mighty one of Jacob," "the shepherd," "the rock of Israel," "the God of your father," and "the Almighty." In Moses's blessing deity is referred to as "the Lord" and "the one who dwells in the bush." This latter title makes sense given the revelation of "the Lord's" name to Moses and the experience of Moses with God at the burning bush. While both the testament and the blessing speak of blessings on the "brow" of Joseph, Jacob describes him as one "set apart from his brothers" while Moses has him as the "prince" among his brothers.

But of perhaps even more significance is what is not said about Joseph. Although he is given a leading role, it is not the leading role in either the testament or the blessing. This is not what one might expect from the Joseph narrative and may indicate, as Turner has noted,[36] that Jacob tries to ensure that Joseph's dreams do not find fulfillment by giving Judah the role of leadership. In the blessing of Moses, Joseph once again comes in second, though this time to the tribe of Levi.

---

34. Is this the Mediterranean or Chinnereth or perhaps both? Cf. Tigay, *Deuteronomy*, 330.

35. Wright, "Zebulun," 912, Zebulun "is rich in terms of water resources, soil and building materials . . . Perhaps more importantly, the tribal inheritance of Zebulun carried a number of important natural routes connecting the seacoast with points inland, including the Great Trunk Road running between Egypt and Mesopotamia . . . [Several of Zebulun's cities] guarded strategic junctures on the main routes as witnessed by their appearance in Amarna texts 8, 224, 225 and 245 (cf. Josh 11:1)." He continues, "Zebulun's eventual control of the northwestern extremity of the Jezreel Valley and of the final bend of the *Via Maris* toward the Mediterranean is adequate to explain Jacob's words."

36. Turner, *Genesis*, 200.

Joseph is a fruitful bough, a fruitful bough by a spring; his branches run over the wall. The archers[37] fiercely attacked him; they shot at him and pressed him hard. Yet his bow remained taut, and his arms were made agile by the hands of the *Mighty One of Jacob*, by the name of the *Shepherd*, the *Rock of Israel*, by the God of your father, who will help you, by the *Almighty* who will bless you with blessings of *heaven above*, blessings of *the deep that lies beneath*, blessings of the breasts and of the womb. The blessings of your father are stronger than the blessings of the *eternal mountains*, the bounties of the *everlasting hills*; may they be on the *head of Joseph*, on the *brow* of him who was *set apart* from *his brothers*.

Gen 49:22–26

And of *Joseph* he said: Blessed by the LORD be his land, with the choice gifts of *heaven above*, and of *the deep that lies beneath*; with the choice fruits of the sun, and the rich yield of the months; with the finest produce of the *ancient mountains*, and the abundance of the *everlasting hills*; with the choice gifts of the earth and its fullness, and the favor of *the one who dwells on Sinai*.[38] Let these come on *the head of Joseph*, on the *brow* of the *prince* among *his brothers*. A firstborn bull—majesty is his! His horns are the horns of a wild ox; with them he gores the peoples, driving them to the ends of the earth; such are the myriads of Ephraim, such the thousands of Manasseh.

Deut 33:13–17

Although Benjamin is, after Joseph, the favorite son of Jacob, ironically the latter's testament does not unambiguously offer a blessing for Benjamin.[39] Moses's blessing is much clearer in this regard. For Moses, Benjamin is no longer a ravenous wolf (Gen 49:27), but the beloved (Deut 33:12).

Conclusion

Contrary to Brueggemann, the testament and the blessing are tied in numerous and various ways to their narrative contexts. We have further found that despite ambiguities and uncertainties the reading of these texts narratively and intertextually bears interpretive fruit which has the potential to yield much theological ore. In particular, we have seen that the internal family tensions which are sown among the sons and daughters of Jacob from

---

37. Turner, *Genesis*, 203: "The reference to those who attacked Joseph is striking (49.23). Within the context of the Joseph story the attackers must surely be his brothers. Thus 49.24 which depicts how Joseph repulsed such an attack with the help of God, would refer to how he trumped his brothers by rising to high office in Egypt."

38. Hebrew סנה "in the bush."

39. Turner, *Genesis*, 203: "The final blessing, that on Benjamin (49.27), continues the flow of short blessings which began with Zebulun's and which was interrupted by Joseph's. As with elements in the blessings on Dan (49.17) and Gad (49.19), it is not clear whether Benjamin's 'devouring' and 'dividing' as a wolf is intended to be positive or negative."

the circumstances of their birth play themselves out throughout their lives up to and on through to their ultimate development into the tribes of Israel. However, the actions and reactions of the sons of Jacob and the tribes which develop from them play a larger role in the working out of their destinies than is often realized. While the testament does seem to anticipate and to an extent control the future destiny of the tribes, what that destiny means in real terms is, to a large extent, determined by the future choices of the tribe. Levi and Simeon are both scattered and effectively disinherited from a normal tribal existence by Jacob, but whether this destiny is a blessing or a curse is determined by the future actions of the Levites and Simeonites. Jacob's personal agenda seems to show up in his testament. But that personal agenda only determines the future within certain limits. Despite Jacob's personal favoritism for Joseph, the oldest son of his only truly legitimate wife, Judah, is given the ruling role over Joseph.

As an announcement of plot for the Pentateuch, Jacob's blessing has the same complex relationship to the ensuing narrative events as the earlier announcements of plot do within the book of Genesis. That complex relationship demonstrates a complex creative tension between destiny and human response which challenges our theological categories.

Bibliography

Brueggemann, Walter. *Genesis*. Interpretation. Louisville: John Knox, 1982.
Christenson, Duane L. *Deuteronomy 21:10—34:12*. Nashville: Nelson, 2002.
Heck, Joel D. "Issachar." In *Dictionary of the Old Testament: Pentateuch*, edited by T. Desmond Alexander and David W. Baker, 458–60. Downers Grove, IL: InterVarsity, 2003.
De Hoop, Raymond. *Genesis 49 in Its Literary and Historical Context*. Oudtestamentische Studiën 39. Leiden: Brill, 1999.
Sailhamer, John H. *The Meaning of the Pentateuch: Revelation, Composition, and Interpretation*. Downers Grove, IL: InterVarsity, 2009.
Sarna, Nahum M. *Genesis*. JPSTC. Philadelphia: Jewish Publication Society, 1989.
Tigay, Jefferey H. *Deuteronomy*. JPSTC. Philadelphia: Jewish Publication Society, 1996.
Turner, Laurence A. *Announcements of Plot in Genesis*. JSOTSup 96. Sheffield: JSOT Press, 1990.
———. *Genesis*. Readings. Sheffield: Sheffield Academic, 2000.
Wright, Paul H. "Naphtali." In *Dictionary of the Old Testament: Pentateuch*, edited by T. Desmond Alexander and David W. Baker, 587–88. Downers Grove, IL: InterVarsity, 2003.
———. "Reuben." In *Dictionary of the Old Testament: Pentateuch*, edited by T. Desmond Alexander and David W. Baker, 691–93. Downers Grove, IL: InterVarsity, 2003.
———. "Zebulun." In *Dictionary of the Old Testament: Pentateuch*, edited by T. Desmond Alexander and David W. Baker, 911–12. Downers Grove, IL: InterVarsity, 2003.

2

Abram as Israel, Israel as Abram

Literary Analogy as Macro-Structural Strategy in the Torah[1]

SETH D. POSTELL

Israel College of the Bible

1. Introduction

MOSHE BEN NAHMAN (RAMBAN, twelfth–thirteenth cent. AD) argued "Everything that happened to the fathers is a sign to the sons."[2] Looking to the Patriarchal narratives for these signs by unpacking allegories could potentially open the door for all kinds of eisegetical interpretations at odds with careful exegesis. At the same time, it would be careless to dismiss Ramban's assertion hastily without consideration, given the presence of manifold literary features such as allusion and literary analogy placed throughout the biblical text.[3]

---

1. This article was originally published in *Tyndale Bulletin* 67.2 (2016) 161–82. I am grateful to the editors of Tyndale for their kind permission to republish this article for this Feschrift in honor of the man who taught me to read the Bible, Dr. John H. Sailhamer, may his memory be blessed (Eccl 7:1).

2. Ramban on Gen 12:6 (all translations is this article are my own). Similarly, see his comments on Gen 12:10 and *Genesis Rabbah* 48.7.

3. Bazak, *Parallels Meet* (Hebrew, translation my own, all translations of Hebrew my own), 10, writes, "[T]he phenomenon of literary parallels in the various books of the Bible is not coincidental or occasional, but is found consistently and systematically in the books of the Bible' (my translation). A literary analogy occurs when one story intentionally alludes to and parallels another story for the purposes of comparison and contrast." See Alter, *The Art of Biblical Narrative*, 21; Sternberg, *Poetics of Biblical*

Both Jewish and Christian scholars have already uncovered many of the literary parallels between Abram's story and what happens later in Israel's story, as will later be discussed, but it seems that the observable interplay of the two stories is far more extensive than may have been previously noticed.

Textual evidence indicates that the individual stories that constitute the Abram narrative (Genesis 11–15) have been strategically arranged to foreshadow Israel's exodus from Egypt, their journey through the wilderness to Mount Sinai, and the making of the Sinai Covenant. The abundance of shared language and themes ranging over such a broad swath of texts strongly suggests the presence of an overarching and unifying textual strategy. Israel came forth from the loins of their father Abram. So too did their history.

Many literary and thematic parallels can be seen between Genesis 1–11 and Israel's story as recorded in the Former Prophets (Joshua–Kings).[4] Adam's story, in terms of its textual strategy, seems to point forward to what would happen to the people of Israel, serving as an interpretive key for understanding Israel's story.[5] For this reason, reading and rereading Adam's story yields a far deeper appreciation of the meaning Israel's story in the Former Prophets. Similarly, I believe that the Torah's author carefully arranged a chain of narrative events in the Abram narrative which were intended to prefigure Israel's story, and that when placed side by side, the texts reveal a macro-structural analogy between the two stories that is worthy of our attention.

The purpose of this paper is to present the textual evidence pointing to an intentional and extended literary analogy, and to offer a few possible explanations of its function in the larger context of the Torah story.[6] In the first part of this article, I contend that Abram's story literally paves the way for Israel's story. In part two of this paper, I attempt to interpret the data by asking three questions:

1. What is the purpose of the Abram–Israel analogy in the Torah story?
2. Is there significance to the point at which the two stories diverge?

Narrative, 114, 132–33, 35, 41, 268–70, 365–66; Zakovitch, *Through the Looking Glass*; Grossman, "Dynamic Analogies," 394–414.

4. Postell, *Adam as Israel*.

5. It is equally correct to reverse the paradigm, i.e., "Israel as Adam," and argue that Israel's story also points back to Adam's story. In other words, each text shines interpretive light on the other. See Ben-Porat, "The Poetics of Literary Allusion," 107–8.

6. This study attempts to understand and interpret the Torah in its final form.

3. What are the implications for our understanding of the NT's figural reading of some of the Torah's narratives?[7]

Many scholars recognise commonly accepted criteria for identifying literary parallels and analogies.[8] I propose the presence of an intentional literary analogy when both stories share unique and/or rare words and phrases as well as corresponding themes and motifs. At times, the rare words and phrases used by the author to signal intertextuality are what Michael Riffaterre calls ungrammaticalities,[9] cogently explained by Daniel Boyarin as "the awkwardness of a textual moment, at any linguistic or discourse level, which by its awkwardness points semiotically to another text which provides a key to its decoding."[10]

2. Literary Data

a) Scattering from a City of Bricks to the Land of God (Gen 11:1–9 || Exod 5)

Abram's call to leave Ur of the Chaldeans (Gen 12:1–3) and then his exodus from Egypt (Gen 12:10—13:4) to go to the Promised Land are preceded by the Babel narrative (Gen 11:1–9). The juxtaposition of the Babel narrative with Abram's call portrays the patriarch's departure as leaving a city built by people (Gen 11:4, 31) to go to a land chosen by God (Gen 12:1; cf. Gen 2:8–14). Parallels with earlier narratives in the Primeval History (Genesis 1–11) not only serve to contrast sinful cities built by men with the land of God, but also echo Abram's westward journey to the Promised Land as a return to the Land of Eden (see Gen 2:8).[11]

An indicator of literary analogy is the repetition of rarely used words and phrases in the context of parallel motifs. In this case, we see a shared use of the word for building bricks connecting the Babel narrative with the

---

7. On NT figural interpretation, see Allison, *The New Moses*; Clifford, "The Exodus in the Christian Bible," 345–61; Hays, *Reading Backwards*; Emerson, "Arbitrary Allegory," 14–21.

8. Garsiel, *The First Book of Samuel*, 25; Grossman, "Dynamic Analogies," 396; Hays, *Echoes of Scripture*, 29–32; Leonard, "Identifying Inner-Biblical Allusions," 241–65; Stanfield, "The Song 'Ha'azinu' and its Presence in Isaiah 1–39," 15–16.

9. Riffaterre, *Text Production*, 12, 51.

10. Boyarin, "Inner Biblical Ambiguity, Intertextuality and the Dialectic of Midrash," 29–30.

11. Compare Gen 4:16–17 with 11:2, 4; Gen 4:26 with 12:8; see Postell, *Adam as Israel*, 88–91; 98–102.

Exodus narrative. It is essential to note that the verb לבן "to make bricks" and the plural noun לְבֵנִים "bricks" are used together only in these two places in the Torah (Gen 11:3; Exod 5:7), and in both places refer to building projects that are antithetical to the purposes of God for his people. Just prior to Abram's exodus from Egypt (Gen 12:10—13:4), the Babel narrative describes the building of a city of bricks (לְבֵנִים, Gen 11:3). God, however, thwarts this building project by scattering its builders over the face of the whole land: וַיָּפֶץ יְהוָה אֹתָם מִשָּׁם עַל־פְּנֵי כָל־הָאָרֶץ (Gen 11:8). Likewise, just prior to Israel's exodus from Egypt and return to the Promised Land, the Israelites build cities of bricks (לְבֵנִים) for Pharaoh (Exod 5:7). This building project, however, is thwarted (Exod 5:14–19) when the Israelites are compelled to scatter over all the land: וַיָּפֶץ הָעָם בְּכָל־אֶרֶץ מִצְרָיִם (Exod 5:12).[12] The nearly identical wording of Exod 5:12 and Gen 11:8 in a matrix of parallel motifs suggest the presence of an intentional analogy.

Scattering from a City of Bricks to the Land of God[13]

And each person said to his fellow, "Let us make bricks (נִלְבְּנָה לְבֵנִים) and fire them by fire." And they had the brick for stone and bitumen for mortar. (Gen 11:3)	And you must not continue giving the people straw for making bricks (לִלְבֹּן הַלְּבֵנִים) as days past. Let them go and gather straw for themselves. (Exod 5:7)
And the LORD scattered them from there upon the face of all the land (וַיָּפֶץ יְהוָה אֹתָם מִשָּׁם עַל־פְּנֵי כָל־הָאָרֶץ) and they ceased building the city. (Gen 11:8)	And the people scattered in all the land (וַיָּפֶץ הָעָם בְּכָל־אֶרֶץ מִצְרָיִם) of Egypt (Exod 5:12)

In both Genesis 11 and in Exodus 5, the scattering upon the face of the land signals an important transition: the cessation of building cities for men (Babylon/Egypt) and a return to the land chosen by God (Canaan).

b) Exodus from Egypt
(Gen 12:10—13:4 || Gen 43:1—Exod 12:38)

Several scholars have pointed to the literary parallels between Abram and Israel's exoduses from Egypt.[14] The Torah's description of Israel's Exodus

---

12. For other commentators who have noted an allusion to Gen 11:8 in Exod 5:12, see Hakham, *The Chumash Shmot*, 79; *Baal HaTorim Shmot* 5.12; *Panim Yafot Shmot* 5.12.

13. All translations of the Bible are my own.

14. See for example, Grossman, *Abraham*, 58; Sailhamer, *The Pentateuch as Narrative*, 37–39, 141–42; Wenham, *Genesis 1–15*, 291–92; Römer, "The Exodus in the Book

story, starting with their arrival to Egypt because of famine, through their escape from Egypt (Gen 43:1—Exod 12:38) repeats key words, phrases, and themes found elsewhere only in Gen 12:10–13:2, where Abram's own exodus story is found. Both accounts describe: (1) a "heavy famine" (Gen 12:10; 43:1); (2) a descent to Egypt (Gen 12:11; 46:6); (3) a "captivity" in Pharaoh's service (Gen 12:15; Exod 1:11); (4) plagues upon the Egyptians (Gen 12:17; Exodus 7–12); (5) expulsion from Egypt because of plagues (Gen 12:20; Exod 12:33); (6) a departure with great wealth (Gen 12:16; 13:2; Exod 12:35, 38); and (7) the accompaniment of Lot/a mixed multitude (Gen 13:1; Exod 12:38).[15]

Exodus from Egypt

Famine in the Land precipitates a sojourn in Egypt	And Abram took (וַיִּקַּח) Sarai his wife, and Lot his brother's son, and all their possessions they had acquired (וְאֶת־כָּל־רְכ֣וּשָׁם֮ אֲשֶׁ֣ר רָכָ֔שׁוּ), and the people they acquired in Haran, and they went out to go to the land of Canaan. And they came to the land of Canaan . . . And there was a famine in the land. And Abram went down to Egypt to sojourn there, because the famine was severe in the land (כָּבֵ֥ד הָרָעָ֖ב בָּאָֽרֶץ). (Gen 12:5, 10)	And all the earth came to Egypt to Joseph to buy grain, because the famine was severe over all the earth . . . And the children of Israel came to buy among the others who came, because the famine was in the land of Canaan . . . And the famine was severe in the land (וְהָרָעָ֖ב כָּבֵ֥ד בָּאָֽרֶץ) . . . And they took (וַיִּקְח֣וּ) their livestock and their possessions they had acquired (וְאֶת־רְכוּשָׁ֖ם אֲשֶׁ֣ר רָכָ֔שׁוּ) in the land of Canaan, and came into Egypt, Jacob and all his offspring with him. (Gen 41:57; 42:5; 43:1; 46:6)
People of promise are taken against their will into Pharaoh's service	And the princes of Pharaoh saw her, they praised her to Pharaoh. And the woman was taken to Pharaoh's house. (Gen 12:15)	And they set taskmasters over them to afflict them with heavy burdens. And they built store cities for Pharaoh, Pithom and Raamses. (Exod 1:11)
God afflicts Pharaoh with plagues and the people of promise are sent away from Egypt	And the LORD plagued (וַיְנַגַּ֨ע) Pharaoh with great plagues (נְגָעִ֣ים) and his house, because of Sarai, Abram's wife . . . And Pharaoh put him in the care of men, and they sent him away (וַיְשַׁלְּח֥וּ) with his wife and all that he had. (Gen 12:17, 20)	And the LORD said to Moses, "Still one more plague (נֶ֚גַע) I will bring upon Pharaoh and upon Egypt. Afterward he will send you away (יְשַׁלַּ֣ח) from here. When he sends you away (כְּשַׁלְּח֔וֹ), he will drive you away from here completely." (Exod 11:1)

---

of Genesis," 7–9.

15. On the analogy of Lot and the mixed multitude, see Sailhamer, *The Pentateuch as Narrative*, 38.

The people of promise and others with them go up from Egypt to the Land of Promise with the wealth of Egypt	And Abram went up (וַיַּעַל) from Egypt, he and his wife and all that he had, and Lot with him (וְלוֹט עִמּוֹ), to the Negeb. And Abram was very heavy in livestock, in silver, and in gold (כָּבֵד מְאֹד בַּמִּקְנֶה בַּכֶּסֶף וּבַזָּהָב). (Gen 13:1–2)	And the people of Israel did as Moses told them, and they requested from the Egyptians silver (כֶּסֶף) and articles of gold (זָהָב) and clothing ... And a mixed multitude (עֵרֶב רַב) also went up (עָלָה) with them, and flocks and herds, very heavy in livestock (מִקְנֶה כָּבֵד מְאֹד). (Exod 12:35, 38)

The juxtaposition of the cessation of a building project with an exodus from Egypt in both stories creates a literary bridge binding the Primeval History to the Patriarchal narratives, and the Patriarchal narratives to the Exodus narrative.

c) Lack of Resources Occasions a Conflict (Gen 13:5–18 || Exod 15:22—17:7)

The accumulation of all these parallels and analogous literary material encourages us to continue seeking further analogies. Having just departed from Egypt, Abram takes his nephew Lot (Gen 13:1) and begins his journey (וַיֵּלֶךְ לְמַסָּעָיו, Gen 13:3) back to the Promised Land. Soon there is a crisis: namely, a lack of resources. This crisis leads to a conflict (מְרִיבָה) between Abram and Lot's shepherds (Gen 13:7–8), whereupon the nephew departs, choosing to live in a place reminiscent of Egypt's luxuries (Gen 13:10).

As is the case with Abram and his nephew Lot, Israel journeys from Egypt (וַיִּסְעוּ, Exod 12:37; 15:22; 17:1) with a mixed multitude (וְגַם־עֵרֶב רַב עָלָה אִתָּם, Exod 12:38). Soon the Israelites find themselves in a place lacking essential resources (Exod 15:22). This crisis provokes two dire reactions from the people, presumably the rabble spoken of in Num 11:4. First, the people long to return to Egypt's luxuries (Exod 16:3). Second, the lack of resources culminates in a conflict (מְרִיבָה) between the people and Moses (Exod 17:7). Though ריב is a commonly used root in the Torah,[16] Nahum Sarna notes that every other time מְרִיבָה is used in the Bible, with the exception of Gen 13:8, it "refer[s] exclusively to the controversies and grumblings of the people against their leader and against God over the lack of water during the wilderness wanderings."[17] Though there is little shared language between Gen 13:5–18 and Exod 15:22—17:7, there are still good reasons for

---

16. Gen 13:7–8; 26:20–22; 31:36; Exod 17:2, 7; 21:18; 23:2–3, 6; Num 20:3, 13, 24; 27:14; Deut 1:12; 17:8; 19:17; 21:5; 25:1; 32:51; 33:7–8.

17. Sarna, *Genesis*, 98. See Exod 17:7; Num 20:13, 24; 27:14; Deut 32:51; 33:8; Ezek 47:19; 48:28; Pss 81:8; 95:8; 106:32.

interpreting Abram's story in light of Israel's wilderness journey. First, the presence of the ungrammaticality (מְרִיבָה) in Gen 13:8 is striking. Why does a word used exclusively for Israel's wilderness wanderings with the exception of Gen 13:8 appear here if not but to signal an allusion? Second, the exact sequence of events in the Abram/Israel stories (exodus from Egypt and conflict due to lack of resources) are difficult to explain apart from intentional allusion.

Conflict Initiated by Lack of Resources

And he went by daily marches (וַיֵּלֶךְ לְמַסָּעָיו) from the Negeb... and the land could not support them to dwell together... And there was a dispute (רִיב) between the herdsmen of Abram's livestock and the herdsmen of Lot's livestock... And Abram said to Lot, "Let there be no strife (מְרִיבָה) between you and me, and between your herdsmen and my herdsmen, for we are brothers..." And Lot lifted up his eyes and saw all the valley of the Jordan, that all of it was well watered–before the LORD destroyed Sodom and Gomorrah–like the garden of the LORD, like the land of Egypt (כְּאֶרֶץ מִצְרַיִם) as you go to Zoar. (Gen 13:3, 6–8, 10)	And all the congregation of the people of Israel moved on from the wilderness of Sin by daily marches (... וַיִּסְעוּ לְמַסְעֵיהֶם) by the LORD's command, and camped at Rephidim, but there was no water for the people to drink. And the people disputed (וַיָּרֶב) with Moses and said, "Give us water to drink." And Moses said to them, "Why do you dispute with me? Why do you test the LORD?" And the people thirsted there for water; and they grumbled against Moses and said, "Why, now, have you brought us up from Egypt (מִמִּצְרַיִם), to kill us and our children and our livestock with thirst?" . . . And he called the name of the place Massah and Meribah (מְרִיבָה), because of the dispute (רִיב) of the people of Israel... (Exod 17:1–3, 7).

d) Victory over the Amalekites (Gen 14:1–16 || Exod 17:8–16)

The conflict narratives in Genesis 13 and Exodus 17 are both immediately followed by battle narratives: Abram against the four kings (Gen 14:1–17) and Israel against the Amalekites (Exod 17:816). Oddly, we find an out of place reference to the Amalekites in Gen 14:7: "Then they turned back and came to En-mishpat (that is, Kadesh[18]) and defeated all the country of the Amalekites, and also the Amorites who were dwelling in Hazazon-tamar." This mention of the Amalekites is clearly anachronistic since the Amalekites

---

18. Sarna, *Genesis*, 106; Wenham, *Genesis*, 311, point out that Kadesh is a word commonly associated with Israel's wilderness wanderings (see Num 13:26; 20:1, 14, 16, 22; 27:14; 33:36–37; Deut 1:46; 32:51).

are descendants of Esau, Abram's grandson (Gen 36:10–16).[19] The interpreter is compelled to explain the purpose of the Amalekites in the text. The most likely explanation for this ungrammaticality in the Abram battle narrative is to anticipate Israel's defeat of the Amalekites in Exod 17:8–16. Another rather seemingly insignificant mention of the Horites (הַחֹרִי) in Genesis 14:6 becomes another indicator of analogy in light of the mention of Hur (חוּר) in the parallel battle account in Exod 17:10, 12.

The larger narrative context in which the two battle scenes occur provides further evidence that the texts are intentionally analogous. Both battle scenes are sandwiched between an "exodus out of Egypt" (Gen 12:10–20; Exodus 1–14) and the appearance of a Gentile priest who blesses God (Melchizedek in Gen 14:18–20 and Jethro in Exodus 18).

Victorious Battle over the Amalekites

And the Horites (הַחֹרִי) in their hill country of Seir as far as El-paran bordering the wilderness. And they turned back and came to En-mishpat (that is, Kadesh) and struck all the country of the Amalekites (וַיַּכּוּ אֶת־כָּל־שְׂדֵה הָעֲמָלֵקִי), and also the Amorites who were dwelling in Hazazon-tamar. (Gen 14:6–7)	And Joshua did as Moses told him, to fight with Amalek (בַּעֲמָלֵק), and Moses, Aaron, and Hur (חוּר) went to the top of the hill. (Exod 17:10)

e) Appearance of a Gentile Priest (Gen 14:18–20 || Exod 18)

Genesis 14 and Exodus 18 are remarkably similar, both in terms of shared language as well as in terms of common themes.[20] In both stories, a Gentile priest appears (Gen 14:18; Exod 18:1) after a successful military campaign (Gen 14:14–16; Exod 17:13) and prior to the making of a very significant covenant (Genesis 15; Exodus 19–24). Melchizedek's appearance bears all the syntactical marks of an "ungrammaticality." If one were to remove verses 18–20 there would be no break between the arrival of the king of Sodom and what he says to Abram. This interruption of the flow of the "king of Sodom" narrative gives evidence that the author has strategically placed it

---

19. Traditional Jewish commentators explain the reference to the Amalekites by appealing to Isa. 46:10; God declared the end of the Amalekites from the beginning. See for example, *Gen. Rab.* 42.7; *Tanchuma* 14.1; *Pesiqta Zutarta* 14.7.

20. See Sailhamer, *The Pentateuch as Narrative*, 280–81; Sailhamer, *The Meaning of the Pentateuch*, 368–74.

here following the successful military campaign. In both stories, the Gentile priest offers and/or eats bread (לֶחֶם) with the victorious party (Gen 14:18; Exod 18:12). In both stories, the Gentile priest blesses God for the divine protection afforded the victorious party (וּבָרוּךְ אֵל עֶלְיוֹן, Gen 14:20; בָּרוּךְ יְהוָה, Exod 18:10). In both stories, the Gentile priest makes an offering in honor of the divine victory (Gen 14:18; Exod 18:12), bread and wine in the former case, a burnt offering and sacrifices in the latter case. And in both stories, the Gentile priest surprisingly is granted a place of greater authority over the victorious party. Abram deferentially offers a tithe to Melchizedek (Gen 14:20). Moses deferentially submits to Jethro's counsel (Exod 18:24).

Ministry of Gentile Priest Prior to the Making of the Covenant

Appearance of a gentile priest after successful military campaign and prior to the making of a covenant.	And the king of Sodom went to meet him after his return from defeating Chedorlaomer, and the kings who were with him, to the Valley of Shaveh (that is, the Valley of the King). And Melchizedek, king of Salem, brought out (הוֹצִיא) bread and wine, and he is a priest of God Most High. (Gen 14:17–18)	'... The LORD will have war with Amalek from generation to generation.' And Jethro, the priest of Midian (כֹּהֵן מִדְיָן), Moses's father-in-law, heard of all that God had done for Moses and for Israel his people, that the LORD brought Israel out (הוֹצִיא) of Egypt. (Exod 17:16–18:1)
Gentile priest offers to/eats bread with the victorious party.	And Melchizedek, king of Salem, brought out bread (לֶחֶם) and wine, and he was priest of God Most High. (Gen 14:18)	And Jethro, Moses's father-in-law, took a burnt offering and sacrifices to God; and Aaron came with all the elders of Israel to eat bread (לֶחֶם) with Moses' father-in-law before God. (Exod 18:12)
Gentile priest blesses God for protecting the victorious party.	And he blessed him and said, "Blessed (בָּרוּךְ) be Abram to God Most High, who created the heave and the earth. And blessed be God Most High who handed over your enemies into your hand" (וּבָרוּךְ אֵל עֶלְיוֹן אֲשֶׁר־מִגֵּן צָרֶיךָ בְּיָדֶךָ). And he gave him a tenth from everything. (Gen 14:19–20)	And Jethro rejoiced about all the good which the LORD did for Israel, how he saved him from the hand of Egypt (הִצִּילוֹ מִיַּד מִצְרָיִם). And Jethro said, "Blessed (בָּרוּךְ) is the LORD who rescued you from the hand of Egypt and from the hand of Pharaoh, who rescued the people out from under the hand of Egypt" (הִצִּיל אֶתְכֶם מִיַּד מִצְרַיִם וּמִיַּד פַּרְעֹה אֲשֶׁר הִצִּיל אֶת־הָעָם מִתַּחַת יַד־מִצְרָיִם). (Exod 18:9–10)

Gentile priest presents an offering in honor of the divine victory.	And Melchizedek, king of Salem, brought out bread and wine, and he was priest of God Most High. (Gen 14:18)	And Jethro, Moses's father-in-law, took a burnt offering and sacrifices to God … (Exod 18:12a)
Gentile priest granted a more authoritative role than the victorious part.	And he gave him a tenth from everything. (Gen 14:20b)	And Moses obeyed his father-in-law and did all that he said. (Exod 18:24)

The ministry of Gentile priests prior to the making of the Torah's two central covenants (Abrahamic and Sinai) is difficult to explain apart from an overt textual strategy designed to depict the making of one covenant in light of the other.

f) Making of the Covenant (Genesis 15 || Exodus 19–24)

Thus far, we have presented a chain of narrative events in the life of Abram that closely prefigure Israel's story. It would appear that these parallels serve as background and props for some main event, and that they are building up to a crescendo. What is it all pointing towards? The apex of the analogy is the making of the covenants—the Abrahamic Covenant in Genesis 15, and the Sinai Covenant in Exodus 19–24. Both narratives are replete with shared language and common themes that hold great significance.[21] First, both narratives emphasise the importance of faith (הֶאֱמִין ב-), faith being a central theme in the macrostructure of the Torah (Gen 15:6; Exod 19:9).[22] Second, in both narratives, God self-identifies to the covenantal recipient in virtually identical terms: "I am the LORD who brought you out of" (אֲנִי יְהוָה אֲשֶׁר הוֹצֵאתִיךָ מ) Ur of the Chaldeans/the land of Egypt (Gen 15:7; Exod 20:2). The fact that this particular divine self-identification formula appears elsewhere only in Deut 5:6 and 6:12 tips the balance strongly in favor of an intentional allusion. Third, both accounts describe the fear of the covenant recipient along with the presence of supernatural darkness (Gen 15:12, 17; Exod 20:18, 21). Fourth, in both accounts, God appears to the covenant recipient in fire (אֵשׁ), smoke (עָשָׁן) and a torch (לַפִּיד) (Gen 15:17;

---

21. See Ramban on Gen 15:17; Wenham, *Genesis*, 333; Sailhamer, *The Meaning of the Pentateuch*, 369; Römer, "The Exodus in the Book of Genesis," 17–20.

22. See Schmitt, "Redaktion des Pentateuch im Geiste der Prophetie," 170–89; Sailhamer, *The Pentateuch as Narrative*, 72–78.

Exod 19:18; 20:18). It is essential to note that this is the only time "smoke" (עָשָׁן) and "torch" (לַפִּיד) are used together to describe a theophany in the Hebrew Bible. Finally, both narratives describe the making of a covenant (Gen 15:18; Exod 24:8).[23]

The Making of the Covenant[24]

Both "covenant narratives" emphasize the importance of "believing."	And he believed the LORD (וְהֶאֱמִן בַּיהוָה), and he reckoned it to him as righteousness. (Gen 15:6)	And the LORD said to Moses, "Behold, I am coming to you in a thick cloud, that the people may hear when I speak with you, and may also believe you (בְּךָ יַאֲמִינוּ) forever." (Exod 19:9)
Both "covenant narratives" include a unique statement of God's self-revelation.	And he said to him, "I am the LORD who brought you out from Ur of the Chaldeans (אֲנִי יְהוָה אֲשֶׁר הוֹצֵאתִיךָ מֵאוּר) to give you this land to possess." (Gen 15:7)	I am the LORD your God, who brought you out of the land of Egypt (אָנֹכִי יְהוָה אֱלֹהֶיךָ אֲשֶׁר הוֹצֵאתִיךָ מֵאֶרֶץ), out of the house of slavery. (Exod 20:2)[X]
In the making of the covenant, the reciprocal party experiences terrible dread and darkness.	As the sun was setting, a deep sleep fell on Abram. And behold, dreadful and great darkness fell upon him ... When the sun had set and there was darkness. (Gen 15:12, 17)	And all the people saw the thunder and the lightning and the sound of the trumpet and the mountain smoking, and the people saw and trembled, and they stood far away ... And the people stood far away, and Moses drew near to the thick darkness. (Exod 20:18, 21)
In the making of the covenant, God appears to the reciprocal party in fire, smoke, and a torch.	When the sun had set and there was darkness, behold, a fire pot of smoke (תַנּוּר עָשָׁן) and a torch of fire (לַפִּיד אֵשׁ) passed between these pieces. (Gen 15:17)	And Mount Sinai was engulfed in smoke (עָשָׁן) because the LORD descended upon it in the fire (אֵשׁ), and its smoke (עֲשָׁנוֹ) ascended like the smoke of a kiln (כְּעֶשֶׁן הַכִּבְשָׁן) ... And all the people saw the thunder and lightning (הַלַּפִּידִם) and the sound of the trumpet and the mountain smoking (עָשָׁן) ... (Exod 19:18; 20:18)

23. There are several other lexical links particularly between Genesis 14–15 and Exodus 18 that fall outside of the parallel plot structure in these narratives, yet whose presence strongly suggests intentional intertextuality: שָׁלוֹם (Gen 15:15; Exod 18:7, 23), גֵּר יִהְיֶה זַרְעֲךָ בְּאֶרֶץ לֹא לָהֶם//גֵּר הָיִיתִי בְּאֶרֶץ נָכְרִיָּה (Gen 15:13; Exod 18:3), צפר (Gen 15:10; Exod 18:2), אֱלִיעֶזֶר (Gen 15:2; Exod 18:4), and עשר (Gen 14:20; Exod 18:21).

24. Deut 5:6; 6:12

The making of the covenant itself.	On that day the Lord made a covenant with Abram . . . (Gen 15:18)	And Moses took the blood and threw it on the people and said, "Behold the blood of the covenant that the Lord has made with you . . ." (Exod 24:8)

3. The End of the Abram–Israel Analogy

In examining the remarkable similarities between the two stories, it is also clear that the parallel tracks of the two stories diverge at a particular point, but this in itself is a literary device not without significance. The Abram–Israel analogy has been consistent since Genesis 11, but after five chapters of parallels, the analogy falls apart. The breakdown of the Abram–Israel analogy comes with the account of Hagar in the desert in Genesis 16. Hagar, rather than Abram, is the primary focus of the storyline,[25] and in place of the Abram–Israel analogy, we find an unexpected analogy between Hagar and Israel.[26] Hagar and Israel are both slaves who have left Egypt (Gen 15:13; 16:1) and are afflicted (ענה) by their masters (Gen 15:13; 16:6, 9).[27] Both flee (ברח) from their cruel masters to the desert (Gen 16:6, 8; Exod 14:5), to springs of water (Gen 16:7; Exod 15:27) in or near the Wilderness of Shur (Gen 16:7; Exod 15:22) and Kadesh (Gen 16:14; Num 13:26). Finally both are heard and visited by God because of their afflictions (Gen 16:11; Exod 3:7; 4:31; see 22:22).[28] Even the name Hagar (הָגָר) is suggestive of Israel's future status as strangers (גֵר) in the land of Egypt.

This sudden shift in analogous characters is attention-grabbing. Yonatan Grossman argues quite convincingly that changeovers of characters in an analogy are a function of literary strategy.[29] He calls these changeovers "dynamic analogies." According to Grossman, the shift in analogous characters purposely "present[s] an obstacle to the reader in maintaining a steady reading of the analogies between the narratives."[30] In this particular case,

---

25. Grossman, *Abraham*, 113.

26. For an extensive treatment of the Hagar–Israel analogy, see Römer, "The Exodus in Genesis," 11–17. Emerson ("Arbitrary Allegory," 19) writes, "What we see, then, from the verbal and conceptual connections between Genesis 16, 21 and Exodus 12–19 is that the Hagar narrative foreshadows the Exodus narrative . . ."

27. Grossman, *Abraham*, 113–14; Emerson, "Arbitrary Allegory," 20.

28. Emerson, "Arbitrary Allegory," 20, further suggests another parallel: Hagar and Israel both receive their promises/covenant in the wilderness (unlike Abram).

29. Grossman, "Dynamic Analogies," 395.

30. Ibid.

Israel's identification with Hagar, rather than Abram, immediately after the "making of the covenant," presents the reader with a substantial obstacle. Why the sudden change in such a sustained and consistent analogy between Abram and Israel?

What is to be gained by seeing this extended analogy?

In light of the literary evidence presented, I want to refer again to the three questions presented at the introduction to the paper. The first two questions are directly tied to the meaning and function of the Abram–Israel analogy in the Torah and the third question relates to the NT's figural interpretation of some of the Torah's narratives.

1. What is the purpose of the Abram–Israel analogy in the Torah Story as a whole?

Literary analogies in Genesis provide a system of intra-connectivity; a means for transposing many individual stories into one big story. The reader who notices the Torah's literary analogies is able to see the forest for the trees, and to see the trees for what they are within the forest.

The ability to hear the echoes of God's promises to Abram in the creation mandate, for example, results in the ability to understand Abram's divine election. "God blessed them; and God said to them, 'Be fruitful and multiply, and fill the earth, and conquer it'" (Gen 1:28). The creation mandate involves blessing, seed, and the subjugation (conquest) of הָאָרֶץ (the land). This three-fold mandate contains all the major provisions of God's promises to Abram: blessing, seed, and the conquest of the land. The literary analogy between Adam and Abram, in this case, provides the interpretive key for understanding Abram's election in the larger story. Adam's sin and exile resulted in a failure to implement God's plan of blessing for creation. Abram is chosen to reestablish and reassert God's blessing over all creation, to make creation "very good" again.

The Abram–Israel analogy, therefore, serves a similar strategic purpose. It binds Israel's story with God's purposes for creation through Abram to Adam. The analogy signals to the reader that Israel's story is vitally important to God's creation purposes. In this light, the Exodus is not merely a story about Israel's national independence, but rather, it is a story about God's commitment to the whole of creation, and to all the families on the earth whom God intends to bless (cf. Exod 1:7; Gen 1:28).

The Abram–Israel analogy means that the Sinai Covenant, by virtue of its correspondence to the Abrahamic Covenant, is also rooted deeply in God's purposes for creation. Oddly, the universal aspects of the Abrahamic Covenant are seemingly absent from the Sinai Covenant. Rather than universal blessing, Sinai focuses on national blessings and curses strictly associated with Israel's obedience to the Sinai Covenant. We find legislation intended to keep Israel separate from the nations.

So how does the Sinai Covenant fit into the Torah's story of blessing for the whole of creation? The strong Abram–Israel analogy invites us to ask about the manner in which the two quite different covenants function in the larger story, and to understand how the Sinai Covenant has a universal as well as national scope. The analogy draws the reader to consider the rich, broader implications of Israel's Tabernacle, priesthood, and sacrificial system for all of creation (cf. Exod 31:17; Gen 2:1–3). It comes as little surprise that Israel's worship system is rich in allusions to creation and to the Garden of Eden.[31] The Abram–Israel analogy, therefore, serves as a literary bridge binding God's concern for Israel with a concern for creation as a whole, indicating God's intention to bless the nations as well. By choosing Israel, God chooses creation.

The Abram–Israel analogy means that godly Gentiles play a significant role in the Torah's story of redemption. The analogy compels the reader to consider the significance of two Gentiles, Melchizedek and Jethro. They move onto centre stage on the eve of two of the most significant events in biblical literature: the making of the Abrahamic and the Sinai Covenants. Both individuals step onto the stage unannounced, and overshadow two of the Torah's leading characters: Abram and Moses. Both individuals bless the bless-er and the bless-ed alike, and are duly rewarded with special honour. These honoured Gentiles preemptively take their stand to praise God and bless God's people Israel as they ready themselves to enter into the redemptive covenants.[32]

Melchizedek and Jethro are the Torah's exemplary Gentiles who pave the way for the unexpected appearance of other honorable Gentiles in the Torah's grand finale. "O Gentiles, cause his people to exalt" (Deut 32:43).[33] Who are these Gentiles and why are they commanded to cause Israel to

---

31. For an excellent treatment of this topic, see Morales, *The Tabernacle Pre-Figured*.

32. Sailhamer, *The Meaning of the Pentateuch*, 371.

33. Of the five instances of the verb רנן in the Hiphil, two clearly have a causative sense (Ps. 65:9; Job 29:13; see *HALOT*). The causative reading of Deut 32:43 also clarifies the syntactical function of "his people" in the clause. "His people" functions as the direct object of the verb, and not as an epexegetical explanation of "Gentiles" ("O Gentiles, his people").

exult? To find answers to these questions, we must look to the larger context of the Song of Moses.[34] In Deut 32:21, we read:

> They [Israel] have made me jealous with what is no god; they have provoked me to anger with their idols. So I will make them jealous with those who are no people; I will provoke them to anger with a foolish nation.

According to this verse, Israel provokes God to jealousy by choosing and cherishing strange gods (Deut 32:16–18). In turn, God provokes Israel to jealousy by choosing and cherishing Gentiles. It makes most sense, therefore, to identify the Gentiles in 32:43 as those referred to in 32:21, i.e., non-Israelites who are divinely chosen to provoke Israel. Surprisingly, the goal of the provocation is worship.[35] At this momentous occasion at the end of the Song, at the conclusion of the Torah, these Gentiles, like Melchizedek and Jethro before them, stand at Abram/Israel's side, praising God for the mighty acts of redemption.

2. Is there significance to the point at which the two stories diverge?

Finding meaning in something that exists is much easier than finding meaning in something that does not. Why does the analogy between Abram and Israel break down? There are a number of possibilities. I would like to suggest three.

One reason the analogy breaks down could be the meaning of Abram's new name, Abraham. Though the promise to Abram is universal in scope (Gen 12:3), the Abram narratives are focused on the fatherhood of one seed, both in its individual as well as its collective sense (see Gen 15:4, 13–14). In Genesis 17, however, God reveals a new and surprising aspect of the promise. Abraham is not only destined to be Israel's father, he is destined to be the father of a "multitude of nations" as well (Gen 17:5; see 17:16). In other words, "Abraham not as Israel," because Abraham now represents Israel and the nations (Gen 17:5, 16).

A second possibility has to do with a shift in focus away from Abraham that begins with Hagar in Genesis 16 as it then transitions onto Isaac in Genesis 17. Of course, this explanation cannot account for the fact that Abraham continues to be the primary focus of the story until Gen 25:11.

There is a third, more likely explanation. The analogy between Abraham and Israel breaks down because Israel's behavior is markedly unlike

---

34. Deut 32:1–43.

35. This is likely how Paul understood the meaning of the Song as well (see Rom 11:11; 15:10).

Abram's after the making of the Sinai Covenant. The Hagar–Israel analogy marks a red flag that something changes after the making of the covenant. Of particular interest is the narrative material that follows immediately after the making of the Sinai Covenant. Exodus 32 marks a major crisis in Israel's spiritual life, a crisis that becomes indicative of their spiritual condition throughout the remainder of the Primary History.[36] The Golden Calf breaks the analogy between Father Abraham and his children because after the making of the covenant, Israel no longer behaves like Abraham (cf. Gen 15:5; Num 14:11; Deut 1:32; 9:23).

3. What are the implications for our understanding of the NT's figural reading of some of the Torah's narratives?

What are the implications of the Abram–Israel analogy for our understanding of the NT's figural interpretation of some of the Torah's narratives? Two passages come to mind, both of which have generated a lot of discussion because of the apparently creative ways the NT refers to the Tanakh. The first passage is Paul's interpretation of the Hagar narratives in Gal 4:21–31. In a recent article, Matthew Emerson argues for a far more nuanced, textually sensitive reading of Paul's allegorical reading of the Hagar narratives in Genesis 16 and 21.[37] He points to numerous intertextual parallels linking Hagar with Israel, and argues that Paul's interpretation demonstrates a careful reading of the Torah's narratives.

Though I make no claim to know exactly how Paul came to identify Hagar as a sign pointing to the Sinai Covenant, it is remarkable to find the sudden and unexpected shift from the Abram–Israel to the Hagar–Israel analogy just after the making of the covenants. In my opinion, the timing of the breakdown of the Abram–Israel analogy and the unexpected presentation of the Hagar–Israel analogy may shed some helpful light on Paul's figural reading of the Hagar narratives. Perhaps Paul's identification of Hagar with the Sinai covenant was mediated through the story of the Golden Calf. Hagar epitomizes the fruit of Abram impatiently trying to achieve God's promises (a son) through the flesh, a sin which is repeated when Israel grew tired of waiting for God's promises (the land) while Moses tarried on the mountain (Exod 32:1). For Paul, both Hagar and the Sinai covenant seemingly represent human effort to gain God's promises through the flesh. Whether or not I have correctly understood Paul's interpretive insights, one thing is clear to me: Paul's figural reading of Genesis, a reading in which characters serve as signs (allegories) for other characters,

---

36. Freedman, *The Nine Commandments*.
37. Emerson, "Arbitrary Allegory," 14–21.

is quite at home in a body of literature where literary analogy is essential to its compositional strategy.

The second passage I want to consider is Matthew's figural interpretation of Hos 11:1 in Matt 2:15. One of the implications of this study is the importance of literary analogy for our understanding of the meaning of the Torah's narratives. The Torah's narratives, by design, have a figural force. It is crucial to note that Matt 2:15, though possibly a citation of Hos 11:1, is also a clear allusion to the Exodus narrative. This is not Matthew's only allusion to the Exodus narrative. Matthew 2 belongs to a series of many individual stories which have been joined together to form an extended Jesus–Israel/Moses analogy.[38] Matthew 2:19–21 is a nearly verbatim quotation of Exod 4:19–20 (LXX/OG).

Jesus–Moses Analogy

Now when Herod died, behold and angel of the LORD appeared in a dream to Joseph in Egypt, saying, "Get up. Take the child and his mother and go to the land of Israel. For dead are those who sought the life of the child." So he got up, took the child and his mother, and he went to the land of Israel (τεθνήκασιν γὰρ οἱ ζητοῦντες τὴν ψυχὴν τοῦ παιδίου. ὁ δὲ ἐγερθεὶς παρέλαβεν τὸ παιδίον καὶ τὴν μητέρα αὐτοῦ καὶ εἰσῆλθεν εἰς γῆν Ἰσραήλ). (Matt 2:19–21)	Now after many days, *the king of Egypt died*. And the LORD said to Moses in Midian, "Go! Depart to Egypt, for dead are all those who sought your life." And Moses took his wife and his children, and put them on the donkeys, and returned to Egypt (τεθνήκασιν γὰρ πάντες οἱ ζητοῦντές σου τὴν ψυχήν. ἀναλαβὼν δὲ Μωυσῆς τὴν γυναῖκα καὶ τὰ παιδία ἀνεβίβασεν αὐτὰ ἐπὶ τὰ ὑποζύγια καὶ ἐπέστρεψεν εἰς Αἴγυπτον). (Exod 4:19–20 LXX).[39]

In fact, Matthew 2 is brimming with other allusions to the Exodus narrative: Herod–Pharaoh, the Magi–midwives, Jesus–Moses, etc. What is more, in the verses immediately following Exod 4:19–20 (the passage to which Matthew alludes) we find an explicit identification of Israel as God's son.

> Then you shall say to Pharaoh, "Thus says the LORD, 'Israel is my firstborn son, and I say to you, "Let my son go that he may serve me." If you refuse to let him go, behold, I will kill your firstborn son.'" (Exod 4:22–23)

Matthew's strategic allusion to Exod 4:19–20 was surely intended to "place the reader within [the] field of whispered or unstated correspondences"[40]

---

38. For an excellent treatment of Matthew's use of typology, see Allison, *The New Moses*. The Abram–Israel analogy further demonstrates that biblical analogies can be quite extensive, unifying many individual stories into a larger whole.

39. Wevers, ed., *Exodus*, Septuaginta.

40. Hays, *Echoes of Scripture*, 20.

with Exod 4:22–23. For the Evangelist, the Exodus tells two stories simultaneously, a tale of two sons coming out of Egypt.[41]

Matthew 2 also finds its place within a more extensive Jesus–Israel/Moses analogy. In Matthew 2, God brings Jesus out of Egypt. In Matthew 3, God brings Jesus through the waters of the Jordan. In Matthew 4, God brings Jesus to the wilderness to be tested. Matthew's three temptations follow the exact order of Israel's wilderness temptations, up to and including the sin of the Golden Calf, where Israel bows down and worships a false god, something Jesus refuses to do. In Matthew 5–7, Jesus goes up a mountain to give his Torah to his disciples. Finally, in Matt 9:36 we find an allusion to Num 27:17, wherein Moses delegates his authority to Joshua to go and conquer the Promised Land. It is likely not coincidental that in Matthew 9–10, Jesus also delegates his authority to the disciples, who are then commanded to go only to the lost sheep of the house of Israel (Matt 10:6). Matthew 2–10[42] follows Israel's story in Exodus, and does so by the use of shared language and common themes. Matthew's quotation of Hos 11:1 is appropriate because it cogently articulates the essence of his understanding of the entire Exodus narrative as a sign to the sons.

How did Matthew come to see Jesus's story in the Exodus narrative? First, the contents of Matthew's Gospel points to an author who knew the Torah well and would likely have been aware of the parallels we have highlighted here. Though he may not have been aware of the axiom "the deeds of the fathers are a sign to the sons" (מעשי אבות סימן לבנים) it is clear he was reading the Torah's narratives as signposts for the future. Second, Matthew's reference to the star (Matt 2:1–2, 9) points to the Evangelist's familiarity with the Balaam narrative (see Num 24:17), where we find an analogy between Israel's exodus with that of Israel's king (cf. Num 23:21–24; 24:7–9, 17).

Because literary analogy is a key feature of the Torah's compositional strategy, I find Matthew's interpretation of the Exodus narrative to be remarkably consistent with the Torah's own inner network of literary analogies. Matthew relates the story of Jesus to the Exodus narrative in a manner that shines light on the rich tapestry of the Torah's potential meanings.

---

41. Because of the J/analogy, scholars frequently refer to Jesus as the "True Israel," i.e., that Jesus replaces Israel. Given the fact that Jesus came to save his people from their sins (Matt 1:21), perhaps the Jesus–Israel analogy is not meant to show that Jesus replaces Israel, but serves as their greatest representative. For this reason, "Truest Israelite" might be more in line with the purposes of the analogy.

42. Matthew 1 functions much like Genesis, i.e., a genealogical trail that leads us from Adam to a king from the tribe of Judah.

4. Conclusion

Though Ramban may have overstated his case when he said, "Everything that happened to the fathers is a sign to the sons," in the case of Abram it is not so far from the truth. Almost everything that happened to Abram did in fact happen to Israel. By means of rare words, ungrammaticalities, and common themes, the Torah depicts Abram and Israel's story simultaneously. Abram's story is Israel's story in a nutshell.

Summary of the Abram–Israel Analogy

Scattering from a City of Bricks to the Land of God	Gen 11:1–9	Exod 5
Exodus from Egypt	Gen 12:10—13:4	Gen 43—Exod 14
Lack of Resources Occasions a Conflict	Gen 13:5–18	Exod 15:22—17:7
Victorious Battle over the Amalekites	Gen 14:1–16	Exod 17:8–16
Appearance of a Gentile Priest	Gen 14:18–20	Exod 18
Making of the Covenant	Gen 15	Exod 19–24

These stories have in common all the major elements of the plot. Abram's story is Israel's; Israel's story is Abram's story, but not in every way. The literary analogy breaks down after the making of the covenant, about the time Abram receives his new name.

I have presented my thoughts on the meaning of the extensive literary analogy between Abram and Israel: that it is designed, above all, to create a metanarrative wherein many stories unite into a single story that tells how the once very good creation will become very good again, through Adam, through Abram, through Israel. I have offered an explanation as to why it breaks down after the making of the covenant: that the Golden Calf narrative is the source and cause of this breakdown. Israel's behavior is radically unlike Abram's after their encounter with God at Mount Sinai. Abram passes the divine test with unflinching obedience and is commended as one who fears the Lord, a man of faith and credited with righteousness,[43] while Israel quickly turns aside to worship other gods and the wilderness generation comes to be identified as a stiff-necked and rebellious people.[44] Unlike Abram, they lack righteousness because they do not believe and do not obey God's voice. In short, the analogy between Abram and Israel is no longer fitting when Israel's stops walking in their father's shoes.

---

43. Gen 15:6, 22:1, 22:12, 26:5.
44. Exod 32:9, 33:3, 5, 34:9; Deut 9:6, 13, 23, 10:16; 31:27

Finally, I argued that attention to the Torah's own use of literary analogy offers a helpful vantage point for viewing the NT's usage of Pentateuchal narratives that are typically regarded as far removed from the literal sense of the original passages: Paul's interpretation of the Hagar narratives in Galatians 4 and Matthew's interpretation of the Exodus narrative. These NT passages are shown to be remarkably sensitive and careful readings of the Torah's story when seen through the lens of the Torah's own inner matrix of literary analogies.

Bibliography

Allison, Dale C., Jr. *The New Moses: Matthean Typology*. Minneapolis: Fortress, 1993.

Alter, Robert. *The Art of Biblical Narrative*. New York: Basic, 1981.

Bazak, Amnon. *Parallels Meet: Literary Parallels in the Book of Samuel*. Alon Shvut, Israel: Hotza'at Tvunot, 2005.

Ben-Porat, Ziva. "The Poetics of Literary Allusion." *Poetics and Theory of Literature* 1 (1976) 107–8.

Boyarin, Daniel. "Inner Biblical Ambiguity, Intertextuality and the Dialectic of Midrash: The Waters of Marah." *Prooftexts* 10 (1990) 29–30.

Clifford, Richard J., SJ. "The Exodus in the Christian Bible: The Case for "Figural" Reading." *Theological Studies* 63 (2002) 345–61.

Emerson, Matthew Y. "Arbitrary Allegory, Typical Typology, or Intertextual Interpretation? Paul's Use of the Pentateuch in Galatians 4:21–31." *Biblical Theology Bulletin* 43 (2013) 14–21.

Freedman, David Noel. *The Nine Commandments: Uncovering the Hidden Pattern of Crime and Punishment in the Hebrew Bible*. New York: Doubleday, 2000.

Garsiel, Moshe. *The First Book of Samuel: A Literary Study of Comparative Structures, Analogies and Parallels*. Ramat Gan, Israel: Revivim, 1985.

Grossman, Yonatan. *Abraham: A Story of a Journey*. Tel Aviv: Yedioth Ahronoth Books, 2014 (Hebrew).

———. "'Dynamic Analogies' in the Book of Esther." *VT* 59 (2009) 394–414.

Hakham, Amos. *The Chumash Shmot with the Commentary Daat Mikrah*. Vol. 1. Jerusalem: Mossad Harav Kook, 1991 (Hebrew).

Hays, Richard B. *Reading Backwards: Figural Christology and the Fourfold Gospel Witness*. Waco, TX: Baylor University Press, 2014.

———. *Echoes of Scripture in the Letters of Paul*. New Haven: Yale University Press, 1989.

Morales, L. Michael. *The Tabernacle Pre-Figured: Cosmic Mountain Ideology in Genesis and Exodus*. Biblical Tools and Studies 15. Leuven: Peeters, 2012.

Postell, Seth D. *Adam as Israel: Genesis 1–3 as the Introduction to the Torah and Tanakh*. Eugene, OR: Pickwick Publications, 2011.

Leonard, Jeffrey M. "Identifying Inner-Biblical Allusions: Psalm 78 as a Test Case." *JBL* 127 (2008) 241–65.

Riffaterre, Michael. *Text Production*. Translated by Terese Lyons. New York: Columbia University Press.

Römer, Thomas. "The Exodus in the Book of Genesis." *Svensk exegetisk årsbok* 75 (2010) 7–9.
Sailhamer, John H. *The Meaning of the Pentateuch: Revelation, Composition and Interpretation*. Downers Grove, IL: IVP Academic, 2009.
———. *The Pentateuch as Narrative: A Biblical-Theological Commentary*. Grand Rapids: Zondervan, 1995.
Sarna, Nahum M. *Genesis*. JPSTC. Philadelphia: Jewish Publication Society of America, 1989.
Schmitt, Hans-Christoph. "Redaktion des Pentateuch im Geiste der Prophetie." *VT* 2 (1983) 170–89.
Stanfield, Yohanan (Ian). "The Song 'Ha'azinu' and Its Presence in Isaiah 1–39." PhD diss., Hebrew University of Jerusalem, 2012 (Hebrew).
Sternberg, Meir. *The Poetics of Biblical Narrative: Ideological Literature and the Drama of Reading*. Indiana Biblical Literary Series. Bloomington: Indiana University Press, 1985.
Wenham, Gordon J. *Genesis 1–15*. WBC 1. Waco, TX: Word, 1987.
Wevers, John W., ed. *Exodus*. Septuaginta: VT Graecum, Auctoritate Academiae Scientiarum Gottingensis editum, 2,1. Göttingen: Vandenhoeck & Ruprecht, 1991.
Zakovitch, Yair. *Through the Looking Glass: Reflection Stories in the Bible*. Tel Aviv: HaKibbutz Hameuchad, 1995 (Hebrew).

3

Wisdom is Worth a Thousand Laws

Legal Insufficiency and Exception as Intentional Compositional Strategy in the Pentateuch

KEVIN CHEN

Union University

Introduction

THE PENTATEUCH DESCRIBES SEVERAL incidents in which Moses needs to make a legal decision but is initially unable to because of the insufficient scope of existing laws. Targum Neofiti to Lev 24:12 counts four such incidents: the case of the unclean men who could not celebrate the Passover on the designated day (Num 9:1–14), the case of the inheritance of Zelophehad's daughters (Num 27:1–11), the case of the punishment of the blasphemer (Lev 24:10–23), and the case of the punishment of the Sabbath-breaker (Num 15:32–36). Jacob Milgrom remarks, "The common denominator in these four cases is that Moses cannot resolve the legal problem either on precedent or on his own, so he seeks divine ... intervention by the sanctioned formal means of an oracle."[1] The Pentateuch also describes exceptions to existing laws, such as Moses' eventual satisfaction with Eleazar and Ithamar's abstention from eating the sin offering after their brothers died (Lev 10:16–20) and the provision of cities of refuge for those who kill someone unintentionally (Num 35:9–15; Deut 4:41–43; 19:1–10; cf. Exod 21:13).

---

1. Milgrom, *Leviticus 23–27*, 2112. Targum Neofiti (trans. McNamara) says that Moses "decided them in accordance with the understanding from above." Cf. Fishbane, *Biblical Interpretation in Ancient Israel*, 98–106.

The thesis of this essay is that these repeated displays of the insufficiency of existing laws and of exceptions to them are an intentional part of the compositional strategy of the Pentateuch. In other words, the author of the Pentateuch is attempting to show that existing laws are regularly unable to account for new situations that arise and that laws sometimes have exceptions. Thus, though laws are generally helpful, right judgments depend not only on strict attention to the so-called "letter of the law" but also to the particular situation (especially the motive involved) and to circumstantial divine guidance. In this way, these situations imply that laws alone are not enough—wisdom is also needed in order to discern the divine will. To modify a familiar phrase, wisdom is worth a thousand laws.

Preliminary Issues

Since this essay deals with issues such as wisdom, law, and narrative, it is necessary first to discuss these terms and to explain their relation to the present thesis and to the Pentateuchal passages under consideration.

Wisdom

Biblical wisdom is a broad subject and is defined by one scholar as "the exercise of the mind as a religious pursuit."[2] Despite its breadth, scholars agree on its key sub-themes: divine retribution for conduct, the choice between living responsibly or recklessly, creation, and citizenship.[3] Biblical wisdom is commonly associated with canonical "Wisdom Literature" of Proverbs, Job, and Ecclesiastes, each of which explores the theme of wisdom in different ways.[4] Nevertheless, Kidner and others note that all of them ground wisdom in the "fear of the Lord" (יִרְאַת יְהוָה) or a slight variation thereof (e.g., Prov 1:7; 9:10; 15:33; Job 1:1, 8; 2:3; 28:28; Eccl 12:13).[5] This healthy respect for the Lord can play out in one's life in a variety of ways, such as a departure from sin (Job 28:28; Prov 8:13; 16:6), a reverent awareness of final judgment by the Lord (Eccl 12:13–14; cf. 2 Cor 5:11; 7:1), honesty (Exod 18:21; Ps 34:12–14; cf. 2 Chr 19:7, 9), and humility (Prov 22:4; cf. 8:13, 15:3), to name a few. The foundation of wisdom in "the fear of the Lord" should be no surprise in view of other passages that describe the Lord as both

---

2. Berry, *An Introduction to the Wisdom and Poetry of the Old Testament*, 2.
3. Ibid., 4.
4. Weeks, "Wisdom in the Old Testament," 30.
5. Kidner, *Proverbs*, 59.

the possessor and giver of wisdom. Job 12:13 states, "with him is wisdom [חָכְמָה] and strength" (Job 12:13; cf. Prov 8:22–31). Thus, it follows naturally that it is he who "gives wisdom; from his mouth [מִפִּיו] come knowledge and discernment" (Prov 2:6; cf. Exod 36:1; 1 Kgs 5:9; Ps 51:8).

Scholars have found that this theme of wisdom can also be found in texts outside of the "Wisdom Literature" corpus. For example, Von Rad's seminal article explored wisdom themes in the Joseph narrative.[6] Likewise, the works of Morgan and others have explored this theme in the prophets, the "Deuteronomistic History," Esther, the Psalter, and the apocalyptic.[7] In the particular case of the Psalter, these efforts are reflected in the classification of some psalms as "wisdom psalms." Furthermore, the key phrase "the fear of the Lord" is found in Pss 19:10; 34:12; and 111:10 (also Isa 11:2; 33:6), where it generally carries the same sense as it does in Wisdom literature. Similarly, Abraham is characterized in the Pentateuch as being one who "fear[s] God" (Gen 22:12). Thus, Kidner aptly remarks that wisdom "is older than Solomon (though he gave it its greatest stimulus) and wider than the books we classify as wisdom."[8]

As will be discussed in further detail below, the theme of wisdom can also be found in the Pentateuch. For the purpose of the present discussion, the relevant aspects of wisdom are decision-making and the fear of the Lord. Just as one of the purposes of the Book of Proverbs was to impart instruction in doing "righteousness and justice and equity" (Prov 1:3), so Moses found himself in situations in which he needed to judge according to these ideals. Second Samuel 23:3 even describes righteous ruling as "ruling in the fear of the Lord" (מוֹשֵׁל יִרְאַת אֱלֹהִים; cf. Isa 11:2–3). Through repeatedly seeking divine help, Moses also demonstrated a "fear of the Lord."

Law, Narrative, and the Pentateuch

The Pentateuch is well-known for its abundance of laws. This has led many readers to view it as a book of laws or a law-book. For example, Rashi asserted that "the main purpose of the Torah is its commandments,"[9] and many have followed him since. As if to reinforce this view, the Pentateuch is often referred to as "the Law" in English translations of the Bible, the

---

6. Von Rad, "The Joseph Narrative and Ancient Wisdom," 292–300. Contra Crenshaw, "Method in Determining Wisdom Influence upon 'Historical' Literature," 129–42.

7. Morgan, *Wisdom in the Old Testament Traditions*. Cf. Day et al, *Wisdom in Ancient Israel*, 94–169.

8. Kidner, "Wisdom Literature of the Old Testament," 117.

9. Rosenberg, *Genesis*, 2. Original: למצותיה אלא אינה התורה עיקר.

Greek word νόμος being uniformly translated as "Law" (e.g., Matt 7:12, "the Law and the Prophets") and the Hebrew word תּוֹרָה likewise (e.g., Mal 3:22, "the Law of Moses"). However, such a view of the Pentateuch does not account well for Genesis 1 through Exodus 11, which contains very few laws. Indeed, this large portion of the Pentateuch is almost entirely narrative. If the Pentateuch is a book of law, why does it begin with such a long stretch of narrative? Moreover, this narrative does not stop with the giving of the first laws to the Israelites in Exodus 12. On the contrary, it continues to the end of the Pentateuch and always provides an overarching narrative context for the giving of various laws. This is true even for lengthy sections of laws, such as those in Leviticus. In these sections, the narrative may be fairly characterized as having "slowed down" considerably, but the important point is that the overarching narrative context is still there.

Thus, the Pentateuch is better understood as a "book with laws" rather than as a law-book.[10] Once this is established, certain questions naturally arise: if the Pentateuch is not a law-book, then what is it and what is its meaning? How do law and narrative relate to the composition of the Pentateuch as a whole and to the meaning that its author wishes to convey through this whole? Does the Pentateuch have a discernible structure, and if so, what, if anything, did the author wish to communicate through it? A thorough treatment of these issues is beyond the scope of this paper, but Sailhamer has dealt with them extensively in several works.[11]

For the present purposes, the crucial point is that the Pentateuch is not simply a law-book but a narrative that describes the giving of laws at various points in the narrative. If this is true, then the reader of the Pentateuch must investigate not only individual laws or collections of laws that were directed to the Israelites but also the author's purpose or intention for including these laws within the narrative whole. In other words, what role do these laws play in the compositional strategy of the Pentateuch as a whole? It is this very question that is being asked regarding the aforementioned passages that concern the insufficiency of laws and exceptions to them. According to Michael Fishbane, this insufficiency is well-known, "Students of biblical law have long noted that neither any one collection of laws, nor all of them together . . . sufficiently cover the numerous areas required for an operative and positive law code."[12] For Fishbane, this insufficiency provided

---

10. Sailhamer, *The Meaning of the Pentateuch*, 27.

11. Ibid.; see also Sailhamer, *The Pentateuch as Narrative*. Works of other scholars also show awareness to these issues to varying degrees, such as Wenham, *Story as Torah*; Clines, *The Theme of the Pentateuch*; Sprinkle, *The Book of the Covenant*.

12. Fishbane, *Biblical Interpretation in Ancient Israel*, 91.

an impetus for "legal exegesis"[13] and serves as evidence for "a much more comprehensive oral law."[14]

From the perspective of a compositional strategy, however, the question is what role the author intends these examples of legal insufficiency to play in the Pentateuch as a whole. It seems likely that the author is not merely reporting these incidents as some of the many that Moses encountered while leading the Israelites through the wilderness. Instead, the author intentionally included them as a part of his compositional strategy in order to say something about the nature of law. Rather than telling the reader directly, the author uses the literary device of repetition to communicate his point. By including multiple passages that contain repeated words and ideas, the author cues the reader into linking these passages together and inquiring into their collective communicative intent. The thesis of this essay is an attempt to answer the question: why did the author of the Pentateuch, in a book with so many laws, include these passages that demonstrate their insufficiency and exceptions? The proposed answer is that through them he wanted to communicate the superior value of wisdom to his readers.

Sailhamer on the Theme of Wisdom in the Pentateuch

Before considering these passages, it is constructive to observe the theme of wisdom in the Pentateuch from a broader perspective so as to provide framework and plausibility for the present thesis. As was mentioned above, wisdom themes are often found outside of Wisdom Literature, the Pentateuch included. This is evident through the appearance of the terms חָכְמָה and חָכָם, most frequently with reference to Bezalel and others involved in the construction of the tabernacle (e.g., Exod 31:2–6; 36:1–2, 4, 8), but also with reference to Joseph (Gen 41:33, 39) and the appointment of tribal heads (Deut 1:13, 15). Furthermore, as Kidner remarks, "some of the favorite wisdom concepts are in the Pentateuch, which opens with the themes of creation, knowledge, and life, and closes in Deuteronomy with fatherly exhortations not unlike those of Prov 1–9."[15]

Sailhamer goes even further and asserts in his article, "A Wisdom Composition of the Pentateuch?," that "the notion of wisdom is a central theme of the Pentateuch, perhaps even *the* central theme."[16] Like Kidner, he

---

13. Ibid., 91–94.
14. Ibid., 95.
15. Kidner, "Wisdom Literature of the Old Testament," 117.
16. Sailhamer, "A Wisdom Composition of the Pentateuch?" 25; emphasis original.

also sees wisdom themes at the beginning and end of the Pentateuch (i.e., Genesis 1–11; Deuteronomy 33–34), and he argues that their presence in such strategic locations shows the importance of the theme of wisdom to the Pentateuch as a whole. After referring to existing literature on wisdom themes in Genesis 1–11, Sailhamer discusses Genesis 2–3 in further detail. He points out that the phrase "good and evil" (Gen 2:9, 17; 3:5, 22) also appears in Eccl 12:14,[17] at the conclusion of Ecclesiastes. Likewise, he observes that the phrase "tree of life" is found not only in Gen 2:9 and 3:24, but also in Prov 3:18; 11:30; 13:12; and 15:4. In Gen 3:6, Eve took of the forbidden fruit after seeing that it was desirable "to make one wise" (לְהַשְׂכִּיל). Thus, Sailhamer remarks, "The central theme of the fall story is humanity's quest for wisdom."[18] He also sees wisdom themes at the end of the Pentateuch, in Deuteronomy 33–34. He notes that whereas the law was given in a special way to Moses by angels (Deut 33:2–3), the written Pentateuch was "the possession of the assembly of Jacob" (v. 4). It is a written source of divine revelation and guidance for Israel as a whole. Thus, Deut 33:4 demonstrates that the Pentateuch has a "focused Wisdom concept of the written Torah,"[19] much like that of Psalm 1. Another important appearance of the wisdom theme at the conclusion of the Pentateuch has to do with the commissioning of Joshua. Although this commissioning was already described in Num 27:18–21, Deut 34:9 refers to it again. Numbers 27:18 says that "the Spirit is on [Joshua]" (i.e., he is a prophet; cf. Num 11:25), but the wisdom theme appears in Deut 34:9 in its statement that he is "full of the Spirit of *wisdom*" (רוּחַ חָכְמָה). As a result, Sailhamer remarks, "The new leadership represented by Joshua at the close of the Pentateuch is thus characterized by wisdom, not prophecy."[20] This view of Joshua as a wise man is consistent with Josh 1:8, in which he is commanded to meditate upon Scripture (וְהָגִיתָ בּוֹ) so that he can become wise (וְאָז תַּשְׂכִּיל). Sailhamer concludes,

> Therefore, both at the beginning of the Pentateuch (Gen 1–11) and at its conclusion (Deut 33–34) one finds a deep interest in wisdom and Wisdom themes. The blessing of life, which was lost in the eating of the tree of knowing [28] good and evil, is regained by meditating day and night on the Torah.[21]

---

17. Ibid., 26, though in a slightly different form. In Gen 2:9, 17; 3:5, 22, the phrase is טוֹב וָרָע, whereas in Eccl 12:14, it is אִם־טוֹב וְאִם־רָע .

18. Ibid.

19. Ibid.

20. Ibid., 27.

21. Ibid., 27–28.

The importance of the theme of wisdom in the Pentateuch is confirmed by Ps 19:8–10. These verses celebrate the Pentateuch ("the law of the Lord") in six parallel lines, beginning with the well-known line, "The law of the Lord is perfect, reviving the soul." They also contain explicit wisdom themes. In language reminiscent of Proverbs, the Pentateuch is described as "making wise the simple" (מַחְכִּימַת פֶּתִי, v. 8). The Pentateuch is even referred to as "the fear of the Lord" (יִרְאַת יְהוָה, v. 10). This is an unusual title for "the law of the Lord," especially in light of the more conventional titles also used in these verses ("testimony," "precepts," "commandment," "judgments"). In calling it "the fear of the Lord," the psalmist has chosen a title that focuses on its message, which he evidently sees as centering on wisdom.[22]

The Case of the Unclean Men and the Passover (Num 9:1–14)

Having set forth the presence and importance of the wisdom theme in the Pentateuch as a whole, the aforementioned Pentateuchal passages may now be considered, which express this wisdom theme in their own ways. The first passage to be investigated is Num 9:1–14, which demonstrates the insufficient scope of existing laws concerning the celebration of the Passover (see Exodus 12).

In this passage, the Lord tells Moses to command the Israelites to celebrate the Passover at its appointed time, the fourteenth day of the first month (Num 9:2–3; Exod 12:1–6). The first Passover had been celebrated in Egypt, and this second Passover was to be celebrated in the wilderness. The celebration was to take place in accordance with all of its "statutes" and "ordinances" (Num 9:3). These instructions were given in Exod 12 and included taking an unblemished, year-old lamb on the tenth day of the first month (vv. 3–5), keeping charge of it until the fourteenth day (v. 6), slaying it at twilight on the fourteenth day (v. 6), spreading its blood on the doorposts of the house (v. 7), and preparing and eating it and other foods in a prescribed way (vv. 8–11). The importance of celebrating it on the prescribed day is highlighted in v. 14: "*This very day* [הַיּוֹם הַזֶּה] will be a remembrance for you and you will celebrate it as a feast, a feast for the Lord, throughout your generations; you will celebrate it as a feast as an everlasting statute" (cf. vv. 17–18). Indeed, it was on this very day (and night) that the

---

22. Clines connects this meditation on wisdom in the Torah in Ps 19:8–10 more specifically to the tree of knowledge in Gen 3. See Clines, "The Tree of Knowledge and the Law of Yahweh," 8–14. Likewise, Ps 111 celebrates the works of the Lord (including redemption) and closes with a commendation of "the fear of the Lord."

Lord brought the Israelites out of Egypt (vv. 41–42, 51). Num 9:5 gives the positive report that the Israelites celebrated the Passover this second time "according to all which the Lord commanded Moses," as they had the first time (Exod 12:28, 50).

However, some men did not participate in this Passover celebration. Num 9:6 explains that they "were not able to celebrate the Passover" (וְלֹא־יָכְל֥וּ לַעֲשֹׂת־הַפָּ֖סַח) because they were unclean (טְמֵאִ֗ים) as a result of contact with a human corpse. The original instructions concerning the Passover did not mention any prohibitions for the "unclean," and membership in the Israelite community indicated by circumcision seemed to be the only requirement for participation (vv. 43–49). Only later would instructions in Lev 7:20–21 forbid the "unclean" from eating the sacrificed meat of peace offerings. In Num 9, this regulation seems to have been extended to other sacrificed meats, such as the Passover lamb.[23] Perhaps with this in mind, these unclean men approach Moses and explain their situation (Num 9:7). They complain that they are being "held back" (נִגָּרַע) from participating in the Passover.

Moses is thus presented with a dilemma: should these unclean men be allowed to celebrate the Passover or not? On the one hand, these men could not celebrate the Passover because they were unclean. On the other hand, their complaint seemed to have some legitimacy, not only in their opinion but also in Moses'. The potential consequences were severe regardless of which option was chosen—eating sacrificed meat while unclean would result in being "cut off" from their people (Lev 7:21) and not celebrating the Passover seemed to unfairly exclude them from this festival. After all, celebration of the Passover by "all the assembly of Israel" (כָּל־עֲדַ֥ת יִשְׂרָאֵ֖ל) had been commanded by the Lord (Exod 12:47).

Moses does not know what to do, so he instructs the men to wait while he seeks the Lord for a solution (Num 9:8). The Lord's response is to issue generalized instructions that those who are unclean because of a corpse or are inhibited due to lengthy travel are to celebrate the Passover instead on the fourteenth day of the second month (vv. 10–12). However, those who do not celebrate the Passover during the first month and do not meet either of these conditions will be guilty of sin and will be cut off from their people (v. 13). Thus, these instructions make legal provision for two groups of people who are prevented from celebrating the Passover through little or no fault of their own. The original Passover laws are still upheld, with the exception that these unclean men and others like them in the future could celebrate the Passover on this alternate date.

---

23. Keil and Delitzsch, *Pentateuch*, 684.

In relation to the theme of wisdom in the Pentateuch, Num 9:1–14 demonstrates that existing laws, despite having been divinely given, are sometimes unable to account for new, complicated situations that arise. The limitations of these laws do not seem to result from an oversight of their originator (the Lord) but from the nature of law itself, especially as it relates to new situations. When the original Passover laws were given, little attention had been given thus far to the "unclean,"[24] and naturally these laws mention nothing about those who might be "unclean." In Num 9:1–14, a wooden application of existing laws would have unfairly excluded the unclean men. Perhaps sensing this, Moses did not immediately issue a decision but instead sought the Lord, whose answer made provision for their inclusion in the Passover celebration on an alternate date. In this way, Moses' actions serve as an example of seeking the Lord when faced with a legal dilemma. Moreover, it is noteworthy that the divine solution to this particular legal dilemma was more laws. From this perspective, this incident may serve as an illustration of the growth and complication of laws.[25]

The theme of wisdom emerges with even greater clarity in view of the strategic location of Num 9:1–14 in the Pentateuch. It is located just before the Israelites leave Mount Sinai in Num 10:12. Their stay at Mount Sinai, which Exodus 19 through Num 10:11 details at length, is finally over, and they have finally finished receiving the many laws given there. But despite having recently received so many laws, Moses and the Israelites immediately encounter a situation for which existing laws are of insufficient scope in Num 9:1–14. The strategic location of this passage just prior to the Israelites' departure from Sinai thus suggests the insufficient scope of the many laws given thus far. Apparently, there were not enough laws. Numbers 9:1–14 also functions to balance a recent instance of the strict application of law in relation to the redemption of 22,273 Israelite firstborn (Num 3:39–53). In that situation, the redemption of the exact number of Israelite firstborn was carried out through the taking of the 22,000 Levites and of a redemption price for the additional 273 firstborn remaining.

The strategic location of Num 9:1–14 is also suggested by what immediately follows it. The next passage describes the descent of a cloud upon the tabernacle (vv. 15–23). This cloud would appear as fire by night (vv. 15–16) and was a constant source of divine guidance for Israel as they traveled

---

24. The adjective טָמֵא ("unclean" or "defiled") does not even appear in the Pentateuch until Lev 5:2. Incidentally, the animals taken into the ark in Gen 7:2, 8 are classified slightly differently as "clean" (טָהוֹר) and "not clean" (לֹא טְהֹרָה in v. 2; אֵינֶנָּה טְהֹרָה in v. 8).

25. The reader might wonder if there could be additional legitimate reasons for not celebrating the Passover on the prescribed date.

through the wilderness (vv. 17-23). This passage dovetails with Num 9:1-14. Just as Moses needed situational guidance (in a legal matter) from the Lord, so the pillar of cloud provided situational guidance (in geographical matters) for the Israelites' travels. Whether for a short stay or a long one, they would travel if and only if the cloud moved (vv. 18-22). Likewise, just as the Lord spoke to Moses in order to guide him in 9:1-14, so Israel's camping and traveling under the guidance of the cloud are done "according to the mouth of the Lord" (עַל־פִּי יְהוָה; vv. 18, 20, 23). In both situations, this additional guidance was necessary despite existing laws.

The Case of the Inheritance of Zelophehad's Daughters (Num 27:1-11; 36:1-12)

The next passage to be considered is Num 27:1-11, which demonstrates the insufficient scope of existing laws concerning the inheritance of land. In this passage, the five daughters of Zelophehad, a Manassite, bring their case to the door of the Tent of Meeting before Moses, Eleazar, the leaders of Israel, and the entire assembly (vv. 1-2). They explain that their father had died in the wilderness and had no sons (v. 3; cf. 26:33). Their concern is that the "name" (שֵׁם) of their father will be "withdrawn" (יִגָּרַע) from his family because his inheritance of land will be given to someone else, probably another relative (v. 4; cf. 26:52-55).[26] The daughters of Zelophehad want the right to inherit their father's land, and they ask Moses directly for it (v. 4). Moses brings their case before the Lord (v. 5), and the Lord answers (vv. 6-11). He agrees with the daughters of Zelophehad and orders that their father's inheritance be given to them (v. 7). He also gives generalized instructions to the Israelites regarding the transferring of a man's inheritance. First priority goes to his son, followed by his daughter, his brother, his uncle, and finally his nearest relative (vv. 8-11).

The similarity of this situation in 27:1-11 to the one in 9:1-14 is apparent. Once again, Moses is faced with a legal decision for which a wooden application of existing laws would be unfair. Both the unclean men and Zelophehad's daughters had legitimate complaints. As before, Moses seeks the Lord for an answer, who responds with new instructions that would deal fairly with the present situation and future similar ones. The connection between these two passages is further strengthened through the repetition of the verb גָּרַע ("to withdraw or restrain") in 27:4 and 9:7.[27] In both situations, the divine decision is against "withdrawing" the interested parties

---

26. Levine, *Numbers 21-36*, 346.
27. This verb occurs 21 times in the OT, 12 of which are in the Pentateuch.

from their respective communities in some way. The unclean men are not "withdrawn" from their fellow Israelites who are celebrating the Passover, and Zelophehad's name is not "withdrawn" from his extended family. In other words, the Lord decides in both cases to include these parties rather than to exclude them through a wooden application of law.

The case of Zelophehad's daughters is picked up again in Num 36:1–12. This time it is the heads of the extended family of Zelophehad who approach Moses and the leaders of Israel (v. 1). They acknowledge the Lord's decision to give Zelophehad's inheritance to their daughters, but they raise the point that if these daughters marry outside of the tribe, then this inheritance will be "withdrawn" (וְנִגְרְעָה) from Manasseh and added to another tribe's inheritance (vv. 3–4). As before in 27:7, the objection is deemed "right" (כֵּן), and Moses responds with another instruction "according to the mouth of the Lord" (עַל־פִּי יְהוָה) that the daughters are to marry within their own tribe to prevent the passing of inheritance from one tribe to another (36:5–7). This same instruction holds for future women who inherit land (vv. 8–9).

In relation to the wisdom theme in the Pentateuch, Num 27:1–11 and 36:1–12, like 9:1–14, show that existing laws are sometimes unable to account for new situations that arise. In both cases, a wooden application of existing laws would have led to an unfair exclusion of the interested parties from their respective groups or the undesirable transfer of inheritance from one tribe to another. Instead, the divine solution made provision for the inclusion of both the unclean men in the Passover celebration and the "name" of Zelophehad in his extended family, and the preservation of each tribe's inheritance. Both passages also suggest that dilemmas should lead one to seek guidance from the Lord, who answers Moses both times.

However, the case of Zelophehad's daughters has an additional dimension because it is revisited in Num 36:1–12. Through this repetition, the growth and complication of laws is demonstrated with greater clarity because new laws are given not just once but twice in response to issues raised by the Israelites. In other words, the Lord's response in Numbers 27 did not sufficiently account for the potential marriage of Zelophehad's daughters outside of their tribe. Assuming that the Lord was aware of this, why didn't he give a more robust set of laws earlier? The biblical text does not directly answer this question. Nevertheless, what can be inferred is that the Lord was content to give laws that did not account for that situation and in so doing preserved the need for circumstantial guidance from him and thus for an ongoing dynamic relationship with him. In any case, it is practically impossible for a system of law to account for every potential situation fairly, and one that attempts to do so would almost certainly be lengthy, tedious, cumbersome, and more trouble than it is worth.

The case of Zelophehad's daughters also appears in strategic locations in this portion of the Pentateuch (Numbers 26–36). Numbers 26 marks a new section of narrative through the taking of a census of a new generation of Israelites. The previous generation also underwent a census (Numbers 1) but were sentenced to die in the wilderness because of their unbelief and disobedience (14:22–35). The census in Num 26 closes with the comment that "among these there was no one numbered by Moses and Aaron the priest who numbered the sons of Israel in the wilderness of Sinai. For the LORD said to them, 'They will surely die in the wilderness'" (vv. 64–65). The case of Zelophehad's daughters is introduced in Numbers 27 immediately after the census in Numbers 26 as the first thing that the new generation encounters. Thus, just as the previous generation of Israelites encountered a legal dilemma just before leaving Sinai and immediately after receiving many laws there, so the new generation encounters one immediately after being introduced into the narrative. Both generations in this way experience the insufficiency of laws at key moments in the Pentateuch. It was evidently an intergenerational experience. Moreover, just as Num 9:1–14 dovetails with the passage that immediately follows it, so does Num 27:1–11. Numbers 27:12–23 concerns the commissioning of Joshua, who, like the pillar of cloud and fire in 9:15–23, would lead the Israelites' travels after Moses' death (27:17, 21; cf. 9:18, 23).[28] The "Spirit" is in Joshua (27:18), and as Sailhamer has already noted above, his commission is revisited at the end of the Pentateuch, where he is characterized as being "full of the spirit of wisdom" (Deut 34:9). Finally, the revisitation of the case of Zelophehad's daughters in Numbers 36 results in its functioning as a sort of inclusio for this section of narrative (Numbers 26–36) that concerns the new generation of Israelites. This structural feature gives even greater emphasis to the themes of wisdom, legal insufficiency, and the growth and complication of law for the new generation.

---

28. Moses asks for someone who "will go out before them" (יֵצֵא לִפְנֵיהֶם) and "will come in before them" (יָבֹא לִפְנֵיהֶם), and "will bring them out" (יוֹצִיאֵם) and "will bring them in" (יְבִיאֵם). Though using different verbs (נָסַע and חָנָה instead of יָצָא and בּוֹא), the pillar of cloud is described similarly. When the cloud lifted, the Israelites "would set out" (יִסְעוּ), and when the cloud remained, "they would camp" (יַחֲנוּ). Furthermore, the LORD says to Moses regarding Joshua that "according to his mouth they will go out and according to his mouth they will come in" (עַל־פִּיו יֵצְאוּ וְעַל־פִּיו יָבֹאוּ; Num 27:21). This corresponds to the description of the Israelites and the pillar of cloud, "according to the mouth of the LORD the Israelites set out, and according to the mouth of the LORD they camped" (עַל־פִּי יְהוָה יִסְעוּ בְּנֵי יִשְׂרָאֵל וְעַל־פִּי יְהוָה יַחֲנוּ; Num 9:18, cf. v. 23). Cf. Deut 31:14–15, 23.

The Case of the Punishment of the Blasphemer
(Lev 24:10–23)

Having considered the previous two passages in which new, complicated situations demonstrated the insufficiency of existing laws, this essay now turns to the consideration of two passages that concern the punishment for a violation of an existing law. Whereas in the previous two cases exceptions were sought for existing laws, no exception is sought in either of the two present cases. Rather, it is the precise punishment that is to be meted out for the violation that is to be determined.

The first of these two cases concerns the punishment of a blasphemer in Lev 24:10–23. The offender was the son of an Egyptian man and an Israelite woman who "blasphemed the Name" (וַיִּקֹּב ... אֶת־הַשֵּׁם) and "cursed" (וַיְקַלֵּל) while fighting with another Israelite (vv. 10–11). This was a clear violation of Exod 22:27, "You shall not curse God" (אֱלֹהִים לֹא תְקַלֵּל), and Exod 20:7, "You shall not take up the name of the LORD in vain" (לֹא תִשָּׂא אֶת־שֵׁם־יְהוָה אֱלֹהֶיךָ לַשָּׁוְא). Although Exod 20:7 states that those who commit this sin will not be acquitted, it does not say precisely how they should be punished. Neither does Exod 22:27 specify what the punishment should be, though Exod 21:17 (and likewise Lev 20:9), which deals with the comparatively lesser offense of cursing one's parents, suggests that it should be severe: "The one who curses his father or his mother will surely be put to death" (וּמְקַלֵּל אָבִיו וְאִמּוֹ מוֹת יוּמָת).[29] Because Moses does not know how to proceed with punishment, he places the blasphemer "in custody" (בַּמִּשְׁמָר) until "the mouth of the LORD" (פִּי יְהוָה) is "made plain to them" (לִפְרֹשׁ לָהֶם; v. 12). The LORD's response is to have the entire assembly stone the blasphemer outside of the camp (vv. 13–14). Such would also be the fate of anyone who committed this sin henceforth (vv. 15–16). After the LORD gives additional laws concerning those who kill or injure a person or an animal (vv. 17–22), the Israelites stone the blasphemer (v. 23).

Although no exception is being sought here, the insufficiency of the existing legal code is apparent again, this time because the punishment for blasphemy is unknown. The existing code had specified that this was a sin, but it did not specify how it should be punished. In view of this uncertainty, Moses seeks the LORD for further direction, as he did in two cases considered above. He even wants to decide "according to the mouth of the LORD" (עַל־פִּי יְהוָה; v. 12), just as he did with Zelophehad's daughters in Num 36:5 (cf. Num 9:18, 20, 23). The LORD responds with instructions not only for the

---

29. Contra Milgrom, also citing 1 Kgs 21:13, concludes that "the death penalty for blasphemy was well-known," and that the issue was whether this death penalty applied to a non-Israelite or half-Israelite. See Milgrom, *Leviticus 23–27*, 2111.

present situation and future similar ones, but also more broadly for situations related to killing or injuring of people and animals.[30] Thus, the topics of the insufficiency of laws, seeking the LORD, and the growth of law appear in the case of the blasphemer as well.

The importance of the case of the blasphemer is elevated when it is recognized that it is one of only two lengthier narrative passages in the book of Leviticus, with the other being Lev 8–10.[31] Although the broader narrative framework of the giving of the law remains, Lev 24:10–23 is thus a rare section of Leviticus in which something happens besides the giving of laws. Indeed, in this book of almost continuous lawgiving, what happens in this distinctive passage is that the numerous laws given so far are implicitly shown to be insufficient because the punishment for blasphemy is unspecified. One is left to wonder whether there can ever be enough laws.

The Case of the Punishment of the Sabbath-breaker (Num 15:32–36)

The second passage that concerns the determination of punishment for a violation of an existing law is the case of the Sabbath-breaker in Num 15:32–36. While in the wilderness, the Israelites find a man gathering wood on the Sabbath, and they bring him to Moses (vv. 32–33). The Israelites had been repeatedly commanded to keep the Sabbath by abstaining from work (Exod 20:8–11; 31:13–16; 35:2; Lev 19:3, 30; 23:3; 26:2; cf. Deut 5:12–15). The penalty for breaking the Sabbath was death (Exod 31:14–15; 35:2). Did this man's actions constitute a breaking of the Sabbath and hence warrant the death penalty? Two passages suggest so. The Israelites previously had been prohibited from gathering (לְקֹט) and from cooking manna on the Sabbath (Exod 16:23–29), a prohibition that would seem to extend to the similar act of gathering (קֹשֵׁשׁ) wood. Furthermore, kindling a fire on the Sabbath was explicitly forbidden (Exod 35:3), and gathering wood, though not in direct violation of this command, was suspicious as an act of preparation to kindle a fire.[32]

---

30. For further discussion of the connection of these laws to the blasphemy laws, see Milgrom, *Leviticus 23–27*, 2119–21.

31. Milgrom, *Leviticus 23–27*, 2102, classifies it as "one of only two narratives in the Book of Leviticus," with the other being Lev 10:1–11. The frequent use of the *wayyiqtol* (narrative) verb form, however, begins in Leviticus 8 and continues through Leviticus 10. These chapters fit together since they narrate the consecration and failure of the priests. Nevertheless, Milgrom's basic point regarding the distinctiveness of Lev 24:10–23 still stands.

32. See Wenham, *Numbers*, 132. Cf. Weingreen, "Case of the Woodgatherer,"

Nevertheless, Moses is unsure of how to proceed with punishment, so he puts the man "in custody" (בַּמִּשְׁמָר; v. 34). The Lord's guidance is clear: the man is to be put to death, and his execution was to take place by stoning (v. 35). In the Lord's eyes, the man had broken the Sabbath. Even though there was no explicit prohibition against gathering wood, the intent of the law had been violated, and the man was held responsible. The immediately preceding context suggests that this man is being cited as an example of someone who commits a sin "with a high hand" (בְּיָד רָמָה; i.e., deliberately and defiantly) and is "cut off" (vv. 30–31).[33]

The correspondence between the case of the Sabbath-breaker and the case of the blasphemer is unmistakable. In both cases, someone is caught in a sin and brought to Moses. Moses then does not know how to proceed with punishment and awaits guidance from the Lord. Next, the Lord gives the guidance sought by Moses. Especially noteworthy is the verbal correspondence between Lev 24:12 and Num 15:34:

Lev 24:12	Num 15:34
וַיַּנִּיחֻהוּ בַּמִּשְׁמָר לִפְרֹשׁ לָהֶם עַל־פִּי יְהוָה	וַיַּנִּיחוּ אֹתוֹ בַּמִּשְׁמָר כִּי לֹא פֹרַשׁ מַה־יֵּעָשֶׂה לוֹ
And they placed him in custody until it was clear to them what was in accordance with the mouth of the Lord.	And they placed him in custody, for it was not clear what should be done to him.

These are the only two verses in the Pentateuch (and in the entire OT) that contain the terms פָּרַשׁ ("to be clear"), מִשְׁמָר ("custody"), and נוח (Hiphil, "to place"),[34] which leaves no doubt that these two passages ought to be viewed together.

One difference between the case of the Sabbath-breaker and the case of the blasphemer (and the other two aforementioned cases) is that the case of the Sabbath-breaker does not result in a legal precedent (see Lev 24:15–16; Num 9:10–13; 27:8–11; 36:8–9). It is only this man who is dealt with here (Num 15:35), and there are no additional laws given to declare the guilt of those who might gather wood on the Sabbath in the future. Perhaps such laws would have been inappropriate or unhelpful because they could have led to an unnecessarily pedantic approach to keeping the Sabbath. After all, if gathering wood on the Sabbath is forbidden henceforth, what

---

361–64.

33. Such an understanding not only fits with the severe punishment decreed but also with the serious failures of Israel in Numbers 14 and of Korah and his followers in Numbers 16.

34. The verb פָּרַשׁ occurs in only two other places in the OT (Ezek 34:12; Neh 8:8; cf. Ezra 4:18), neither of which contain either of the other two terms.

else is forbidden? The questions are seemingly endless.³⁵ Instead, the lack of a precedent here suggests that the point is that the intent of the Sabbath law was not to be violated. This emphasis on the intent of the Sabbath highlights the importance of wisdom in understanding this intent over against a detailed listing of additional Sabbath laws. To be sure, additional laws are given in Num 15:37–41, but they are of a more general nature. Israel is instructed to make tassels on their garments to help them "remember [וּזְכַרְתֶּם] all the commandments of the Lord" (v. 39), one of which was, of course, the Sabbath. Indeed, the Sabbath-breaker had failed to "remember [זָכוֹר] the Sabbath day" (Exod 20:8).

The Case of the Uneaten Sin Offering (Lev 10:16–20)

In the four passages considered so far, Moses seeks the Lord because he faces a legal decision for which the existing legal code does not provide sufficient guidance. In the cases of the unclean men on the Passover and of Zelophehad's daughters, complex situations gave rise to exceptions to existing law. The next two examples to be considered also concern exceptions. Though different from the previous four cases because Moses does not seek direct guidance from the Lord, these two examples and the exceptions they describe contribute to the general theme of the necessity of wisdom in reaching just decisions.³⁶

The first of these two examples concerns Aaron, Eleazar, Ithamar, and an uneaten sin offering in Lev 10:16–20. After the ordination of Aaron and his sons as priests (Lev. 8) and an appearance of the glory of the Lord (Lev 9), two of Aaron's sons, Nadab and Abihu, offer "strange fire" (אֵשׁ זָרָה), for which they are put to death by the Lord (Lev 10:1–2). Their father Aaron and their two brothers, Eleazar and Ithamar, are forbidden by Moses from mourning and from leaving the tent of meeting, on penalty of death (vv. 6–7). Moses also instructs Aaron, Eleazar, and Ithamar to eat their rightful portions of the grain offering and of peace offerings (vv. 12–15; 9:17, 21; cf. 2:3; 6:9; 7:10, 28–36). However, when Moses inquires about the goat

---

35. The Talmud attempts to answer some of these questions at extreme length in its tractate concerning the Sabbath (*Shabbat*).

36. Fishbane connects this passage to Lev 24:10–14 (the case of the blasphemer), Num 9:6–8 (the case of the unclean men and the Passover), and Num 27:1–5 (the case of Zelophehad's daughters). See Fishbane, *Biblical Interpretation in Ancient Israel*, 227. Likewise, Milgrom, *Leviticus 23–27*, 2102, connects it to the case of the blasphemer, noting that these two passages are the "only two narratives in the Book of Leviticus" and share "a similar structure." Both passages also concern a major sin.

offered recently as sin offering (9:3, 15), he discovers that it had been entirely burned up (10:16). Moses becomes angry with Eleazar and Ithamar because the sin offering was supposed to be eaten (vv. 17–18; cf. 6:19–23). Leviticus 6:19 states, "The priest who offers it as a sin offering shall eat it; in a holy place it shall be eaten."

Aaron's response to Moses is that he did not feel that it was appropriate to eat of the sin offering on the same day that two of his sons died (v. 19).[37] In other words, in spite of the Lord's instructions for the priest to eat of the sin offering, Aaron believed that his situation called for an exception. He even asks, "If I ate the sin offering today, would it be pleasing in the eyes of the Lord?" Aaron's rhetorical question shows that he actually believed that eating the sin offering in this case would *not* have been pleasing to the Lord, Lev 6:19–23 notwithstanding.[38] Upon hearing this, Moses is satisfied (v. 20).

The approval of Aaron's abstention from eating the sin offering as prescribed in Lev 6:19 is a clear demonstration of an exception to an existing law. To put it even more sharply, it was a divinely approved exception ("would it be pleasing in the eyes of the Lord?") to a divinely given law. This law was thus not absolute but limited, despite its divine origin. Because of the recent deaths of two of his sons, Aaron exercised his own judgment in abstaining from partaking of the sin offering. It was a bold move in light of the clear instructions in Lev 6:19–23, but he reckoned that eating the sin offering in this situation would not please the Lord. He seems to have weighed the competing claims of eating the sin offering and conducting himself appropriately in view of the deaths of two of his sons, and he rightly chose the latter. Rather than slavishly following the law, Aaron exercised wisdom, as did Moses with his approval.[39]

Cities of Refuge

The next example of an exception to existing laws is the set of passages that concerns cities of refuge. Although these passages do not deal with a specific legal decision, the provision of these cities serves as an exception

---

37. Fishbane, *Biblical Interpretation in Ancient Israel*, 227. See also Milgrom, *Leviticus 1–16*, 635–636: "It is apparent from Aaron's enigmatic response . . . that he did not change the rite inadvertently. He acted deliberately . . ."

38. This response seems to exclude the possibility that the tragic events of the day were so overwhelming that he forgot to eat the sin offering.

39. Laws were also added after this incident as in the cases discussed above (see Leviticus 11–15), but Lev 16:1 associates them with the sin of Nadab and Abihu, not the uneaten sin offering.

for existing laws against killing another human being. Cities of refuge are discussed in several places in the Pentateuch (Num 35:9-15; Deut 4:41-43, 19:1-10; cf. Exod 21:13).

The starting point for understanding the provision of cities of refuge as an exception to an existing law is the Sixth Commandment, "You shall not kill" (לֹא תִרְצָח; Exod 20:13; Deut 5:17). Although this commandment is often translated, "You shall not murder," a survey of the usage of the verb רָצָח in the Qal (as it appears in the Sixth Commandment and frequently elsewhere) suggests that this is not the best translation.[40] To be sure, it can be used with reference to murder (e.g., Num 35:16-21), but it can also be used of capital punishment (Num 35:30) and of unintentional killing (see below). In view of this broader usage, the sense of רָצָח in the Qal is more accurately translated, "to kill (a human being)," than, "to murder."[41]

The provision of cities of refuge had been foretold in Exod 21:12-13, which promises a "place" to flee for a person who accidentally strikes a person to death. This promise is fulfilled in Num 35:9-15, which contains the LORD's instructions to set aside six cities of refuge, three on each side of the Jordan. The purpose of these cities is to protect a person who "kills" someone (רֹצֵחַ)[42] unintentionally (בִּשְׁגָגָה) from being slain by the "avenger" (גֹּאֵל) before standing trial (v. 12). In Deut 4:41-43, Moses follows these instructions by setting apart the three cities of refuge on the east of the Jordan. They are for the protection of "one who kills someone, who kills his neighbor accidentally" (רוֹצֵחַ אֲשֶׁר יִרְצַח אֶת־רֵעֵהוּ בִּבְלִי־דַעַת; v. 42). Deuteronomy 19:1-10 likewise contains a charge to set aside the remaining three cities of refuge on the west of the Jordan (vv. 1-7; cf. Josh 20).[43] As in the other two passages, these are for the sake of "the one who kills someone ... accidentally" (הָרֹצֵחַ ... בִּבְלִי־דַעַת; Deut 19:4). Thus, although the Sixth Commandment is clear that one should not "kill" (רָצָח), the instructions concerning the cities of refuge show that "one who kills someone" (רֹצֵחַ) unintentionally is an exception to the rule and deserves protection. In other words, the motive matters. In fact, the close proximity of passages related to cities of refuge

---

40. רָצָח appears 40 times in the Qal, twice in the Niphal, four times in the Piel (2 Kgs 6:32; Isa 1:21; Hos 6:9; Ps 94:6), and once in the Pual (Ps 64:2). In the Piel (and thus the Pual probably also), usage does suggest that רָצָח means "to murder."

41. See the helpful discussion in Durham, *Exodus*, 292-93. רָצָח may exclude killing in war, however, since it is never used in military contexts. See McConville, *Deuteronomy*, 129.

42. The sense of the Qal participle רֹצֵחַ here is clearly "one who kills," not "one who murders," since this person has "killed," not "murdered," someone unintentionally.

43. Verses 8-10 state that an additional three cities were to be added "if the LORD your God increases your boundary," bringing the total number of cities of refuge to nine. See McConville, *Deuteronomy*, 227.

(Exod 21:12–13; Deut 4:41–43) to both listings of the Ten Commandments (Exodus 20; Deuteronomy 5) suggests that at least part of their purpose is to qualify the Sixth Commandment.[44] Along similar lines, the discussion of cities of refuge in Num 35:9–15 is in close proximity to the revisitation of the case of Zelophehad's daughters in Num 36. These consecutive passages dovetail with one another in their nuancing of existing law.

In contrast with the previous five cases considered thus far, this time there is no complicated situation that gives rise to an exception or the need for additional divine guidance. Instead, the Lord himself accounts for unintentional killing beforehand through setting aside cities of refuge. The consideration for motive in this legislation resonates with other laws that do this as well (e.g., Lev 4; Num 15:22–29). Indeed, the Lord tests the heart (Jer 11:20; Prov 17:3) and does not look merely on the outward appearance (1 Sam 16:7). The provision of the cities of refuge is thus a demonstration of the Lord's own wisdom.

Wisdom is Worth a Thousand Laws

The preceding discussion has highlighted that the Pentateuch, despite having so many laws, recounts several situations for which the existing legal code was insufficient. The four situations, which occur from Lev 24 onward, did not arise when there were still very few laws but after many laws had already been given. Two of these situations, ironically, concerned the punishment of serious sins—blasphemy and breaking the Sabbath. These were certainly not obscure concerns, but the numerous existing laws did not account for the situations that arose. Likewise, existing laws concerning the Passover and the rights of inheritance did not adequately account for the unclean men and for Zelophehad's daughters, and both groups were granted exceptions so that they could be rightfully included in the community. Exceptions were also granted to Aaron, Eleazar, and Ithamar because of the recent deaths of Nadab and Abihu and to anyone who might kill someone accidentally.

These examples serve to illustrate the inherent limitations of laws through their inability to account for every potential situation adequately. New, complex situations arose in the Pentateuch that warranted special consideration. The unclean men and Zelophehad's daughters would have been treated unfairly through a wooden application of existing law. Their respective situations, though perhaps less common, resulted in the granting

---

44. *Contra* Christensen, *Deuteronomy 1–21:9*, 99, who calls Deut 4:41–43 a "disjunctive element."

of exceptions. Exceptions were also granted to grieving family members and to anyone who unintentionally takes the life of another human being. If exceptions were granted for a divinely-given, lengthy legal code, then one would expect the same for other legal codes. Indeed, any legal code that attempted to account for every situation fairly would probably be unsuccessful, ineffective, and exceedingly cumbersome. It was already seen above how new situations often gave rise to more laws in the form of legal precedents.

Just as these examples demonstrate that laws are inherently limited because of their inability to account for every situation fairly, they also show how just decisions can be made. The giving of the law evidently did not remove the need for additional guidance from the LORD. On four occasions in which Moses did not know how to proceed, he sought and received such guidance. He demonstrated a "fear of the LORD" and was given divine wisdom. The case of the uneaten sin offering and the laws concerning the cities of refuge also showed consideration for situational factors like grief and motive.

If these considerations are received as a part of an intentional compositional strategy, then the author of the Pentateuch is deliberately highlighting the limitations of laws and the greater value of wisdom. This may seem counterintuitive in a book with so many laws, but the author is nevertheless careful to demonstrate these inherent limitations repeatedly and strategically in this book. Thus, right decisions are made not on the basis of laws alone, but with the help of wisdom. It takes wisdom to know what to do when the law is silent and when an exception should be made. This wisdom is rooted in "the fear of the LORD," which is naturally expressed through seeking and receiving divine guidance, as Moses exemplified. Wisdom also takes into account situational factors, such as motive.

This prioritization of wisdom over law, however, should not be taken as an attempt to drive a wedge between the two. After all, the law itself is "wisdom" (Deut 4:6–8). The laws concerning the cities of refuge, with their emphasis on motive, are an example of divine wisdom, as discussed above. Likewise, Gershon Brin observes that some laws make special allowances for the poor,[45] and thus have situational considerations "built-in." Similarly, Moshe Weinfeld has pointed out wisdom motifs in Deuteronomy.[46] Law and wisdom, then, are closely related. But they are not identical. The law is an expression of wisdom, but it is an incomplete expression (Deut 29:28). This is because wisdom is broader than law. Wisdom also includes the careful application of law to new, complex situations, the ability to recognize excep-

---

45. Brin, *Studies in Biblical Law*, 74ff.
46. Weinfeld, *Deuteronomy and the Deuteronomic School*, 244–81.

tions to law, and the ability to decide well when there is no law. Wisdom does not supersede law, but it encompasses and surpasses law.

Two passages from other parts of Scripture may serve as additional illustrations, starting with Solomon's decision concerning the two prostitutes in 1 Kgs 3:16–28. Having asked the Lord for wisdom in the passage immediately preceding (vv. 5–15), Solomon is confronted with a maternity dispute. His suggestion to cut the disputed child in two effectively revealed the true mother, but this was *ad hoc* and not based on an existing law. Indeed, there was no law for this situation, and Solomon decided in accordance with "the wisdom of God" (חָכְמַת אֱלֹהִים; v. 28). A second example deals with exceptions. In a dispute related to his disciples picking grain on the Sabbath, Jesus cites two relevant exceptions to law. David and his companions entered the house of God and ate forbidden showbread because they were hungry, and priests break the Sabbath by performing their duties yet are innocent (Matt 12:4–5; cf. John 7:22–23). As his justification, Jesus cites the intent of the Sabbath as being for the benefit of man (Mark 2:27; cf. Matt 12:12).

Along these same lines, Joseph Blenkinsopp observes that the prophets tend to focus on the essence of laws, "We also detect a generalizing tendency in prophetic preaching whereby the essence of the laws, and of the individual, itemized demands they lay on their contemporaries, is expressed in a brief and compendious way."[47] He cites Mic 6:8; Hos 4:2; and Jer 7:9–10 as examples. Hosea 8:12 might be added, in which the Lord laments that rebellious Israel regards "the many things of my law" (רֻבֵּי תּוֹרָתִי) as something "foreign." Given the situation, David Hubbard comments, "More law is not the answer."[48] Instead, the book of Hosea concludes with a call for wisdom (Hos 14:9). This emphasis on the limitations of law and of the surpassing value of wisdom can also be derived from the Pentateuch alone, as argued above. The Pentateuch is thus consistent on these points with the prophets, Solomon, and Jesus.

Conclusion

The Pentateuch contains not only many laws but also several examples for which the limitations of these laws are demonstrated, either through their insufficiency in treating new situations, the granting of an exception to them, or both. In four of these examples, Moses does not know what to do and subsequently seeks and receives the Lord's guidance. In two others, consideration is made for situational factors such as grief and motive.

---

47. Blenkinsopp, *Wisdom and Law*, 105.
48. Hubbard, *Hosea*, 152.

Taken together, these observations suggest that the author of the Pentateuch uses these examples as part of his compositional strategy to communicate the limitations of law and the surpassing value of wisdom, the beginning of which is "the fear of the LORD." Understood in this way, the Pentateuch is not a mere law-book or book of laws but a book that teaches wisdom through laws, to be sure, but also distinctively through their insufficiency and exceptions.

Bibliography

Berry, Donald K. *An Introduction to the Wisdom and Poetry of the Old Testament*. Nashville: Broadman & Holman, 1995.

Blenkinsopp, Joseph. *Wisdom and Law in the Old Testament: The Ordering of Life in Israel and Early Judaism*. Rev. ed. Oxford Bible Series. Oxford: Oxford University Press, 1995.

Brin, Gershon. *Studies in Biblical Law: From the Hebrew Bible to the Dead Sea Scrolls*. Translated by Jonathan Chipman. JSOTSup 176. Sheffield: Sheffield, 1994.

Christensen, Duane L. *Deuteronomy 1—21:9*. 2nd ed. WBC 6A. Nashville: Nelson, 2001.

Clines, David J. A. *The Theme of the Pentateuch*. JSOTSup 10. Sheffield: Sheffield Academic, 1978.

Clines, David J. A. "The Tree of Knowledge and the Law of Yahweh." *VT* 24 (1974) 8–14.

Crenshaw, James. "Method in Determining Wisdom Influence upon 'Historical' Literature." *JBL* 88 (1969) 129–42.

Day, John, et al. *Wisdom in Ancient Israel: Essays in Honour of J. A. Emerton*. Cambridge: Cambridge University Press, 1995.

Durham, John I. *Exodus*. WBC 3. Waco, TX: Word, 1987.

Fishbane, Michael. *Biblical Interpretation in Ancient Israel*. New York: Oxford University Press, 1985.

Hubbard, David Allen. *Hosea*. TOTC. Downers Grove, IL: InterVarsity, 1990.

Keil, C. F., and Franz Delitzsch. *Pentateuch*. Commentary on the Old Testament. Translated by James Martin. Peabody, MA: Hendrickson, 1996.

Kidner, Derek. *Proverbs*. TOTC. Downers Grove, IL: InterVarsity, 1964.

Kidner, Derek. "Wisdom Literature of the Old Testament." In *New Perspectives on the Old Testament*, edited by J. Barton Payne, 117–131. Waco, TX: Word, 1970.

Levine, Baruch A. *Numbers 21–36*. AB 4A. New York: Doubleday, 2000.

McConville, J. Gordon. *Deuteronomy*. Apollos Old Testament Commentary. Downers Grove: InterVarsity, 2002.

Milgrom, Jacob. *Leviticus 1–16*. AB 3. New York: Doubleday, 1991.

———. *Leviticus 23–27*. AB 3B. New York: Doubleday, 2001.

Morgan, Donn F. *Wisdom in the Old Testament Traditions*. Atlanta: John Knox, 1991.

Rad, Gerhard von. "The Joseph Narrative and Ancient Wisdom." In *The Problem of the Hexateuch and Other Essays*, 292–300. Translated by E.W. Trueman Dickson. Edinburgh & London: Oliver & Boyd, 1966.

Rosenberg, A. J. *Genesis: A New English Translation*. Vol. 1. New York: Judaica Press, 1993.

Sailhamer, John H. "A Wisdom Composition of the Pentateuch?" In *The Way of Wisdom: Essays in Honor of Bruce K. Waltke*, edited by J. I. Packer and Sven K. Soderlund, 15–35. Grand Rapids: Zondervan, 2000.

———. *The Meaning of the Pentateuch: Revelation, Composition, and Interpretation*. Downers Grove, IL: InterVarsity, 2009.

———. *The Pentateuch as Narrative: A Biblical-Theological Commentary*. Grand Rapids: Zondervan, 1995.

Sprinkle, Joe M. *The Book of the Covenant: A Literary Approach*. JSOTSupp 174. Sheffield: JSOT Press, 1994.

Stahl, Nanette. *Law and Liminality in the Bible*. JSOTSup 202. Sheffield: Sheffield Academic, 1995.

Weeks, Stuart. "Wisdom in the Old Testament." In *Where Shall Wisdom be Found? Wisdom in the Bible, the Church and the Contemporary World*, edited by Stephen Barton, 19–30. Edinburgh: T. & T. Clark, 1999.

Weinfeld, Moshe. *Deuteronomy and the Deuteronomic School*. 1972. Reprint, Winona Lake, IN: Eisenbrauns, 1992.

Weingreen, Jacob. "The Case of the Woodgatherer (Numbers XV 32–36)." *VT* 16 (1966) 361–364.

Wenham, Gordon. *Numbers*. TOTC. Downers Grove, IL: InterVarsity, 1981.

———. *Story as Torah: Reading the Old Testament Narrative Ethically*. Grand Rapids: Baker, 2000.

4

What's in a Name

*Shear Yashub and the
Sign of Immanuel*

JAN VERBRUGGEN

Western Seminary

Introduction

THIS IS, I REALIZE, a very popular topic to write on and to try to write something new or from a different perspective might be very hard and may even be foolish. The struggle in the interpretation of this passage has more to do with how it has been quoted in Matthew, and the problems that that quotation creates with the interpretation of this text in its original historical context.[1] Nevertheless, I am hoping to throw something new in the mix and I hope that this will bring some clarity to our understanding of this passage and hopefully also in the discussion of single or double fulfillment.

The Call of Isaiah
(Isaiah 6)

The book of Immanuel begins with Isaiah's vision of the LORD enthroned in his heavenly temple[2] and with the installation of Isaiah as the LORD's

---

1. Wegner, "How Many Virgin Births are in the Bible? (Isaiah 7:14)," 467.

2. See also the similarity in which the LORD is described as high (רוֹם) and exalted (נָשָׂא) and the parallel with Isa 52:13 the Servant of the LORD. The reference to a shoot and a branch which we find in Isa 11:1 is also picked up in the suffering servant section

messenger. As Isaiah encounters the vision of the Holy God, he realizes his own sinfulness and he cries out, "Woe is me, for I am ruined! Because I am a man of unclean lips, and I live among a people of unclean lips" (Isa 6:5, NASV) His confession is both personal and corporate.[3] He receives symbolic personal "redemption" through the act of an angel who touches the offending part of his body that he had mentioned (vv. 6–7). In the next verse (v. 8), a call goes out from the Lord for a volunteer to go out for Him and Isaiah volunteers. The content of his message to the people is not very encouraging. Isaiah has to deliver his message to the people who won't be able to comprehend it (v. 9). The aim of his ministry is even to render the hearts of the people insensitive, their ears dull and their eyes dim. While the message, if understood, would lead to repentance and restoration, at this time, the Lord does not want this to happen. Jesus also quotes this passage and states that Isaiah is now being fulfilled, as He preaches to the crowd in parables. We see here an example of a type of prediction that will even be even more pronounced in Isa 7:14, a prediction which has its real fulfillment in Messiah, but until He comes, the prediction reverberates with echoes in history. Isaiah, a prophet of the Lord brings his message of salvation and judgment, but the people are too hard hearted to comprehend it. How much more tragic will it be that when Messiah comes, the true salvation of the Lord, the people will still be too hard hearted that they will not understand the full extent of His message and ministry and will fail to submit to His authority.[4] Isaiah is startled with his mission and asks how long this deafness, hard heartedness will last. God's response to this question is not comforting or reassuring, but contains a clear judgment on the people and the announcement of the exile:

> "Until cities are devastated and without inhabitant, Houses are without people and the land is utterly desolate The Lord has removed men far away, And the forsaken places are many in the midst of the land. Yet there will be a tenth portion in it, and it will again be subject to burning, Like a terebinth or an oak Whose stump remains when it is felled. The holy seed is its stump." (Isa 6:11–13, NASV)

But within this devastating judgment there is also a first clear reference to the remnant: even a felled tree leaves a trace, so also after the expulsion of the people from the land, there will be stump left, and this stump is the holy

---

of Isa. 53 (see v. 2).

3. Isaiah uses here synecdoche, *pars pro toto*, where in the unclean lips stand really for the sinfulness of man.

4. See Matt 13:14–15; Mark 4:12; Luke 8:10; John 12:40; Acts 28:26.

seed, that will continue its allegiance to the LORD, and it is this remnant which will be mentioned throughout the book of Immanuel.

The Threat from the North
(Isa 7:1–9)

While it is unclear when this first encounter with Ahaz took place, it is clear this must be before the subjugation of Aram (Syria) by Assyria.[5] Judah, beleaguered by Aram and Israel because of its refusal to join them in their fight against Assyria, is greatly discouraged. So Isaiah is ordered to go and meet king Ahaz. Isaiah is expressly told by the LORD to take his son She'ar Yashub (שְׁאָר יָשׁוּב) with him. So, both of them stand at a public place to deliver the message from God to the king.[6] This message to the king is one of encouragement in which the prophet relays in no uncertain terms that the actions of these two kings will come to naught. Israel and Aram had been trying to install a new regime in Judah, a regime more inclined to their policy of hostility and resistance towards the rising power of Assyria. The prophet makes it clear through his message that the might of Aram and Israel is really the might of just two people, namely their kings and that these two kings are not invincible. The LORD then adds a time table, the first of three in the book of Immanuel, to the destruction of the northern kingdom and states that within 65 years, Ephraim will be too shattered to be a people. It ends with the perplexing statement, "If you will not believe, you surely will not be established," in which the prophet twice uses the root אמן with different *binyanim* which creates a word-play. So, while the message from Isaiah doesn't seem to ask for a clear response, the ending statement of Isaiah, seems to indicate that his message was not received in faith by the king.[7]

In this first passage, the premise that is expressed later on in Isa 8:18[8] is clearly established. The names of the prophet and his children are signs

---

5. The text just states, "in the days of Ahaz . . ." Ahaz started to rule as coregent with his father Jotham in 743 BC, and since this deals with the threat from Israel and Aram, it must be before the destruction of Damascus in 733 BC.

6. This public place, "the conduit of the upper pool, on the highway to the fuller's field," is also mentioned later on Isaiah when the three emissaries from Assyria came to Jerusalem to talk to king Hezekiah (Isa 36:2 = 2 Kgs 18:17).

7. Rice, "Neglected Interpretation of the Immanuel Prophecy," 221: "The political and spiritual life of Judah hangs in the balance. If Ahaz will not believe he will not be established (7:9b)."

8. "See, I and the children whom the LORD has given me, are for signs and wonders in Israel from the LORD of hosts, the one who dwells on mount Zion."

and bear part of the message to the people of Judah.⁹ In this light, I want to look again at the command given to Isaiah when God orders him to speak to Ahaz. Here comes Isaiah (meaning Salvation is of the LORD, or the LORD's salvation) and his son Shear Yashub (a remnant shall return) to give a message to the king.¹⁰ This is the only reference to this son of Isaiah.¹¹ Why did he have to come with Isaiah but to give a clear message to the king that exile is part of their future? Salvation belongs to the LORD, even if exile comes, since God will cause a remnant to return.¹² In his message also, Isaiah is encouraging the king of Judah to stand firm, in that the rise and fall of Judah is in the LORD's hands, not in the hand of these two kingdoms, who if one would analyze it properly, are really only two men that stand against the plan of God.¹³

---

9. I disagree here with the otherwise excellent commentary on Isaiah of Smith, *Isaiah 1–39*, 207–8, where he states, "Although Shear-Jashub was instructed to go with Isaiah, God never addresses the significance of his being there. Thus he appears to play a very minor role in the narrative. His name means 'a remnant will return,' which probably complemented Isaiah's positive message of hope. Since the story never reveals how Shear-Jashub's name was employed in this conversation, the most appropriate thing for the interpreter to do is to admit that no one knows how his presence actually assisted in communicating God's message to Ahaz." Isaiah 8:18 clearly states that the children are given as signs with the names of both of his children making up short little sentences that carry a clear message to the original hearers. Rice, "Neglected Interpretation of the Immanuel Prophecy," 220, further states, ". . . Shear-Yashub is vitally related to God's will for the king on this occasion."

10. Blank, "The Current Misinterpretation of Isaiah's *She'ar Yashub*," 15, wants to read it, not as an encouragement, but as a stern warning: "'No more than a remnant, a mere remnant' will return, will come back alive."

11. We do see the phrase שְׁאָר יָשׁוּב later on again but not as reference to the son of Isaiah, but as a phrase expressing that the remnant shall return (Isa 10:21 [2x], 22).

12. The name שְׁאָר יָשׁוּב can of course be translated in a number of ways as Irvine, "Isaiah's She'ar-Yashub and the Davidic House," 79, has demonstrated already: (a) A remnant indeed will return (to the LORD); (b) A remnant indeed shall return (i.e. survive); (c) Only a remnant will return (to the LORD); (d) Only a remnant will return (i.e. survive). Irvine takes it as a hopeful message and opts for (a). Killan, "Der Verstockungsauftrag Jesajas," 215–25, sees it more as a reference to (d): only a small insignificant number of people will survive. Others see the threat more against Israel and Syria, that only a remnant of their forces will return. See Day, "Shear-Jashub (Isaiah 7:3) and 'the Remnant of Wrath' (Psalm 76:11)," 76–78. Clement, *Isaiah 1–39*, 83. Wildberger, *Isaiah 1–12*, 296–97, sees a combination of meaning in the name: doom and deliverance, that although only a remnant will return for them there will be salvation.

13. I even wonder if Isaiah is not also sending a message in the way he uses the name of the king of Israel. The name פֶּקַח normally refers to the opening of the eyes, which is exactly what God has said will not happen. See Isa 6:10: "Render the hearts of this people insensitive, Their ears dull, And their eyes dim, Otherwise they might see with their eyes, Hear with their ears . . ." (Isa 6:10, NASB). It is also remarkable that Isaiah uses the name of the king of Israel (פֶּקַח) only once, but refers to him normally as

The Sign Given to Ahaz
(Isa 7:10–22)

In a subsequent message to the king, the king is offered a sign.[14] It is a sign[15] of his own choosing, giving him the permission to make it a truly supernatural sign.[16] He responds with the hypocritical statement, "I will not ask nor test the LORD" (v. 13).[17] While his response was supposed to reflect a certain piousness on behalf of the king,[18] from the reaction of the LORD we know that it only reveals his unbelief in the LORD. Instead of relying on deliverance from the LORD, Ahaz had put his hope on the king of Assyria.[19] So, the LORD then gives him a sign, which leads to the famous prophecy of Isa 7:14–16:

> "Therefore the LORD himself will give you a sign: The virgin will conceive and give birth to a son, and will call him Immanuel. He will be eating curds and honey when he knows enough to reject the wrong and choose the right, for before the boy knows enough to reject the wrong and choose the right, the land of the two kings you dread will be laid waste." (Isa 7:14–16, NIV)

Lots of ink has been spilled trying to determine the semantic range of the word עַלְמָה, and who this child is historically, but it is not my intention to rehash all the arguments.[20] I am just going to give you my position and move

---

the son of Remalliah (see Isa 7:1, 4, 5, 9; 8:6).

14. While not stated, the message is most likely delivered by Isaiah.

15. Smith, *Isaiah 1–39*, 211–212, writes, "a sign is merely a symbolic representation of something else and does not have to be miraculous."

16. The supernatural nature of the sign is expressed here by the merism, "Make it as deep as the deepest depth, or as high as highest height."

17. By itself it might not necessarily be hypocritical, but together with v. 9 that is already hinting at his lack of faith, the king is declining it because he doesn't believe that the LORD is willing or has the power to deliver him from the two kings.

18. Deut 6:16.

19. 2 Kgs 16:7–8, 10; 2 Chr 28:16, 21.

20. As to the possibilities of who this child is the following suggestions have been given: (a) The son of the king (see Scullion, "Approach to the Understanding of Isaiah 7:10–17," 292) and some even more specifically referring to Hezekiah (see Hammershaimb, "The Immanuel Sign," 124–42); (b) the son of the prophet (see Gottwald, "Immanuel as the Prophet's Son," 42). Archer, "Isaiah," 618, names Maher-Shalal-Hash-Baz as the fulfillment and further Wolf, "Solution to the Immanuel Prophecy in Isaiah 7:14—8:22," 451–454, sees the references to the scroll and the witnesses as a reference to the marriage ceremony, and marriage contract; (c) Immanuel is the remnant, and the mother is Zion personified (Rice, "Neglected Interpretation of the Immanuel Prophecy," 222–223).

on with my argument. I hold that the word עַלְמָה refers to a young woman of marriageable age:[21] most often this refers to young woman who has had no children yet, possibly even one who has not had sexual relations.[22] The word בְּתוּלָה refers to a woman who has known no man: most often this refers to young women. So, I do take it that there is a possible semantic overlap. Yet, I do not believe that Isaiah was thinking here of a miraculous birth,[23] where a virgin is found pregnant without having had intercourse with a man. The revelation of that miracle is left for Matthew.[24] What the LORD is saying through Isaiah, that as long as you see young women having children, even though you might be under attack from these two kings, you realize that you are not yet done as a people, and that God is still protecting you. As long as your young women get married and have children, you know that God is still with us, and that is why the child is named עִמָּנוּ אֵל "God with us." Too often we end the prophecy here, while vv. 15 and 16 form an integral part of this prophecy. So, in the second part of prophecy, the LORD again establishes a timeline: before the boy born to a young woman knows the difference between good and evil, the land of these two kings (Aram and Israel), will be cleaned out, forsaken. Here the prophecy ends related to the two northern kings. So, I don't take the prophecy to refer to one particular woman, but to young maidens in general who are able to get married and have children, this means that the nation will continue. The time line can refer to a period of up to 20 years when a person was considered able to determine between good and evil and was old enough to be counted among the warriors. So, from a time line of 65 years, we now go to a time line of up to 20 years.

From verses 17 onto the end of the chapter, the prophecy shifts to a prophecy concerning Judah. In Deuteronomistic language he announces

---

21. In agreement with the identification of whom the child is, some have opted that the עַלְמָה refers to the wife of the king, the wife of the prophet or to an undetermined amount of mothers who call their child Immanuel to celebrate the liberation of the land (see McKane, "Interpretation of Isaiah 7:14–25," 214) or women are crying for God's help in distress (Fohrer, *Das Buch Jesaja*, 102–103).

22. I take the definite article on the word הָעַלְמָה as being generic, referring to the class of "young women" than to any individual specific young woman. Gesenius sees the definite article being used here "to denote a single person or thing (primarily one which is as yet unknown, and therefore not capable of being defined) as being present to the mind under given circumstances.... (הָעַלְמָה, i. e. *the* particular *maiden*, through whom the prophet's announcement shall be fulfilled; we should say a *maiden*)" (GKC, 407–408).

23. Wolf, "Solution to the Immanuel Prophecy in Isaiah 7:14—8:22," 455–456. Wolf sees the word עַלְמָה referring to a girl soon to be married (450), but must mean "virgin" (455), but not that she was a virgin at childbirth.

24. Although it should be noted that the LXX clearly translates the term as "ἡ παρθένος / the virgin."

the devastation of Judah that comes to fulfillment in the times of Ahaz and Hezekiah. The acts of the king of Assyria will lead to a great humiliation: with the imagery of shaving, it is stated that the hair of the head, beard and legs will be removed by a razor, which is identified as being done by the king of Assyria.[25] What in Deuteronomy was a great blessing, namely that land was flowing with milk and honey, becomes here a judgment. Where there had been vines, there will now be briars and thorns (v. 23), because the people had been taken away into exile. The people who remain in the land, their diet will change. They will eat what they can get through shepherding, looking for wild honey, or through hunting.[26] Where at the present time people would eat all kinds of food staples, when the king of Assyria is done, people will be lucky to have heifer and a pair of sheep, because that is all that is left to produce food. Verse 22 gives a clear outcome of the devastation: everyone who is left will eat curds and honey.

I understand thus that this prophecy of Isa 7:14 has its real fulfillment in Messiah, when God really dwelled with us. But up until then, the encouragement of the people is that although tough times are ahead, even the exile, they know God will not abandon them as long as young women are able to get married and have children, and the nation lives on, even if it is just in a remnant that will return to the land, in a time of the LORD's own choosing. The prophet's second child is kind of an example of this, and as such he is again a sign that God is still with us.

Maher-Shalal Hash-Baz (Isa 8:1–8)

As a demonstration of the hope, but also of the certainty of God's judgment upon the land, Isaiah is first instructed to write upon a tablet the words, מַהֵר שָׁלָל חָשׁ בַּז "swift is the booty and speedy the prey." In order to attest to the truthfulness of God's plan, God summoned two faithful witnesses who are supposed to back up the truthfulness of what is written on the tablet, namely Uriah the priest and Zechariah the son of Jeberchiah.[27] Isaiah then approaches a prophetess.[28] Then God produced a second sign of the coming

---

25. The shaving of the head and the beard is normally a sign of mourning (see Isa 15:2; Jer 7:29; 48:37; Mic 1:16).

26. That is why v. 24 has the reference to the bow and arrow.

27. Wolf, "Solution to the Immanuel Prophecy in Isaiah 7:14–8:22," 451, sees them actually as witnesses of the marriage of Isaiah to the prophetess.

28. Presumably his wife; maybe he wants to demonstrate his faith in God, in response to the prophecy of Isa 7:14, that as long as young women are getting pregnant

devastation, by asking the prophet to name his child born to the prophetess in the same way as what he wrote on the tablet: *Maher Shalal hash baz*. The child is also a sign that God is still not done with his people, because again a young woman has given birth to a son. The nation continues to produce a new generation. This child is now used to give a third timeline, although a much shorter timeline than the ones that went before, probably to indicate the time that has passed since the last prediction, and this time indicating the time range for the destruction of Aram and Israel: before the child will be able to say father or mother, the wealth of Damascus and the wealth of Samaria will be carried away to Assyria (Isa 8:4). This time line seems to be limited to 1 or 2 years.

But the judgment on Aram and Israel has also ramifications for the life in Judah. God first states that they have rejected Him, the Lord who is metaphorically represented here by the gentle waters of Shiloah. Secondly, they have rejoiced in Rezin and the son of Remaliah. This is a difficult section. Who is doing the rejoicing here? Who is being referenced here with the phrase "this people"? The context seems to demand that we are still talking about Judah. Since in vv. 1–4 we find a clear prophecy concerning the destruction of these two countries, the rejoicing is most probably referring to the rejoicing over the destruction of Aram and Israel. So, verse 6 gives the two reasons for judgment, vv. 7–8 brings the actual judgment. In a metaphor of flooding, Judah is described to be flooded by the waters of Assyria up until the neck. This is probably a reference to the assault of Assyria upon Judah during the time of Hezekiah, when all of the land of Judah was taken except for the city of Jerusalem (see Isaiah 36–39).

Immanuel Again
(Isa 8:8–22)

The metaphor then refers to the land as the land of Immanuel (Isa 8:8). This brings out the constant contrast that we see here, and that we often find in many of the prophets: even in the judgment of God, one can see the promises of God and the hope in God. While they are being overwhelmed by the armies of Assyria, this land is still the land of Immanuel: God has not reneged on his promises and the name of the land, the land of Immanuel, testifies to the fact that God is with them and still faithful to the covenantal promises. In v. 9, we see a clear contrast with what goes before. Isaiah's reaction to the devastation that Judah will undergo is in no way a rejection of the people of

---

and giving birth in Judah or Israel, it is a clear sign that God has not rejected them as a people and that a remnant shall return.

Israel by God. He boldly challenges even the nations and orders them to be shattered and that any plan they might devise against God's people will not stand, because God is with them (עִמָּנוּ אֵל, Isa 8:10).

While vv. 9–10 are directed at the nations, vv. 11–15 are directed at the people of God, Israel and Judah. Instead of repenting and turning to God when they see the calamity that God has promised come their way, the people forget God's plan and promises, and focus on solely on the calamity. As the prophet clearly states in v. 13; it is the Lord who should be feared and dreaded. If they fear God, they indeed will find him to be a sanctuary, if they do not, then God will become a stumbling block towards them.

In vv. 16–22, Isaiah is making clear what he intends to do and he directs his disciples to do the same: namely, he will wait for the Lord and he will hope in Him, but at the same time, he orders the testimony and the law sealed. The order is probably to his disciples, and John Oswalt sees in this command a withdrawal by Isaiah from public ministry, because he had been unable to have a real effect in directing the king's actions in the conflict with Israel and Aram.[29] Isaiah looks back to all that has transpired, and he clearly recognizes that he and his children are signs and wonders or symbols from the Lord God for Israel. Isaiah's message and his name testify that salvation is from the Lord. The name of Isaiah's son "Shear Yashub" testifies that although the exile is coming, God is not done with his nation, and a remnant will return from exile. Isaiah's younger son's name testifies to the speed of the judgment that is coming upon the people of God.[30] Some have opted to see this pericope of Isa 8:16–18, as referring to Christ and his disciples. I am not inclined to do this for three reasons: (a) One would have to spiritualize the words in v. 18, in reference to the children, that this is really referring to the spiritual children of the Messiah. (b) Verse 17 seems to me more something that a mortal man would say, not the incarnate Christ; (c) I do not see any passage in the New Testament, referring back to these verses as being fulfilled in Christ.[31]

In the next pericope, there are differences of opinion as to who speaks these words. It is either the Lord speaking to Isaiah and his disciples or it is advice Isaiah is giving to his disciples. It presents at least a message to the disciples in both approaches, which explains the possible scenarios of how people might try to entice them to apostasy and it really describes well the majority of the people of their time who have abandoned following after

---

29. Oswalt, *The Book of Isaiah*, 235.
30. Young, *The Book of Isaiah*, 316.
31. See further Oswalt, *The Book of Isaiah*, 235–236, but contra Young, *The Book of Isaiah*, 316–17. Although in all fairness to Young, he does make it a hypothetical possibility: "If, however, the reference is to Christ . . ." (317).

God but instead are looking for answers in all the wrong places like mediums, necromancers instead of approaching the living God (v. 19). Isaiah's reaction is to affirm that the only true source of knowledge is namely God himself, here represented by the testimony and the teaching (v. 20). These inquiries will be of no account and will give them no answers, leading them to distress and hunger which will further infuriate them to the point that they will curse king and God (v. 21).[32] While maybe the king definitely has not been the righteous king that they had hoped for, instead of looking up in hope to God, they will curse Him, and when they look down at the earth, they only find gloom and anguish there.

The Future Hope
(8:23—9:6)

This brings us to a new pericope, which is in stark contrast with the previous one, the passage of the birth of the prince of peace. This is a well known passage which has been treated often and well in other places, so I will limit my remarks here. Still, it is crucial a building block for the understanding of how the proper nouns are being used in the book of Immanuel.

The conjunction כִּי connect with what was stated before, while the negation לֹא makes a contrast with what went before. The gloom of the previous verse is not final. While the people deserve the just result of their rebellion, God is not satisfied with that and shows here a work that he will do in an undetermined future time. When every human attempt to bring light has failed, God will bring light to an oppressed and a humbled area which has not been esteemed: the region of Galilee.

By way of a special clausal construction,[33] the contrast of what was with what will be is brought forth in the strongest possible way. The past gloomy condition is contrasted with the glorious work that God will do in the land. The usage of "darkness" and "light" in Isaiah, is always used in a sense of moral evil, distress, calamity over against moral good, righteousness and salvation. So, a lost people is really promised salvation here. The appearance of the light marks the change to the people's despairing situation by God who presents his light. Because of this light, there is now rejoicing, joy and gladness presented to us with a series of similes. Instead of depopulation the nation now increases.

---

32. Notice the paronomasia between the words עָבַר and the word רָעֵב.
33. Casus pendens.

In the following verse, the reason for joy is explained in three כִּי clauses: they rejoice because (a) God has freed them; (b) warfare would be done away with; (c) a child is born to "us."

The "us" is foremost the nation, but we will see that the salvation brought by the child is much broader than just the nation of Israel. Who is this child? He is definitely a ruler, (see the references to kingdom, government, and throne) but he is not called a king. In our text, he is presented as a child. But the language used for this child, makes it clear that he is not a mere human. This is clearly the eschatological figure, the Messiah.[34] This figure will experience a human birth. But looking at the epitaph's one must also conclude that the person is also divine: he is called a wonderful counselor (פֶּלֶא יוֹעֵץ) but only God does פֶּלֶא. Throughout the book of Isaiah, human wisdom is derided, insufficient to give them counsel which leads to salvation (1:26; 3:3; 5:21; 19:11–15). By contrast, this child will give wonderful counsel, counsel which is divine, beyond the merely human counsel. Further he is called אֵל גִּבּוֹר, a term that is only used in the Tanakh to describe the God of Israel.[35] He is called אֲבִיעַד. Many kings claim to be father to their people, but this royal person is different. This person's fatherhood is claimed to be forever. שַׂר שָׁלוֹם is the climax of the titles. He is a king who will deal differently with his people. While he will be a valiant warrior, this child will also be a king, who establishes peace, who brings reconciliation between God and man and man and man (Isa 53:5; 57:19; 66:12). In the last verse of this pericope, the nature of the child is further revealed by what he will do: His government will increase and to the peace of his rule is no end.[36] He will reign from David's throne with justice and righteousness forever. These are incredible statements that seem to be very much out of place if we are dealing with a mere human ruler. Again this is a clear indication that this child, this ruler is an eschatological figure. Lastly, Isaiah identifies the agent who will establish and sustain the son's coming kingdom: קִנְאַת יְהוָה צְבָאוֹת תַּעֲשֶׂה־זֹּאת "the zeal of the LORD of Hosts will accomplish this" (Isa 9:6). The only other place where this idea of the zeal of the LORD is mentioned again we find again a clear reference to the remnant of God's people (Isa 37:32).[37]

The contrast with the children mentioned in chapter 8, or even the echo of Isa 7:14, promises deliverance from contemporary oppression. The deliverance brought about here, is worded in much stronger terms and

---

34. At least one witness, Targum Jonathan, identifies him so explicitly.

35. Cf. Deut 10:17; Neh 9:32; Isa 9:5; 10:21; Jer 32:18.

36. Look at the incredible peace depicted in Isa 11:1ff.

37. This phrase is of course also found in 2 Kgs 19:31 although the consonantal text is a little different as it is marked with a Ketib-Qere note.

seems to indicate an ultimate deliverance which will never end. It seems then that the prophecy of 7:14 has its ultimate referent in this child, while all the other children were just echoes or shadows of the real one to come who will really deliver his people. Again, the names of the child are the window into the plan of God. The names declare to us what He really is planning to do. This child delivers his people in a much more complete manner than what was envisioned in 8:3. This promised child will be mentioned again in 11:1.

Back to the Present
(Isa 9:7—10:34)

In the rest of chapter 9 and the first four verses of chapter 10, the Lord is announcing clear judgment again on Israel. While their society is falling apart, they boastfully claim they will rebuild (vv. 9–10). So, the Lord will use the Arameans and the Philistines to devour Israel (vv. 11–12), but in spite of this, Israel does not repent or turn back and seek the Lord (v. 13). With the same imagery as he had used in Deuteronomy, the Lord promises that Israel will be cut down: both the head (the elder and honorable man) and the tail (the prophet who teaches falsehood) (vv. 14–16).[38] Even the weak of society will undergo judgment since not even they are following the Lord, since sin has spread like a cancer in this society (vv. 17–19) even encompassing the orphan and the widow. The end result is a society upon which the wrath of God rests and from which God has withdrawn his gracious influence. This is revealed in the fact that this society devours itself as expressed in vv. 18–21: wickedness burns like a fire . . . no man spares his brother . . . each of them eats the flesh of his own arm . . . Manasseh devours Ephraim, and Ephraim Manasseh. The passage makes then a link to the next pericope: both will turn against Judah, which is really the focus in chapter 10 from v. 5ff. But first we have in the beginning of chapter 10 (vv. 1–4), a woe is expressed over those who oppress the helpless: the poor, the oppressed, the widow and the orphans are especially named.

The focus then shift to Judah and Jerusalem but there is still a clear connection with the previous section, in that this new section again starts with a woe. This new woe focusses on Assyria, the country on whom Judah really had built their hopes. In v. 5, we clearly see an affirmation, that actually, instead of Assyria being the deliverer of Judah, first Assyria is used by God to express his indignation with Judah. But Assyria goes beyond what God had sent them to do, namely to humble the nation, it sets out to destroy

---

38. See Deut 28:13; 28:44.

the nation of Judah. It also became prideful and thought that it had accomplished all the conquests by its own strength (vv. 7–11). God therefore also pronounces judgment upon Assyria (vv. 12–19). After the judgment of Assyria, the restoration of Israel will take place by a remnant, expressed by the word שְׁאָר, a remnant that has now learned to trust in God and not in men (v. 20). The return of the remnant (שְׁאָר יָשׁוּב) is explicitly repeated in v. 21 and v. 22. So, in v. 20 we have שְׁאָר יִשְׂרָאֵל, in v. 21 we have שְׁאָר יָשׁוּב and שְׁאָר יַעֲקֹב who will return to the אֵל גִּבּוֹר, and in v. 22 we find again the phrase שְׁאָר יָשׁוּב. We will find one more reference to the remnant after the Messianic passage of chapter 11 referring to the return a second time from the exile by the LORD as the remnant of his people שְׁאָר עַמּוֹ. The references to remnant are always filled with double entendre: on the one hand, it is stressing that the people are not finished; on the other it is communicating that only a small number has survived the period of judgment that God has allowed to come over his people (see v. 22). It is meant to teach them that they should not fear foreign nations who are often used by God to discipline his people, but they should fear the God of heaven and earth who has brought these foreign kings upon them: it is a sign of His anger but his Anger is just for a moment (v. 25). Discussions vary as to how to take vv. 28–34. Does this refer to Assyria or Judah? If it refers to Judah, then the imagery of being cut down like tree connects well with the imagery of the shoot that comes up in chapter 11. But even if it does not refer to Judah, but to Assyria, there is similar imagery used here: the cutting of the tree as a referent to the destruction of Assyria flows into the imagery of God's salvation plan for all the nations through the shoot of Jesse (11:1).

The Shoot of Jesse (Isa 11:1–16)

What we find in chapter 11 is again a remarkable description of a young, delicate beginning, through which God will work a mighty act of salvation. He is named a shoot (חֹטֶר) or a blossom (נֵצֶר) which will bear fruit. Isaiah indicates that a shoot will spring from the root of Jesse and a branch from that root will bear fruit. This probably refers back to Isa 4:2 and its reference to the Branch of the LORD. The clear reference to the line of David comports well with the reference to the throne and kingdom of David in Isa 9:6. The use of some of the same ideas in Isa 53:2[39] may serve to connect this theme to the idea of the suffering Servant. His endowment with God's Spirit, His

---

39. "For He grew up before Him like a tender shoot, And like a root out of parched ground" (Isa 53:2).

connection with wisdom, knowledge and the fear of the LORD lead to many other Messianic ties and passages (e.g. Isa 61:1, 48:16; Joel 3:1[2:28]; Jer 23:5) and clear eschatological settings (see Isa 2:4; Mic 4:3; Isa 9:7) of a righteous ruler who will rule as kings were supposed to rule: taking care of the poor, the weak and the afflicted of the earth and who will judge the wicked of the earth and give them their due (Ps 2:9), because he is a holy warrior (Isa 59:17) who slays the wicked. His actions will lead into a supernatural peace (Isa 65:25; Ezek 34:25; Hos 2:18). This supernatural peace has it origin in Israel but its reach is worldwide (Isa 11:9). The whole earth will be full of the knowledge of the LORD: this is clearly how it was in the beginning, when God was walking with man. The nations will rally to Him. His resting place will be glorious. Again the return from exile is being mentioned for the remnant of his people (Isa 11:11): the remnants of both Judah and Israel are brought back and the enmity between the two nations will cease (v. 13). The נֵצֶר (shoot) will cause no more יָצֹר (harassment) between Judah and Ephraim. The remnant of Israel is again mentioned in v. 16 again with the phrase the remnant of his people, again stressing that a remnant has survived but it is only a remnant.

Isaiah and Immanuel
(Isa 12:1–6)

The book of Immanuel ends in chapter 12 with a song of thanksgiving and praise. The remnant is really thanking God that although He was angry with them, His anger has turned away and in v. 2 we read that The LORD has become my salvation (יְשׁוּעָה) which is exactly what the name of Isaiah is expressing: Salvation belongs to the LORD and it ends in v. 6 with the words for "great in your midst is the Holy One of Israel" which is really saying, indeed God is with us, עִמָּנוּ אֵל. This song of thanksgiving, praise and faith is what we had expected king Ahaz to say when he was offered a clear sign of God's sure deliverance.

Conclusion

In this book of Immanuel, Isaiah and his children are signs to the nation: on the one hand there is judgment coming, through the exile. On the other hand, God is not done with his people. He remains their salvation and a remnant will return from exile. Their ultimate salvation resides in this eschatological figure, this prince of peace who will reign over them with righteousness and justice. In this figure, they will truly realize that God is with them. Then they will indeed break forth in thanksgiving and say,

> I will give thanks to You, O Lord; for although You were angry with me, Your anger is turned away, And You comfort me. ² "Behold, God is my salvation, I will trust and not be afraid; For the Lord GOD is my strength and song, And He has become my salvation." ³ Therefore you will joyously draw water from the springs of salvation. ⁴ And in that day you will say, "Give thanks to the Lord, call on His name. Make known His deeds among the peoples; Make them remember that His name is exalted." ⁵ Praise the Lord in song, for He has done excellent things; Let this be known throughout the earth. ⁶ Cry aloud and shout for joy, O inhabitant of Zion, for great in your midst is the Holy One of Israel. (Isa 12:1–6)

Bibliography

Archer, Gleason. "Isaiah." In *Wycliffe Bible Commentary*, edited by Everett Harrison and Charles F. Pfeiffer, 605–54. Chicago: Moody, 1990.

Blank, Sheldon H. "The Current Misinterpretation of Isaiah's *She'ar Yashub*." *JBL* 57 (1948) 211–15.

Clements, R.E. *Isaiah 1–39*. New Century Bible. Grand Rapids: Eerdmans, 1981.

Day, John. "Shear-Jashub (Isaiah 7:3) and 'the Remnant of Wrath' (Psalm 76:11)." *VT* 31 (1981) 76–78.

Fohrer, Georg. *Das Buch Jesaja*. Vol. 1. Zürcher Bibelkommentare. Zurich: Zwingli, 1960.

Gesenius, W. *Gesenius' Hebrew Grammar*. Edited by E. Kautzsch. Translated by A. E. Cowley. 2nd ed. Oxford: Clarendon, 1910.

Gottwald, Norman K. "Immanuel as the Prophet's Son." *VT* 8 (1958) 36–47.

Hammershaimb, Erling. "The Immanuel Sign." *Studia theologica* 3 (1951) 124–42.

Irvine, Stuart A. "Isaiah's She'ar-Yashub and the Davidic House." *Biblische Zeitschrift* 37 (1993) 78–88.

Killan, R. "Der Verstockungsauftrag Jesajas." In *Bausteine biblischer Theologie: Festgabe für G. Johannes Botterweck zum 60. Geburtstag*, edited by Heinz-Josef Fabry, 215–25. Bonner biblische Beiträge 50 Bonn: Hanstein, 1977.

McKane, William. "Interpretation of Isaiah 7:14–25." *VT* 17 (1967) 208–19.

Oswalt, John. *The Book of Isaiah, Chapters 1–39*. NICOT. Grand Rapids: Eerdmans, 1986.

Rice, Gene. "Neglected Interpretation of the Immanuel Prophecy." *ZAW* 90 (1978) 220–27.

Scullion, John J. "Approach to the Understanding of Isaiah 7:10–17." *JBL* 87 (1968) 288–300.

Smith, Gary. *Isaiah 1–39*. The New American Commentary. Nashville: Broadman & Holman, 2007.

Wegner, Paul. "How Many Virgin Births Are in the Bible? (Isaiah 7:14): A Prophetic Pattern Approach." *JBL* 54 (2011) 467–84.

Wildberger, Hans. *Isaiah 1–12*. Translated by Thomas H. Trapp. Continental Commentaries. Minneapolis: Fortress, 1991.

Wolf, Herbert Martin. "Solution to the Immanuel Prophecy in Isaiah 7:14–8:22." *JBL* 91 (1972) 449–56.

Young, Edward J. *The Book of Isaiah*. Vol. 1. Grand Rapids: Eerdmans, 1992.

5

Persuasion and Allusion

The Rhetoric of Text-Referencing in Ezekiel

Michael A. Lyons

Simpson University

Introduction[1]

The book of Ezekiel is a fruitful area for the study of techniques for persuasion in communication.[2] Indeed, the prophet after whom the book is named is depicted as one who attempts to persuade his audience: his contemporaries describe him as one who uses tropes (משלים, Ezek 21:5), and they gather to hear his speeches like they would the love-songs of a popular singer—but fail to act upon what he says (Ezek 33:30–32). Of course, this literary depiction of rejection is itself an argument, one that is meant to persuade the *reader* of the book.

The rhetorical goals and techniques of the prophet Ezekiel and of the book that bears his name have received significant attention in the last thirty-five years. This focus can be traced back to Michael Fox's 1980 article

---

1. It gives me great pleasure to dedicate this essay to John Sailhamer, who introduced me to the study of Biblical Hebrew, innerbiblical text-referencing, and the history of interpretation.

2. Dale Patrick and Allen Scult define rhetoric as "the means by which a text establishes and manages its relationship to its audience in order to achieve a particular effect"; see Patrick and Scult, *Rhetoric*, 12. Compare Michael V. Fox: "Rhetoric is persuasive discourse (persuasive in intent if not in accomplishment). Rhetorical criticism may be defined first of all as the examination and evaluation of such discourse for the nature and quality of its suasive force"; Fox, "Ezekiel's Vision," 2.

on the rhetoric of Ezekiel's vision of the valley of bones,[3] and numerous other studies have been produced since then.[4] Most recently, Dalit Rom-Shiloni has examined the rhetoric of communal exclusion in the exilic and post-exilic period. Her analysis includes a description of how the book of Ezekiel functions as a response to the Jerusalemites who were marginalizing those deported in 597 BCE.[5] Yet another way in which the rhetorical function of prophetic speech and literature is being studied is in the application of trauma theory.[6] It is increasingly appreciated that the prophetic books represent an attempt to grapple with the trauma of deportation and resettlement, provide answers to the questions arising from this trauma (Why did this happen to us? What is the status of our relationship with Yhwh?), and instill hope for the future.[7] Still, there is much room for further research.

The question I would like to answer in this essay is: How does Ezekiel's attempt to persuade his audience influence the way he alludes to earlier traditional priestly material? Specifically, how do his rhetorical goals affect his selection and modification of locutions from the Holiness Code (Leviticus 17–26)? By "allusion" I mean instances where an author deliberately uses material from another literary work without overt mention of the act of referencing, the title of the literary work referenced, or the name of its author.[8] Of course, while the relationship between the Holiness Code and Ezekiel is widely recognized, the direction of dependence is a contested issue. I have addressed this matter elsewhere, and in this essay I will take the position that Ezekiel is borrowing from the Holiness Code.[9]

---

3. Fox, "Ezekiel's Vision."

4. See for example Matties, *Rhetoric of Moral Discourse* (1990); Stevenson, *Vision of Transformation* (1996); Friebel, *Jeremiah's and Ezekiel's Sign-Acts* (1999); Renz, *Rhetorical Function* (1999); Kelle, "Dealing with the Trauma of Defeat" (2009).

5. Rom-Shiloni, *Exclusive Inclusivity*, 139–97.

6. See Garber, "Traumatizing Ezekiel," 215–35; Garber, "Vocabulary of Trauma," 309–21; Smith-Christopher, "Ezekiel in Abu Ghraib,"141–58; Smith-Christopher, "Reading War and Trauma," 253–74.

7. See Floyd, "Prophetic Books," 276–97.

8. See Miner, "Allusion," 13–15; Ben-Porat, "Literary Allusion," 105–28. On different approaches to the study of allusion, see Hebel, "Allusion," 135–64.

9. For arguments that Ezekiel borrows from H, see Lyons, *Law to Prophecy*, 61–67, 76–145; Levitt Kohn, *A New Heart*; Milgrom, *Leviticus 23–27*, 2348–65; Driver, *Introduction*, 47–50, 145–51. For arguments that H in its current form borrows from the book of Ezekiel, see Nihan, *Priestly Torah*, esp. 543–45; Nihan, "Holiness Code," 81–122; Grünwaldt, *Heiligkeitsgesetz*, 349–51, 365–66; Wellhausen, *Prolegomena*, 379–84. For arguments that both texts borrowed from each other during a complex process of literary development, see Zimmerli, *Ezekiel 1*, 46–52.

Situation and Rhetorical Goals

The situation to which Ezekiel the prophet speaks is clear from the book: he and his contemporaries were deported from Jerusalem in 597 BCE and have been resettled in Babylon; ten years later, Jerusalem and its temple were destroyed and its remaining citizens deported. Ezekiel describes his fellow-exiles as "rebellious" and "unwilling to listen" (Ezek 2:3–8; 3:7). They refuse to admit culpability (18:2–3), are tempted to assimilate (20:32), and are in despair about the possibility of national restoration (37:11). The prophet's task is to explain the reason for the exile, justify the destruction of Jerusalem as Yhwh's punishment for the people's behavior, prevent assimilation and despair, and convince his fellow-exiles that national restoration is possible.

It is important to note that the persuasive techniques of Ezekiel the speaking prophet are often different than the persuasive techniques of the literary product that bears his name. For example, the rhetorical function of a prophetic sign act must be distinguished from the function of a sign act report. What we have in e.g. Ezekiel 4–5 is a literary composition: originally separate oral sign acts have been juxtaposed, combined, re-arranged, and augmented. In fact, it must be recognized that the entire book of Ezekiel is not a mere transcript of prophetic speech, but is actually a narrative about what Yhwh told the prophet to say.[10] For this reason I will not attempt to reconstruct the oral message of the prophet. But given that the book of Ezekiel is a late-exilic composition,[11] the rhetorical *situations* addressed by the prophet and by the book—and the persuasive goals of each—are largely the same.[12]

---

10. Note the comments of Renz, *Rhetorical Function*, 16: "The book of Ezekiel develops its argument with the reader by narrating the story of a prophet's unfolding argument with his exilic audience. In this way the book addresses its own audience by having the audience in the book addressed by the prophet. In other words, it is a communication by being a narrative about a communication."

11. On the composition and date of the book of Ezekiel, see Albertz, *Israel in Exile*, 351–54; Zimmerli, *Ezekiel 1*, 68–74. Many identify redactional additions to the earliest form of the prophetic book. As I understand these, they are largely examples of *Fortschreibungen*—that is, editorial extensions of existing contextual arguments. The rhetorical function of these is a worthy topic of study in its own right. In the examples I consider below, however, it will not be necessary to distinguish between various levels of the book's editorial history.

12. See Renz, *Rhetorical Function*, 42.

The Rhetorical Role and Techniques of Allusion in Ezekiel

According to Thomas Renz,

> the book aims at a renewal which begins with the reading in exile, but will only be complete when Israel worships Yahweh "on a very high mountain" without again defiling the land ... At first, the readers were only asked to see the end of Jerusalem as the result of her sin, then they were asked to "judge" Jerusalem, and with Jerusalem their own rebellious behavior. In the oracles against the nations the readers were invited to see the same pattern of rebellion against Yahweh at work which had brought Jerusalem to its end. The readers are encouraged to see that rebellion against Yahweh reduces Israel to the level of other nations and does not have a future, since Yahweh will destroy pride against him everywhere. Thus they will realise that assimilation into other nations will only continue the rebellious history of the past and consequently will not open up a future for their community. Chaps. 33–48 then show that the beginning and end of New Israel is the acknowledgement of Yahweh's kingship which has the promise of transformation.[13]

As I will demonstrate, each of the arguments described above by Renz are built from locutions that have been borrowed from the Holiness Code.

Evaluating Israel's Actions

Ezekiel must first convince his contemporaries of their guilt. Without making this case, he has no grounds from which to argue for the necessity of spiritual restoration. Moreover, the notion of guilt plays the central role in Ezekiel's attempt to explain the destruction of Jerusalem and the deportation (see, e.g., Ezek 5:11; 7:9; 8:17–18; 9:10; 15:8; 16:36–43; 23:30; 36:17–19). As he borrows locutions from the Holiness Code (H) for this purpose, he uses several techniques to make his arguments more persuasive. The primary technique is *genre transformation*: Ezekiel transforms H's laws into accusations. For example, in Ezek 22:7–12 the prophet takes locutions from the laws in Leviticus 18–20 and frames them as the "abominations" of what he calls "the bloody city" (cf. Ezek 22:2):

---

13. Ibid., 229–31.

> *They treat father and mother with contemp*t among you; they act with extortion towards the alien in your midst; they oppress orphan and widow among you (Ezek 22:7 // Lev 20:9). You despise *my sacred contributions*, and you *profane my sabbaths* (Ezek 22:8 // Lev 19:3, 8). *Slanderous* men are among you in order to shed *blood*, and they eat on the mountains among you; they commit lewdness in your midst (Ezek 22:9 // Lev 19:16). *The nakedness of a father one uncovers* among you; *the woman unclean in her menstrual period* they rape among you (Ezek 22:10 // Lev 18:7–8, 19; 20:11). And one *commits abomination* with *the wife of his neighbor*, and in *lewdness* another *defiles his daughter-in-law*; and another among you rapes *his sister, the daughter of his father* (Ezek 22:11 // Lev 18:9, 15, 17; 20:10). They take bribes among you in order to shed blood; *you take interest and accrued interest*; and you violently profit from *your neighbor* by *extortion*. And you forgot me—utterance of Lord Yhwh. (Ezek 22:12 // Lev 19:13; 25:36)

Other techniques that Ezekiel employs for persuading his audience of their guilt include the *repetition* and *patterning* of the borrowed locutions. For example, in Lev 18:4–5 we find the following command:

> My ordinances you shall do and *my statutes* you shall keep so as to *walk in* them; I am Yhwh your God. And you shall keep my statutes, and *my ordinances by which a man will live if he does them*; I am Yhwh. (Lev 18:4, 5)

In Ezekiel 20, the prophet turns this into an accusation and repeats it (with minor variations) in Ezek 20:13, 16, 21, 24:

> They did not *walk in my statutes* and they rejected *my ordinances, by which a man will live if he does them*.

This repeated accusation is placed in a chronological framework moving from the exodus out of Egypt (note that according to vv. 7–9, the people rebel even before they leave!) to the journey through the wilderness to the entry into Canaan. This repetition and patterning creates the argument that Ezekiel's contemporaries are incorrigible, and that they perpetuate the same pattern of behavior as their ancestors (20:4, 30).

Another example of repetition and patterning occurs in chap. 18. Here, Ezekiel's contemporaries have refused to admit their own guilt; they find it easier to explain their exilic condition as the result of their parents' sins (18:2–3). To persuade them of their own culpability, the prophet transforms prohibitions from Lev 18, 20, and 25 into the legal scenario in Ezek 18:5–9:

If a man is righteous and does justice and righteousness—if he does not eat on the mountains, and does not lift up his eyes to the idols of the house of Israel, and does not *defile the wife of his neighbor, and does not come near a woman in her menstrual period* (Ezek 18:6 // Lev 18:19–20; 20:10), and does not oppress anyone (but restores to the debtor his pledge), does not commit robbery, gives his bread to the hungry and covers the naked with a garment, *does not give at interest, and does not take accrued interest*; withholds his hand from iniquity; does true justice between one man and another; *walks in my statutes, and has kept my ordinances* so as to act faithfully—he is righteous; he will surely live. Utterance of Lord Yhwh. (Ezek 18:8–9 // Lev 18:4–5; 25:36–37)

This language is repeated and arranged in a three-generation pattern in which Ezekiel attributes the keeping or breaking of H's laws to a righteous father (vv. 5–9), a wicked son (vv. 10–13), and a righteous grandson (vv. 14–17) in order to argue that righteousness and guilt are not transferred across generations. Rather, Ezekiel argues, God will hold the present generation responsible for its own sinful actions.

Yet another technique that Ezekiel employs when convincing his audience of Israel's guilt is that of repeating a locution from H while *creating puns* on its various meanings.[14] The use of wordplay increases the audience's level of engagement with the material. It can also elicit admiration, which would have the effect of creating a bond between the prophet and his audience, increasing the persuasive force of the argument. For example, in Ezek 5:5–8 the prophet borrows from Lev 18:4–5, "you shall do my ordinances (משפטים), and you shall keep my statutes so as to walk in them." He first turns this into an accusation in Ezek 5:7a: "you did not walk in my statutes, and you did not do my ordinances (משפטים)." But he then plays on the word משפטים, using it in two different senses in the following clauses: in v. 7b he accuses the people of not even[15] following the *customary practices* (משפטים) of the nations, and in v. 8, he claims that God will respond by carrying out *acts of judgment* (משפטים) against the people.

---

14. In Greco-Roman rhetoric, this would be labelled *antanaclasis* or *refractio*. See Quintilian, *Institutio oratoria* 9.3.68. For a typology and description of rhetorical figures and their function in modern advertisements, see McQuarrie and Mick, "Figures of Rhetoric."

15. On the text of 5:7b, see Zimmerli, *Ezekiel 1*, 151, who notes that the absence of the negative in some textual witnesses "is an attempt to soften the severity of the original statement in line with 1:12."

Ezekiel's use of repetition in crafting his accusations is, as ancient rhetoricians argued, a technique that increases the clarity and force of argument.[16] But the repetition itself constitutes an accusation, demonstrating that his arguments have not been taken to heart. Had his audience accepted his initial indictments, there would be no need to continue to repeat the accusations that he had fashioned from H's laws. Repetition can therefore be an attempt to underscore the *veracity* of the argument: as Lewis Carroll's Bellman says, "What I tell you three times is true."

Linking Actions to Consequences

Throughout the book, Ezekiel makes the argument that the fall of Jerusalem was both necessary and justified, and that it must be seen as Yhwh's judgment for the people's actions (e.g., Ezek 8:17–18; 9:8–10). In making this argument, Ezekiel attempts to persuade his audience that certain actions have consequences, thereby providing a rationale for their own exilic condition. This is a harsh message; but those who research trauma are aware that for survivors of a disaster, a negative explanation can be better than no explanation at all.[17] This argument is conveyed through a number of rhetorical techniques: first, the reader watches the prophet being told to act out the exile of the Jerusalemites for the sake of his own audience in an attempt to make them "see" (Ezek 12:1–11; note the repetition of the word (ראה). Second, Ezekiel creates a play on words (Ezek 14:22–23) to argue that the arrival of survivors from the fallen city will constitute a "comfort" (נחם) to his own community: the survivors will function as evidence that the disaster was not arbitrary or undeserved (חנם).[18] By this argument he forges an explicit causal connection between "the ways and deeds" of the Jerusalemites and "the disaster which [Yhwh] brought upon Jerusalem." Of course, this linkage of actions to consequences is paradigmatic for the condition of Ezekiel's own community.[19]

---

16. So Quintilian, *Institutio oratoria* 8.2.24: "Consequently we shall frequently repeat anything which we think the judge has failed to take in as he should."

17. On the human impulse to explain disaster, and on certain kinds of self-blame as coping mechanisms, see Janoff-Bulman, "Aftermath of Victimization," 28–30; Janoff-Bulman, "'Adaptive' Strategies," 180–92. Regarding the impulse to rationalize disaster, Gillian Mezey points out that "there is a marked reluctance to accept the accidental nature of violent crime"; see Mezey, "Psychological Responses," 176.

18. See Block, *Ezekiel 1–24*, 451–52.

19. The attempt to link actions to consequences appears in the book's emphasis on causality, seen in the repeated use of the word "because" (יען; this occurs 40x in Ezekiel, almost half of the entire occurrences in the Hebrew Bible. Cf. Ezek 5:7–8, 9, 11; 13:8;

Ezekiel also borrows and transforms locutions from the Holiness Code in order to convince the exiles that their disaster was warranted and divinely planned judgment. The primary technique that Ezekiel uses here is to *transform* H's conditional and remedial covenant punishments into oracles of imminent or present judgment. The punishments in Lev 26 are presented as God's actions to induce repentance. The author creates this effect by listing the punishments in order of increasing intensity, and by separating them into groups with refrains that clearly state their restorative purpose: "if despite this you will not obey . . ." (Lev 26:18, 27); "if you continue hostile to me, and are not willing to listen . . ." (26:21); "if in spite of these you are not disciplined back to me . . ." (26:23). However, when Ezekiel uses the threats from H, he argues that the judgment against Jerusalem is final and total: the punishments are *not* restorative, and there is *no* room for appeal. For example, note Ezekiel's argument in Ezek 5:11–12, where he uses H's locutions to make an explicit causal link between their actions and judgment:

> Therefore, as I live—utterance of LORD Yhwh—surely, because (יען) *you have defiled my sanctuary* with all your detestable things and with all your abominations, so also I will shave off, and my eye will not have pity, and also I will not have compassion. A third of you will die by the *plague*, and by famine they will be finished off in your midst; a third will fall by the *sword* around you; and a third *I will scatter* to every wind, *and I will unsheathe a sword after them*. (Ezek 5:11–12 // Lev 20:3; 26:25, 33)

Ezekiel also combines the technique of transformation with the techniques of *repetition* and *patterning* of borrowed locutions. The locutions he repeats most frequently come from H's covenant punishments in Lev 26:22, 25, and 33.[20] As I noted above, repetition was a technique that ancient

---

15:8; 16:36–37; 20:15–16; 21:29 [ET v. 24]; 23:35; etc.). It can also be seen in the book's emphasis on equivalence in punishment, where Yhwh promises that he will (or did) punish the people "according to their/your ways" (Ezek 7:3, 8, 9; 18:30; 24:14; 33:20; 36:19; 39:24).

20. "And *I will send wild animals* into you, and *they will bereave you*, and *they will cut off your cattle* and diminish you, and your roads will be desolate" (Lev 26:22 // Ezek 5:17; 14:13, 15, 17, 19, 21; 25:13; 29:8; 33:27); "*And I will bring against you the sword* that avenges the covenant, and you will gather yourselves into your cities, *and I will send a plague* into your midst, and you will be given into the hand of the enemy" (Lev 26:25 // Ezek 5:12, 17, 6:3, 11–12; 7:15; 11:8; 12:16; 14:17, 19, 21; 28:23; 29:8; 33:2, 27); "*And I will scatter you among the nations, and I will unsheathe a sword* after you; and *your land will become a desolation, and your cities will be a waste*" (Lev 26:33 // Ezek 5:2, 12; 6:6, 8, 14; 11:16; 12:14, 15, 20; 14:15, 16; 15:8; 19:7; 20:23; 22:15; 29:9, 10, 12; 30:7, 12, 23, 26; 32:15; 33:24+27+28, 29; 35:3–4; 36:4, 19, 34, 35).

rhetoricians spoke of as a way to increase the force of one's argument.[21] Accordingly, Ezekiel repeats these locutions and patterns them in an attempt to persuade his audience of the *extent* and *severity* of judgment. For example, he takes H's punishments in Lev 26:22, 25, 33 and distributes them into a three-part pattern in Ezek 5:12 ("a third by plague/a third by sword/a third scattered"), and into merismic patterns in Ezek 6:12 ("far off/close by/left over"); in 7:15 ("outside/inside"); and in 33:27 ("in waste places/on the surface of the field/in strongholds and caves").

Limiting the Options of His Audience

Ezekiel refers explicitly to two potential problems for the exiles—the temptation to assimilate (Ezek 20:32) and the temptation to trust in foreign powers (29:16). A third problem would be the temptation to despair in the face of the arrogance and hostility of surrounding nations. The oracles against the nations in Ezekiel represent an attempt to prevent these potential problems from becoming realities.[22] In these oracles, the surrounding nations are condemned for their hostility to Jerusalem and joy at its fall (e.g., Ezek 25:3, 6, 8, 12, 15; 26:2) and for their pride (e.g., Ezek 27:3; 28:2–6; 29:3; 32:2). Remarkably, locutions from the Holiness Code are used even here: Ezekiel tries to convince his audience of Egypt's downfall by applying the language of H's covenant punishments to Egypt![23]

Creating Hope

Finally, Ezekiel must convince his audience to move from despair to hope. Because they have no obvious and empirical grounds for believing in national and cultic restoration, Ezekiel must appeal to things other than current or imminent political events. To accomplish this, he borrows and transforms the traditional language of the Holiness Code in order to propose a radical and permanent solution.

---

21. In his treatise titled *On Style*, the ancient rhetorician Demetrius suggested of the use of repetition to create "elevation" (μέγεθος, §66), "vividness" (ἐνάργεια, §211), and "forcefulness" (δεινότης, §267–268) in one's arguments. Brian Vickers traces the rhetorical use of repetition throughout history as a way to "express passion"; see Vickers, "Repetition and Emphasis," 85–113. See also McQuarrie and Mick, "Figures of Rhetoric," 429–32.

22. See Raabe, "Ezekiel's Oracles against the Nations," 187–207.

23. See e.g. Ezek 29:8, 10, 12; 30:6, 18, 23. See also OAN Edom (Ezek 25:13) and OAN Sidon (28:23).

The first technique that Ezekiel uses to provoke hope is the *transformation* of H's conditional covenant blessings into unconditional guarantees. To the degree that Ezekiel has been successful in convincing his audience of their incorrigibility, he has created a new problem for himself: what reason does he have for thinking that they might be willing—or even able—to repent? Or worse: supposing they do repent, what would prevent them from lapsing into apostasy yet again? Ezekiel's radical solution is to present the idea of an unbreakable covenant (Ezek 16:60). While borrowing H's covenant blessings to describe future restoration in Ezek 34 and 36, Ezekiel strips them of their conditional character, and makes them unconditional. Moreover, the book simply omits H's covenant punishments when describing future hope: these will be unnecessary, because Yhwh will transform the people. So H's "*If* you walk in my statutes . . ." (Lev 26:3) is turned into "I will give them a heart of flesh, *in order that they will* walk in my statutes" (Ezek 11:19–20). Or even more forcefully, in Ezek 36:27: "I will put my Spirit within you and *make* you walk in my statutes."

This need for a permanent solution is reflected in the book's repetition of the phrase "never again" (לא עוד): the people will "never again profane [Yhwh's] holy name" (Ezek 20:39; 43:7); there will "never again be a prickly thorn or painful briar among all those around them" (28.24); they will "never again be prey" (34:22, 28); "never again be consumed by hunger" (34:29); "never again experience the insults of the nations" (34:29; 36:15); "never again experience the disgrace of famine" (36:30); "never again be two nations, and never again be divided into two kingdoms" (37:22); "never again defile themselves with their idols, detestable things, and transgressions" (37:23). The land will "never again" bereave its people of children, devour them, or cause them to stumble (36:12, 14, 15). Finally, Yhwh will "never again hide his face" from the people (37:29).

Other techniques that Ezekiel uses to provoke hope are the *reversal* of H's punishments and the *heightening* of H's covenant blessings. For example, H's punishment "I will scatter you among the nations" (Lev 26:33a) is reversed into "I will bring them out from the peoples and gather them from the lands" (Ezek 34:13; cf. 11:17; 20:34, 41). H's punishment "your lands will be desolate and your cities a waste" (Lev 26:33b) is reversed into "the cities will be inhabited, and the waste places rebuilt" (Ezek 36:10; cf. 36:33–36). But Ezekiel does not simply reverse H's punishments; he also modifies H's blessings in order to make his own model of restoration more extravagant than the description of the relationship in H. Not only will Israel "live securely in the land" (Lev 26:5), but they will "live securely in the wilderness and sleep in the forests" (Ezek 34:25). The word "securely" is repeated three times (Ezek 34:25, 27, 28) to underscore its importance as a solution to the problem of the harassed flock described in Ezek 34:1-6. Not only will there be "rain in its season" (Lev 26:4; Ezek 34:26b), but these will be "rains of blessing" (Ezek 34:26c). Ezekiel not only repeats H's blessing about the elimination of wild animals (Lev 26:6; Ezek 34:25), but he also reverses H's punishment of destructive wild animals (Lev 26:22; Ezek 34:28). He describes both people and land as a "blessing" (Ezek 34:26), and reverses H's punishment of enemy attack (Lev 26:25, 32) to claim that the people will "no longer be plunder for the nations" (Ezek 34:28). So by borrowing the traditional imagery of peace and plenty, he appeals to emotion; but he attempts to make his appeal even more persuasive by heightening the imagery.[24] And to address the potential counter-argument that such hope is unrealistic given the people's checkered past, Ezekiel makes future hope contingent on divine initiative rather than on human initiative (Ezek 36:22),[25] and turns H's conditional blessings into guaranteed blessings.

Conclusion

In this essay I have identified Ezekiel's text-handling techniques: the transformation of the genre and modality of material from his source text; the reversal and heightening of material from his source text; and the use of repetition, patterning, and wordplay in the presentation of material from his source text—in these cases, traditional priestly material found in Leviticus 17–26. I have argued that Ezekiel's techniques of allusion can be explained in terms of rhetorical effect: that is, they represent attempts to increase the force of his arguments, or to counter the attitudes and arguments of his contemporaries.

To what extent was Ezekiel successful in his rhetorical endeavor? Was his audience "ashamed of their iniquities" (Ezek 43:10)? We can only guess at the reaction of the first exilic readers of this book. But what we do know is that the book of Ezekiel had a profound effect on later readers in the Second Temple period. These readers looked forward to the restoration described in Ezekiel 37 (4Q385 2.9; 4Q386 1.ii.2–3) and welcomed the spiritual transformation promised in Ezek 36:25–27, 33 (1QS 3.7–9; 4.21–22; John 3:5; Titus 2:14; 3:5–6; Heb 10:22). And the details of Ezekiel's vision in Ezek 40–48 (a very high mountain with God's city on it; life-giving water and trees for healing; a place where God himself dwells with his people) appear in John's vision of cosmic transformation (Revelation 21–22). Ezekiel's powerful use of earlier texts as scripture lie behind what

---

24. See Lyons, "Extension and Allusion."

25. Joyce, *Divine Initiative*, 126: "Israel's obedience will be the result rather than the cause of deliverance, part and parcel of the restoration and certainly not a condition upon which it depends."

later readers recognized: the explosive potential of the book of Ezekiel to create hope for God's work in the future.

Bibliography

Albertz, Rainer. *Israel in Exile: The History and Literature of the Sixth Century B.C.E.* Translated by David Green. Studies in Biblical Literature 3. Atlanta: Society of Biblical Literature, 2003.

Ben-Porat, Ziva. "The Poetics of Literary Allusion." *Poetics and Theory of Literature* 1 (1976) 105–28.

Block, Daniel I. *The Book of Ezekiel: Chapters 1–24.* New International Commentary on the Old Testament. Grand Rapids: Eerdmans, 1997.

Demetrius. *Demetrius on Style: The Greek Text of Demetrius De elocutione Edited after the Paris Manuscript.* Translated by W. Rhys Roberts. Cambridge: Cambridge University Press, 1902.

Driver, S. R. *An Introduction to the Literature of the Old Testament.* 6th ed. New York: Scribner, 1897.

Floyd, Michael H. "The Production of Prophetic Books in the Early Second Temple Period." In *Prophets, Prophecy, and Prophetic Texts in Second Temple Judaism*, edited by Michael H. Floyd and Robert D. Haak, 276–97. LHBOTS 427. New York: T. & T. Clark, 2006.

Fox, Michael V. "The Rhetoric of Ezekiel's Vision of the Valley of the Bones." *Hebrew Union College Annual* 51 (1980) 1–15.

Friebel, Kelvin G. *Jeremiah's and Ezekiel's Sign-Acts: Rhetorical Nonverbal Communication.* JSOTSup 283. Sheffield: Sheffield Academic, 1999.

Garber, D. G., Jr. "Traumatizing Ezekiel, the Exilic Prophet." In *Psychology and the Bible: A New Way to Read the Scriptures.* Vol. 2: *From Genesis to Apocalyptic Vision*, edited by J. Harold Ellens and Wayne G. Rollins, 215–35. Praeger Perspectives. Westport, CT: Praeger, 2004.

———. "A Vocabulary of Trauma in the Exilic Writings." In *Interpreting Exile: Displacement and Deportation in Biblical and Modern Contexts*, edited by Brad E. Kelle et al., 309–21. Ancient Israel and Its Literature 10. Atlanta: Society of Biblical Literature, 2011.

Grünwaldt, Klaus. *Das Heiligkeitsgesetz Leviticus 17–26: Ursprüngliche Gestalt, Tradition und Theologie.* BZAW 271. Berlin: de Gruyter, 1999.

Hebel, Udo J. "Towards a Descriptive Poetics of Allusion." In *Intertextuality*, edited by Heinrich F. Plett, 135–64. Research in Text Theory 15. Berlin: de Gruyter, 1991.

Janoff-Bulman, Ronnie. "Esteem and Control Bases of Blame: 'Adaptive' Strategies for Victims versus Observers." *Journal of Personality* 50 (2006) 180–92.

———. "The Aftermath of Victimization: Rebuilding Shattered Assumptions." In *Trauma and Its Wake.* Vol. 1, *The Study and Treatment of Post-Traumatic Stress Disorder*, edited by Charles Figley, 15–35. Brunner/Mazel Psychosocial Stress Series 4. London: Routledge, 1985.

Joyce, P. M. *Divine Initiative and Human Response in Ezekiel.* JSOTSup 51. Sheffield: JSOT Press, 1989.

Kelle, Brad E. "Dealing with the Trauma of Defeat: The Rhetoric of the Devastation and Rejuvenation of Nature in Ezekiel." *JBL* 128 (2009) 469–90.

Levitt Kohn, Risa. *A New Heart and a New Soul: Ezekiel, the Exile, and the Torah.* LHBOTS 358. London: Sheffield Academic, 2002.

Lyons, Michael A. "Extension and Allusion: The Composition of Ezekiel 34." In *Ezekiel: Current Debates and Future Directions*, edited by William A. Tooman and Penelope Barter. FAT 112. Tübingen: Mohr/Siebeck, 2017.

———. *From Law to Prophecy: Ezekiel's Use of the Holiness Code.* LHBOTS 507. New York: T. & T. Clark, 2009.

Matties, Gordon H. *Ezekiel 18 and the Rhetoric of Moral Discourse.* SBLDS 126. Atlanta: Society of Biblical Literature, 1990.

McQuarrie, Edward F. and David Glen Mick. "Figures of Rhetoric in Advertising Language." *Journal of Consumer Research* 22 (1996) 424–38.

Mezey, Gillian "Psychological Responses to Interpersonal Violence." In *Psychological Trauma: A Developmental Approach*, edited by Dora Black et al, 176–98. London: RCPsych Publications, 1997.

Milgrom, Jacob. *Leviticus 23–27.* AB 3B. New York: Doubleday, 2001.

Miner, Earl. "Allusion." In *The New Princeton Handbook of Poetic Terms*, edited by T. V. F. Brogan, 13–15. Princeton: Princeton University Press, 1994.

Nihan, Christophe. *From Priestly Torah to Pentateuch. A Study in the Composition of the Book of Leviticus.* FAT 2/25. Tübingen: Mohr/Siebeck, 2007.

———. "The Holiness Code between D and P: Some Comments on the Function and Significance of Leviticus 17–26 in the Composition of the Torah." In *Das Deuteronomium zwischen Pentateuch und Deuteronomistischem Geschichtswerk*, edited by Eckart Otto and Reinhard Achenbach, 81–122. Forschungen zur Religion und Literatur des Alten und Neuen Testaments 206. Göttingen: Vandenhoeck & Ruprecht, 2004.

Patrick, Dale, and Allen Scult. *Rhetoric and Biblical Interpretation.* Bible and Literature Series 26; JSOTSup 82. Sheffield: Almond, 1990.

Quintilian. *Institutio oratoria.* Translated by H. E. Butler. Loeb Classical Library. Cambridge: Harvard University Press, 1920–22.

Raabe, Paul R. "Transforming the International *status quo*: Ezekiel's Oracles against the Nations." In *Transforming Visions: Transformations of Text, Tradition, and Theology in Ezekiel*, edited by William A. Tooman and Michael A. Lyons, 187–207. Princeton Theological Monograph Series 127. Eugene, OR: Pickwick Publications, 2010.

Renz, Thomas. *The Rhetorical Function of the Book of Ezekiel.* VTSup 76. Leiden: Brill, 1999.

Rom-Shiloni, Dalit. *Exclusive Inclusivity: Identity Conflicts between the Exiles and the People Who Remained (6th–5th Centuries BCE).* LHBOTS 543. London: T. & T. Clark, 2013.

Smith-Christopher, D. L. "Ezekiel in Abu Ghraib: Rereading Ezekiel 16:37–39 in the Context of Imperial Conquest." In *Ezekiel's Hierarchical World: Wrestling with a Tiered Reality*. Edited by Stephen L. Cook and Corrine L. Patton, 141–58. Society of Biblical Literature Symposium Series 31. Atlanta: Society of Biblical Literature, 2002.

———. "Reading War and Trauma: Suggestions toward a Social-Psychological Exegesis of Exile and War in Biblical Texts." In *Interpreting Exile: Displacement and Deportation in Biblical and Modern Contexts*, edited by Brad E. Kelle et al., 253–74. Ancient Israel and Its Literature 10. Atlanta: Society of Biblical Literature, 2011.

Stevenson, Kalinda Rose. *The Vision of Transformation: The Territorial Rhetoric of Ezekiel 40–48*. SBLDS 154. Atlanta: Scholars, 1996.
Vickers, Brian "Repetition and Emphasis in Rhetoric: Theory and Practice." In *Repetition*, edited by Andreas Fischer, 85–113. SPELL Swiss Papers in English Language and Literature 7. Tübingen: Narr, 1994.
Wellhausen, Julius. *Prolegomena to the History of Ancient Israel*. Translated by J. Sutherland Black and Allan Menzies. 1885. Reprint, New York: Meridian, 1957.
Zimmerli, Walther. *Ezekiel 1: A Commentary on the Book of the Prophet Ezekiel, Chapters 1–24*. Translated by Ronald E. Clements. Hermeneia. Philadelphia: Fortress, 1979.

6

Edom's Desolation and Adam's Multiplication

Parallelism in Ezekiel 35:1–36:15

Tracy McKenzie

Southeastern Baptist Theological Seminary

Introduction[1]

Ezekiel 35 presents a rather unique problem to the book's interpreters with its judgment concerning Edom. Commentators often ask why this second prophecy against Edom is situated within the context of prophecies concerning Israel's restoration. This question would not be so vexing were it not for the section of prophecies against the nations from Ezekiel 25–32, one of which names Edom as an antagonist. A second perplexing issue for Ezekiel 35 concerns its relationship to Ezek 36:1–15. Commentaries commonly indicate in their assessment some type of coordinating relationship between Ezek 35:1–15 and 36:1–15.[2] This assessment stems from the fact that Ezek 35:1 begins a messenger formula that recurs not at 36:1 but at 36:16. Meanwhile, 36:1 repeats the vocative "son of man" and command to prophesy found in 35:2.[3] In addition, there are many parallel elements

---

1. This article was originally written for the 2011 society meeting of the Evangelical Theological Society.

2. Below, I refer to this as "halving." For the notion of "halving" see Greenberg, *Ezekiel 1–20, 25–26*. Although Greenberg does not cite Ezekiel 35 and 36 as an example of "halving," it appears to approximate his description (Greenberg, *Ezekiel 21–37*, 722–25). See also Block, *Ezekiel: Chapters 1–24*, 23.

3. Of this chapter division, Hummel says, "It must rate as one of the most egregiously

between these two halves, Ezek 35:1–15 and 36:1–15.[4] What is the purpose for the possible "intentional dovetailing" of these two subunits?[5] A third complexity stems from the composite nature of the two units. Even such a conservative commentator as Block says, "If ch. 35 seems disjointed, 36:1–15 is even more so. Numerous repetitive and disruptive prophetic formulae appear to chop it up into little fragments . . . The result looks like a patchwork quilt, except that quilts usually reflect more deliberate design."[6] The question must be asked how such a textual unit would develop and what its communicative content would be.

In response to these questions regarding Ezekiel 35, commentators typically explain that before Israel can be restored to its rightful place, her enemies must be destroyed (from her land?).[7] Attempts to historically reconstruct Edom's foray into Israel dominate the discussion in order to supply a cause for Edom's second condemnation. From this perspective, Ezekiel 35 indicates that the eradication of Israel's enemies from the land goes hand in hand with her restoration to the land. This answer falls short for at least four reasons. First, according to Ezekiel 35, Edom will be 'desolated' on the mountain of Seir, not the mountains of Israel where "*adam*" will be multiplied. In this case, Israel could be restored whether or not Edom is desolated or not. Second, there is little evidence that the Edomites actually infiltrated numerically and geographically far enough into the land of Israel to prohibit Israel from returning.[8] Third—and most incisively, Ezekiel 25–32 has just condemned Edom and Israel's other enemies and therefore, the reader is already aware that the nations' condemnation goes hand in hand with Israel's restoration. If the explanation for the second mention of Edom is merely

---

misleading chapter divisions in the OT." Hummel, *Ezekiel 21–48*, 1017.

4. Block, *Book of Ezekiel*, 1:308–10 lists eleven corresponding details. See the list below for more parallel elements.

5. Regarding the use of "Edom" in both texts, Zimmerli concludes, "Since . . . the behavior of Edom is once again expressly mentioned (36:5), one cannot disregard the possibility, at least as far as the final form of M is concerned, that the two sections have been intentionally dovetailed." Zimmerli, *Ezekiel 2*, 232.

6. Block, *Book of Ezekiel*, 1:322.

7. Woudstra, "Edom and Israel in Ezekiel," 21–35 concludes with this reasoning and discusses other details related to Edom's antagonism towards Israel. He also sees Edom as representative of all nations. For this latter notion, see below. For other commentaries who espouse a similar reciprocal judgment/salvation theme, see Allen, *Ezekiel 20–48*, 171; Block *Ezekiel 25–48*, 310; Cooke, *The Book of Ezekiel*, 381–82; Eichrodt, *Ezekiel*, 486–86; Greenberg, *Ezekiel 21–37*, 723–25; Hummerli, *Ezekiel*, 1017. For a cautious rejoinder to this conclusion, see Hals, *Ezekiel*, 260, who follows Zimmerli, *Ezekiel 2*, 232, 239. See also Klein, *Schriftauslegung im Ezechielbuch*, 320–24.

8. An issue which Ezek 35:10, 36:2, and 5 address and to which I return below.

to state that Israel's enemies will be judged when she is restored, how does this extend beyond the purpose of the oracles against the nations within the structure of the book? Fourth, this explanation also fails to address the second and third complexity above: The numerous, parallel, linguistic correspondences between Ezek 35:1-15 and 36:1-15 and the composite makeup of these texts. Any explanation of Edom's second denunciation in Ezekiel 35 must treat the intentional coupling of this subunit with 36:1-15 into a composite whole.

As for this latter issue, a thorough analysis of the literary growth and redaction of these chapters is beyond the limits of this paper.[9] However, it is clear that these chapters accrue from prophecies against other nations and Jerusalem and from other texts and do not, therefore, isolate Edom primarily for their supposed infiltration or even their hatred and envy. Consequently, as the analysis below will demonstrate, a second denunciation against Edom must result from more than mere correspondence to a hypothetically reconstructed reality. Such a complex textual model in conjunction with the many parallel correspondences between the halves strongly suggests a further reason for Edom's second denunciation. It is the thesis of this paper that Edom was explicitly named as a representative for all Israel's enemies because it phonologically corresponds to *adam*, a key term in 36:1-15 representing Yhwh's multiplication, i.e. restoration of all mankind.

This paper will analyze examples of linguistic parallelism between Ezek 35:1-15 and 36:1-15 in order to demonstrate the purpose of a second prophecy against Edom within the context of Israel's restoration. It will do so in three steps. First, it will consider the phenomenon of parallel elements in non-poetic texts in order to substantiate this analysis of Ezek 35:1—36:15. Second, it will examine two cases of parallel, linguistic elements and their coherence with a composite literary makeup of these two subunits. Third, it will briefly mention three literary contexts with related linguistic and content-related elements suggesting interpretive association with Ezekiel 35:1—36:15.

Parallelism and Non-Poetic Texts

Parallelism has been a traditional term used in the modern study of biblical poetry at least since 1778 when Robert Lowth published his work on Isaiah.[10] In recent years, linguists have moved the discussion from tradi-

---

9. See Zimmerli, *Ezekiel*; Klein, *Schriftauslegung*; and Pohlmann, *Ezechiel*.

10. McKane, *Hebrew Bible/Old Testament*, 960-61. For analysis of biblical poetry, including features now called parallelism, see Kugel, *The Idea of Biblical Poetry*. For an

tionally understood 'parallel lines' to that of parallel linguistic elements in language.[11] In *The Dynamics of Biblical Parallelism,* Adele Berlin analyzes various linguistic factors constituting parallelism. Focusing predominantly upon parallel lines, she analyzes similarities and differences within linguistically equivalent categories in order to discern parallel elements within poetry. She attempts, however, to move the discussion of parallelism beyond that of parallel lines to parallelism between linguistic aspects, e.g. lexemes, phonemes, morphemes, or syntagmata. If linguistic aspect is the basis for parallelism rather than parallel lines, then one can analyze non-poetic texts for parallel structures within a textual unit.

Linguists have also examined the artificial dichotomy of poetry and prose genres. Linda Waugh, in "The Poetic Function and the Nature of Language," discusses the distinction between poetry and non-poetic texts based on the functions of different types of texts.[12] Based on the assumption that a primary function of poetry is artistry—what Roman Jakobson calls the poetic function, Waugh reasons that similarities within a linguistic aspect, e.g. two lexemes, within close proximity to one another help to produce an aesthetically pleasing poem.[13] She writes, "[T]he signs and sign-matrices selected from are usually (but not always) related to each other by a variety of similarity relations, including equivalence, similarity, dissimilarity, contrast . . . On the other hand, the signs and sign-matrices combined are usually (but not always) related to one another by contiguity."[14] It is the phenomenon of "similarity relations" in close proximity through which a poetic-type text is created and which gives the 'poetry' its aesthetic properties.

If similarity within contiguity constitutes the poetic function, any sharp dichotomy between prose and poetic texts becomes a matter of degree rather than strict bifurcation. As Waugh indicates, it is the nature of texts to utilize more than one function, e.g. a poetic function and

---

illuminating search for pre-Lowth contributors to the discussion of "parallelism," see Lundbom, *Jeremiah*, 121–27.

11. Roman Jakobson, "Linguistics and Poetics," 350–77, quoted in Berlin, *The Dynamics of Biblical Parallelism, passim*; Linda R. Waugh, "The Poetic Function and the Nature of Language," 143–68, also quoted in Berlin, *Dynamics,* 10–11. A biblical scholar, David Howard, indicates a similar sentiment, "A paradigm shift has also taken place in studies of Hebrew poetry, where linguistic analysis . . . now occupies an important—if not dominant—position." "Recent Trends in Psalms Study," 329–68.

12. Based on Jakobson's work, she lists 6 functions: emotive (expressive), conative (appellative), metalingual (metalinguistic, 'glossing'), poetic (aesthetic), referential (cognitive, denotative, ideational), and phatic. See Waugh, "The Poetic Function," 144.

13. Roman Jakobson, "Linguistics and Poetics," 350–77.

14. Waugh, "The Poetic Function," 150.

referential function.[15] She writes specifically of prose, "Prose . . . is a transitional phenomenon, admitting of various gradations on the continuum between 'ordinary' language with an orientation toward the referential function and the poetic function. As a transitional phenomenon, prose evidences a more complex type, a type in which the poetic and referential modes are intertwined in various ways and to varying degrees."[16] Prose, while lacking the pervasive parallelism constitutive of poetry, retains yet a degree of poetic function.[17]

Ezekiel 35:1—36:15 exhibits this transition between prose and poetic language because of the large number of similar and contrasting elements. These elements contribute to scholars' assessment of "halving." For a thorough understanding of this transitionally oriented text, it will be necessary to ascertain how the poetic function cooperates with the referential function. Berlin elicits an application of parallelism to such texts saying,

> The definition of parallelism offered here is much broader than that found in most biblical studies, in which parallelism is usually considered to involve only semantic and/or grammatical equivalences and to operate only between two or more consecutive lines . . . Once we admit smaller segments as being parallel—e.g., words, phrases, even sounds—though the lines to which they belong are not parallel, we raise the incidence of parallelism within a text. And if we do not restrict our search for linguistic equivalences to adjacent lines or sentences, but take a global view, finding equivalences anywhere within a text, we raise the incidence of parallelism still more.[18]

Berlin's understanding of parallelism substantiates a comprehensive application of parallelism to biblical structures. Moreover, it helps the reader discern intentionally associated elements within a text.[19] Commenting on Roman Jakobson, she continues,

---

15. "[T]he predominance of the poetic function and the subordination of the other functions does not mean that the other functions are subordinated to the extent of being excluded. On the contrary, any one or more of the functions may be present in a variety of ways and with more or less importance vis-à-vis the poetic function." Ibid., 145.

16. Ibid.

17. Depending upon the type of prose and the method and purpose of production, it may contain a significant number of parallelisms that contribute to its different functions. At the very least I have in mind here commonly understood 'parallelisms' within prose such as chiasm and inclusio.

18. Berlin, Dynamics, 3.

19. Shemaryahu Talmon discusses the propensity of biblical authors and editors for

[His] view is preferable because *it enables us to unify phenomena whose relationships have not been perceived* . . . Furthermore, Jakobson's approach allows us to see more readily that the parallelism touted as indicators of poetry are no different from the linguistic equivalences in prose texts. Certain *linguistic usages, including a systematic exploitation of equivalences*, are a mark of biblical style as a whole. They are not limited to one genre, although they may be more prominent in the one usually called poetry.[20]

In an examination of Ezek 35:1—36:15, the perception of equivalences compels the reader to associate the halves with one another and to discern the intent behind their association. The relationships that are perceived from the poetic function, i.e. parallelisms, will guide an understanding of the referential function of Ezek 35:1—36:15.

Parallel Linguistic Elements

The following discussion is an attempt to apply Berlin's definition of parallelism to Ezek 35:1—36:15. Each example in the list below may contain

---

what he calls the "principle of "inversion."" Talmon, *Text and Canon of the Hebrew Bible* (Winona Lake: Eisenbrauns, 2010), 53. He mentions numerous cases in which biblical writers invert or use "distant parallelism." Talmon uses this nomenclature quoted from James Muilenburg "A Study in Hebrew Rhetoric: Repetition and Style," 99. Using the notion of "word pairs," Dahood comments on "distant parallelism" saying, "By supplying new instances of paired words, the tablets enable the biblical literary critic to appropriate rhetorical devices that had heretofore escaped his attention." For Dahood, even though several cola might intervene between word pairs, "[T]he paired verbs create an inclusion. The ancient listener or reader would doubtless have recognized the parallel brace and mentally linked the separated cola together" ("Ugaritic Hebrew Parallel Pairs," 80). Talmon goes on to discuss over twenty cases of distant parallelism of which several are from the book of Ezekiel. He writes, "There is no need to illustrate in detail the abundantly employed technique of parallelistic chiasm in adjacent cola, which prevails in poetic passages, but is found also in prose compositions which often exhibit this distinct literary characteristic" (*Text and Canon*, 54). The "distant parallelism" occurs not in contiguous lines of poetry but across intervening chapters of prose. Talmon's purpose in the analysis deals with elucidation of authors', editors', and scribes' practices in passing along their texts. His conclusion relates to this analysis as well. He states, "In some of the above examples, inversion serves not only as a stylistic phenomenon, *sensu stricto*, but also as a structural principle which ties together 'distant parallels.'" (*Text and Canon*, 60).

20. Berlin, *Dynamics*, 3. Italicized words represent my emphasis regarding the use of equivalences in order to give evidence of intentional parallelisms which create the "halving" and the subsequent message.

parallel linguistic elements. I will limit the ensuing discussion to two cases that are particularly pertinent to a referential function.

Parallel linguistic elements between Ezek 35:1–15 and 36:1–15[21]

The following table enumerates linguistic elements in Ezek 35:1–15 and the corresponding material in Ezek 36:1–15.[22]

Ezekiel 35	Ezekiel 36
35:2 against Mount Seir	36:1 to the mountains of
על הר שעיר	אל־הרי ישראל
35:2, 3 Mount Seir	36:1 mountains of Israel
הר שעיר	הרי ישראל
35:3 behold, I am against you	36:9 behold, I am for you
הנני אליך	הנני אליכם
35:3 I will stretch out my hand	36:7 I will lift up my hand
נטיתי ידי	נשאתי את־ידי
35:3 a desolation and a devastation[23]	36:3dα desolate and hounded
שממה ומשמה	שמות ושאף
35:7 for waste and desolation	
לשממה ושממה	
35:4 your cities, I will make a waste	36:10 and the waste places will be built
עריך חרבה אשים	והחרבות תבנינה

---

21. Some terms and collocations from Ezek 35:1–15 and 36:1–15 are prophetic formulae found throughout the book of Ezekiel and consequently have less value as parallel features between 35:1–15 and 36:1–15: "son of man," "prophesy," "and say," "thus says the Lord GOD," "because," "therefore," and "and you will know that I am the LORD."

22. Similarities and differences within equivalent linguistic aspects parallel one another and may demonstrate an intentional comparison or contrast and therefore, may be significant for understanding the communicative intent. Not all of the parallel cases are of the same value for measuring an intentional relationship between Ezekiel 35:1–15 and 36:1–15. Moreover, in some manner, Jakobson's six factors reveal the multi-functionality of the text. Neither the poetic function nor the referential function excludes other functions from operating in the text such as the attitude of Mount Seir to Israel's misfortune and God's vengeance that will be meted against Mount Seir.

23. For the usage of these terms, see Zimmerli, *Ezekiel*, note B, 1:477 and 2:35. This expression is also found in *Ezek 36:34*.

Ezekiel 35	Ezekiel 36
35:5 because you have eternal enmity	36:3bβ because ... so that you were a possession
יען היות לך איבת עולם	יען ... להיותכם מורשה
35:8 And I will fill its mountains with its slain; your hills and your valleys and all your channels, those slain by the sword will fall in them	36:4b ... to the mountains and to the hills, to the channels and to the valleys
ומלאתי את־הריו חלליו גבעותיך וגאותיך וכל־אפיקיך חללי־חרב יפלו בהם	להרים ולגבעות לאפיקים ולגאיות
	36:6b ... to the mountains and the hills, to the channels and the valleys
	להרים ולגבעו לאפיקים ולגאיות
35:9[24] desolations forever	36:4bβ and to the desolate wastes
שממות עולם	ולחרבו השממות
35:9 and your cities will not be inhabited[25]	36:4b and to the abandoned cities
ועריך לא תישבנה	ולערים הנעזבות
	36:10 and the cities will be inhabited
	ונשבו הערים
35:10 Because you said	36:2 because the enemy said concerning you
יען אמרך	יען אמר האויב עליכם
35:10b two nations and two lands will be mine and we will possess it	36:2b and the ancient high places are our possession
את־שני הגוים ואת־שתי הארצות לי תהיינה וירשנוה	ובמות עולם למורשה היתה לנו
	36:5b ... gave my land for themselves as a possession
	אשר נתנו־את־ארצי להם למורשה

---

24. See below 35:12, 14, and 15.

25. BHS notes a few manuscripts of Cairo Geniza read from the root שוב rather than ישב. Zimmerli notes that in spite of Qumran also containing the same, one "should think of a derivation from ישב." See Zimmerli, 2:225.

Ezekiel 35	Ezekiel 36
	36:12b and they will possess you
	וירשוך
35:11 And I will do according to your anger and according to your jealousy	36:5aβ in the fire of my jealousy, I spoke
ועשיתי כאפך וכקנאתך	באש קנאתי דברתי
	36:6 in my jealousy and in my rage, I spoke
	בקנאתי ובחמתי דברתי
35:11 from your hatred against them	36:2 because the one hating said about you
משנאתיך בם	יען אמר האויב עליכם
35:12b I heard all your aspersions[26]	36:15 and I will not cause to hear among you again the reproach of the nations
שמעתי את־כל־נאצותיך	ולא־אשמיע אליך עוד כלמת הגוים
35:12d saying, they are desolated	36:3dα and 4bβ (see above)
לאמר שממה	
35:12e they are given to us for food	36:13 you devour *adam*
לנו נתנו לאכלה	אכלת אדם
	36:14 you will no longer devour *adam*
	אדם לא־תאכלי עוד
35:14b desolation, I will make you	36:3bα and 4bβ (see above)
שממה אעשה־לך	
35:14b as all the land rejoices(ed)	36:5 with wholehearted rejoicing
כשמח כל־הארץ	בשמחת כל־לבב
35:15a as you rejoiced over the inheritance of the house of Israel	
כשמחתך לנחלת בית־ישראל	
35:15a–c as you rejoiced over the inheritance of the house of Israel concerning which it is desolate; thus I will make you, a desolation you will be	36:3bα and 4bβ (see above)
כשמחתך לנחלת בית־ישראל על אשר־שממה כן אעשה־לך שממה תהיה	

Ezekiel 35	Ezekiel 36
35:15a as you rejoiced over the inheritance of the house of Israel	
כשמחתך לנחלת בית־ישראל	
35:15a–c as you rejoiced over the inheritance of the house of Israel concerning which it is desolate; thus I will make you, a desolation you will be	36:3bα and 4bβ (see above)
כשמחתך לנחלת בית־ישראל על אשר־שממה כן אעשה־לך שממה תהיה	
35:15a … over the inheritance of the house of Israel	36:12c and you will be an inheritance for them
לנחלת בית־ישראל	והיית להם לנחלה
35:15c a desolation you will be, Mount Seir, and all Edom, all of it[27]	36:5b I spoke concerning the rest of the nations, and concerning Edom, all of it
שממה תהיה הר־שעיר וכל־אדום כלה	דברתי על־שארית הגוים ועל־אדום כלא
	36:10 I will multiply upon you *adam*, all the house of Israel, all of it
	והרביתי עליכם אדם כל־בית ישראל כלה

Two Cases of Parallel, Linguist Elements

Parallelism and Composition

The notions of "selection" and "combination" are important for understanding parallelism.[27] These terms express the contiguous arrangement of linguistic phenomena that are similar to one another, e.g., an author chooses a word pair and combines them by means of syntactical or semantic relationship into parallel lines. Selection and combination effectuate parallelism and yield a text with poetic function. As it relates to Old Testament studies, these two notions cohere with a mode of biblical authorship in which an author/redactor selected and arranged his textual materials, adapted them as necessary, and wrote additional material in order to combine them into a larger textual unit.[28] In this manner, the author/redactor of Ezekiel 35:1–36:15 was active in selecting material from other prophecies and texts, arranging

---

26. Zimmerli, *Ezekiel*, 2:229 n. 5c.

27. Jakobson, "Linguistics and Poetics," 358.

28. For more on this understanding of biblical authorship, see McKenzie, *Idolatry in the Pentateuch*, 27–59; and Forher, *Exegese des Alten Testaments*, 139–47.

them into corresponding halves, and adapting those texts for his purpose, writing additional material, and thus creating a parallel structure through the two subunits.[29] Although distinct from the traditional understanding of parallelism due to its absence of parallel lines, it nevertheless coheres with linguists' understanding of parallelism in a broader sense of selection and combination of linguistic elements. In this case, the combination is not in parallel lines; rather, it is in contiguous oracular subunits.

The Mountain of Seir and the Mountains of Israel

From the many examples in the list above, this examination will only consider two cases which demonstrate the parallel and purposeful arrangement of Ezek 35:1–15 and 36:1–15. The first case involves the structurally significant equivalences between the opening verses of each subunit in Ezek 35:2 and 36:1 related to "Mount Seir" and the "mountains of Israel." The repeated word "mountain(s)" involves lexical parallelism.[30] However, more is at work here than mere lexical parallelism or repetition of terminology; more also than mere reference to the distinct geographical entities of Mount Seir and the mountains of Israel.[31] Although geographically distinct lexemes, it is by means of their opposite denotation that the author more sharply points to the significance of the parallelism. The familial nomenclature of the mountain(s), "Seir" and "Israel," is pregnant with biblical history and enmity.[32] At one opposition, "Mount Seir" will experience a "desolation and waste" because of their speech directed against the "mountains of Israel" in 35:12. At the opposite pole, conveyed by the antithesis of "Seir," the "mountains of Israel" will realize God's restoration by means of multiplication. The lexical equivalence and morphological (dis)similarity of "mountain(s)"

---

29. It is the selection, arrangement, adaptation, and writing of words, phrases, clauses, and, in this case, textual subunits, which are coherent with the entire textual unit and not merely a layer of redaction within the unit that suggests that the author/redactor is concerned for the sense of the whole unit. However, it is only by discerning the textual pieces, the stages of growth, and their coherence with the whole that leads the reader to share the ideational content with the one who generated the whole. It is ideal to discern the diachronic expansions in a text in order to understand the constructive theology or meaning between an expanded gloss or textual unit and what was extant prior to the gloss. However, that is not my purpose here.

30. The repeated lexeme also involves morphological parallelism through the contrasting singular and plural forms. For the use of a repeated term in parallel lines, see Berlin, *Dynamics*, 68–69.

31. For the geographical denotation of "Mount Seir," see E.A. Knauf, *Anchor Bible Dictionary*, 1072–73.

32. Ibid., for list of passages.

coupled with the contrasting word pair, Israel and Seir, heightens the contrast between God's plans for each entity.

Moreover, the reader discerns an additional parallel aspect between these two phrases involving morphologic parallelism. In 35:3 and in 36:1, the phrases, "Mount Seir" and "the mountains of Israel" are used in a vocative sense. In these clauses, the identically parallel 'case' heightens the parallel connection between the two passages.

Another case of parallelism involving the two mountains is the preposition used to relate the mountain with the imperative "Prophesy." Seemingly a minor detail, nevertheless, the different prepositions demonstrate the purposeful contrast for the two prophecies. In Ezekiel 35:2, the prophet is told to prophesy "against" (על) Mount Seir. Ezek 36:1 uses the preposition "to" (אל) subtly indicating a less confrontational speech to the mountains of Israel.

Furthermore, the mountains of Israel play an important role in the structure of the book.[33] Significantly, the mountains of Israel receive both warnings of desolation and promises of multiplication. After the messenger formula, Ezek 6:2 says, "Son of man, set your face towards the mountains of Israel and prophesy against them."[34] Ezekiel 36:1 seemingly rejoins 6:2 and 35:2 saying, "And you, son of man, prophesy to the mountains of Israel." Significantly, the topographical locations "mountains, hills, channels, and valleys" mentioned as the place in which the slain will fall upon Mount Seir (Ezek 35:8) but mentioned positively concerning the mountains of Israel (Ezek 36:4, 6) are the same topographical locations that are mentioned as the place upon which the LORD will bring the sword on the mountains of Israel in Ezek 6:3. Moreover, in Ezek 36:10–12, the multiplication of *adam* upon the mountains of Israel reverses the judgment of "desolation and waste" against the mountains of Israel which was prophesied in Ezekiel 6 and 33. To be precise, in Ezek 6:14 and 33:28, 29, the mountains of Israel will lie desolate because the land would experience the linguistically identical "desolation and devastation" (שממה ומשמה) that Mount Seir would experience in Ezek 35:3. Upon the mountains of Israel, however, Yahweh will soon multiply *adam* so that the desolation and devastation of Ezekiel 6 and 33 (but not 35?) are forgotten.

In connection with Mount Seir, the similar syntax between the phrase "Mount Seir and all Edom, all of it" (35:15) parallels two similar phrases in

---

33. See Allen, *Ezekiel*, 2:171; Klein, *Schriftauslegung*, 324–36; Parunak, "Structural Studies in Ezekiel."

34. Author's translation throughout; in 6:2, the *lamed* preposition is used. However, the context of the chapter clearly indicates that Ezekiel is to prophesy against them rather than merely to them.

Ezekiel 36. Ezekiel 36:5 indicates that in jealous fire, God spoke against "the remnant of the nations and Edom, all of it." In contrast, God promises to multiply "*adam*, all the house of Israel, all of it" in Ezek 36:10. The similarity in syntax is obvious: a nominal form, conjunction (in 35:15 and 36:5), the adjective "all" plus another nominal form, and the repeated adjective "all" plus pronominal suffix.[35] These similarities compel the reader to link or parallel the phrases and consider the denotative value in the linkage. Furthermore, the important notion of inheritance is at the center of these parallel phrases. On the one hand, "Mount Seir and all Edom, all of it" will become a desolation because they rejoiced over the desolation of Israel's inheritance. (Ezek 35:15) Similarly, in Ezek 36:5, the LORD rages against "the remnant of the nations and Edom, all of it."[36] On the other hand, in Ezek 36:10, the LORD will multiply "*adam*, all the house of Israel, all of it" upon the mountains of Israel and they "will be an inheritance for them." (Ezek 36:12)

Parallelism between Edom and Adam

Phonological Parallelism

These parallel phrases lead to the second case, the lexemes "Edom" (אדום) and "*adam*" (אדם). What is the nature of the linguistic relationship of these two terms? With the addition of the historically long vowel, *holem-waw*, the phonemes which make up "Edom" parallel the phonemes of "*adam*," a term used five times in Ezek 36:10–15.[37] Berlin calls such phonological phenomena "sound pairs" and describes them "as the repetition in parallel words or lines of the same or similar consonants in any order within close proximity."[38] Immanuel Casanowicz, in his classical study of paronomasia calls a phonological relationship that has significance beyond mere sound a "play upon word."[39] For Casanowicz, this relates to the broader term of paronomasia and says this type of paronomasia "implies the combination

---

35. The lack of a conjunction, distinct nominal and pronominal forms, and the lack of "all" plus nominal form in 36:5 comprise differences in the phrase.

36. For the text critical issues concerning this construction, "all of it," see Zimmerli, *Ezekiel*, 2:229–30.

37 The relationship of these two words in 35:1–15 and 36:1–15 leads to a fuller examination of these two terms within the larger unit encompassing these chapters as well as the book of Ezekiel. See Ezek 34:31 and 36:28.

38. Berlin, *Dynamics*, 104.

39. I. M. Casanowicz, *Paronomasia in the Old Testament* (Boston: Norwood, 1894), 15.

of two words of like or similar sound, but with different meanings.[40] Later, as he demonstrates this phenomenon from Old Testament passages, he reiterates that paronomasia is the "union of similarity of sound with dissimilarity of sense."[41] Wilfred Watson, in his study of Hebrew poetry defines paronomasia as "The deliberate choice of two (or more) different words which sound nearly alike."[42] The terms "Edom" and "*adam*" sound alike but are they deliberately chosen to parallel one another? Moreover, in the absence of traditional Hebrew poetry with parallel lines, does their usage qualify for word play?

As stated earlier, parallelism activates various linguistic levels, one of which is the phonological level. A phonologically parallel relationship has greater validity when it takes place within the presence of other parallelisms.[43] Moreover, proximity between the two words that sound alike has been essential for parallelism. This standard explains why Hebrew poetry with traditionally understood parallel lines has drawn most of the attention. However, other types of word plays also utilize sound and do not occur in traditionally understood parallel lines. Perhaps the most common of these are what Casanowicz classifies simply as "plays upon proper names."[44] In order to heighten the case for a parallel relationship between the two terms, there must be similar phonemes and contiguity. As discussed above, even though the two terms are not in parallel lines, they occur within parallel units in the presence of other parallel elements. This type of contiguity in conjunction with the same phonemes strongly suggests that the terms "Edom" and "*adam*" are related to one another intentionally even though not in typical parallel lines or in an etymological pun.[45]

---

40. Casanowicz, *Paronomasia*, 15.

41. Ibid., 26, quoted in Berlin, *Dynamics*, 111.

42. Watson, *Classical Hebrew Poetry*, 242.

43. Casanowicz, *Paronomasia*, 27; Berlin, *Dynamics*, 152, note 2.

44. Casonowicz, *Paronomasia*, 36–40; These etymological puns use words that are related by root as well as words related only by phonemes. An example of the former is the name of Eve in Gen 3:20; the latter, the name of Noah in Gen 5:29.

45. Allen says of these two terms, "It is probably too that we are meant to see the occurrences of אדום "Edom" (36:5) and the repeated אדם "human beings" in 36:10, 11, 12 and in 36:14, 14 as intentional wordplays." Allen, *Ezekiel 20–48*, 171.

The Development and Coherence of Edom
towards Adam within Ezekiel 35:14–36:10

Moreover, other evidence suggests the construction of an intentional parallel relationship between these two terms. This paper began by asking why Edom, in particular, was chosen for this passage. Edom, like other nations, had already received prophetic judgments against them earlier. Furthermore, an unnamed "enemy" seems to be the culprit in Ezek 36:2–4 where the phrase "remnant of the nations" is twice mentioned before a third occurrence is connected to Edom when the LORD speaks against "the remnant of the nations and Edom, all of it." Interestingly, the words spoken by the unnamed enemy and associated with Edom in 36:5 more closely resemble prophetic judgments against other nations. Zimmerli says it well, "The scornful "aha!" (האח) with which the speech of the enemy begins in 36:2a has its correspondence in the words of the Ammonites in 25:3b (האח) and of the inhabitants of Tyre in 26:2a (האח)."[46] Ammon and Tyre are the culprits here, not Edom. Additionally, Ezek 36:5 explicitly mentions only Edom for "scorn of soul" but Ezek 25:6 and 15 accuse the Philistines and sons of Ammon for this precise attitude. Why take another opportunity to blame Edom when in fact it appears that other nations were the ones with this precise attitude?

In connection with an attempt to understand why Edom was spoken against a second time, scholars have tried to explain Edom's supposed attempt to possess the mountains of Israel.[47] In spite of their efforts, no evidence exists for Edomite infiltration into Israel. Zimmerli says of the issue, "In the light of actual historical circumstances the claim seems very strange. Edom never penetrated beyond Jerusalem . . . That, once again, this is not really a geographical statement, but a theological one is clear . . ."[48] Daniel Block in his commentary on Ezekiel goes to considerable lengths to understand the sentiment against Edom in Ezekiel 35. After considering the historical, geographical, and archeological evidence for an incursion into Israel, Block is forced to say, "However, to date there is no evidence for Edomite penetration north of Jerusalem. The prophet is speaking of

---

46. Zimmerli, *Ezekiel*, 2:236; concerning "Edom" in 36:5, he states, "The specific reference to Edom has been added only secondarily in v 5." Zimmerli, *Ezekiel*, 2:233. This construction seems to suggest an expansion here upon the prophecies concerning the Ammonites and Tyre.

47. Block, *Ezekiel*, 2:319; Johan Lust, "Edom—Adam in Ezekiel, in the MT and LXX," in *Studies in the Hebrew Bible, Qumran, and the Septuagint: Presented to Eugene Ulrich* (Boston: Brill, 2006), 391; Zimmerli, *Ezekiel*, 2:234–35.

48. Zimmerli, *Ezekiel*, 2:235.

Edomite aspirations rather than historical reality."[49] Historical factors alone are unable to account for a second denunciation against Edom. Indeed, as Zimmerli has suggested, the basis for which the term Edom has been used is not primarily geographical or historical but theological in conjunction with its poetic and referential functions.

The connection between Edom, Mount Seir, and Israel can be traced to the book of Genesis and the portrayal of the relationship between Esau and Jacob.[50] More specific to the point here, however, is Edom's relationship to "all the land" and "the rest of the nations" in Ezekiel 35 and 36.[51] This relationship is expounded upon in Ezek 35:14–36:5. Ezekiel 35:14b begins saying "as all the land rejoices(ed?), a desolation, I will make you."[52] As pointed out above regarding the phrase "scorn of soul," Ammon is actually accused of "rejoicing with scorn of soul," not Edom. Moreover, the remnant of the nations and Edom are accused of rejoicing in 36:5. An apparent attempt to clarify 35:14b, Ezek 35:15 begins in similar manner as 35:14b, "As you rejoiced over the inheritance of the house of Israel because it was desolated, thus I will do to you. A desolation you will be, Mount Seir and all Edom, all of it." Prior to the appellation "Edom" in Ezek 35:15, Mount Seir had been the explicit object of judgment in the chapter. Here, however, "Mount Seir" is related to "Edom, all of it."

In further explanation, Ezek 36:1–4 makes clear that the "from every side, the remnant of the nations" pursued the mountains of Israel as a "possession." Two explicit references to both phrases, "from every side" and "the remnant of the nations" in Ezek 36:3 and 4 and their repeated usage through 36:7, suggest that a much wider object of retribution lies at hand than only "Mount Seir" or "Edom." In Ezek 36:5, God speaks in fiery jealousy and will soon act "against the remnant of nations and Edom, all of it." Here, "Edom, all of it" is conjoined to "the remnant of the nations." God speaks against these entities because they appropriated his land as a possession. God's oath against the nations and Edom in 36:5 parallels Mount Seir's words in Ezek

---

49. Block, *Ezekiel*, 2:319.

50. Dicou, *Edom*.

51. "Edom" is mentioned previously in the book in 32:29 at the end of the chapters concerning judgments upon the nations. Moreover, it is used 4 times in Ezekiel 25:12–14 in a section of judgment against Edom.

52. It is quite possible that Ezek 35:15 comments on the connotation of "all the land" in 35:14. To put the matter a different way, "Mount Seir, Edom, all of it" is parallel to "all the land." The question is whether the infinitive should be considered a past or present tense verb. For the issues surrounding text and translation, see Parunak, "Structural Studies."

35:10, "We will possess it."⁵³ Indeed, Edom seems to be a hinge upon which Mount Seir and "the rest of the nations" turn. Judgment is pronounced upon Edom, not because ethnic Edomites alone are the denotative referent but because "Edom" is used in association with "Mount Seir" and "the rest of the nations."

This paper has shown the relationship "Mount Seir," "Edom," and "the rest of the nations" in Ezekiel 35:14—36:5. The LORD spoke "in the fire of my jealousy" against "the rest of the nations and Edom, all of it." This section will demonstrate the coherence of "the rest of the nations and Edom, all of it" to the parallel nominal phrase "*adam*, all the house of Israel, all of it." (Ezek 36:10) In spite of the composite nature of the unit, Ezek 36:5–10 advances this "nations'" theme and develops other themes found within 36:1–4. First, in Ezek 36:6, Ezekiel was to prophesy to the land of Israel and speak "to the mountains and to the hills, to the channels, and to the valleys," four types of terrain which are also addressed in Ezek 36:4.⁵⁴ Second, in Ezek 36:6, Ezekiel was to speak to the terrain because the LORD had spoken in his anger and "in my jealousy," the precise reason for which he spoke in Ezek 36:5. Finally, the topic of the nations recurs at the end of 36:6 where he says to the terrain "because you have borne the reproach of the nations." The "nations around you" appears again in 36:7 demonstrating the emphasis of "nations" to the unit.

Ezekiel 36:7 begins with "therefore" signaling coherence with verse 6 in addition to two other links to 36:6b by means of the term, נשׂא "to lift up." First, in response to the terrain "lifting up" (נשׂא) the reproach of the nations in 36:6b, God will lift up (נשׂא) his hand in an oath. Second, Ezek 36:7b reads, "Indeed the nations which are all around you, they, they will lift up (נשׂא) their reproach." In other words, because the mountains of Israel bore (נשׂא) the reproach of the rest of the nations, God bore (נשׂא)

---

53. In Ezek 36:12, *adam*, will possess the mountains of Israel.

54. This case would be another example of Talmon's distant parallelism in which the order of words is inverted in order to connect passages together. In Ezek 35:8, the LORD will fill the mountains of Mount Seir with its slain and they will fall into the hills, valleys, and channels. With lexical and semantic similarity, the author contrasts this desolation that will take place on Mount Seir with the multiplication that will take place on the mountains of Israel. Ezekiel 36:4 reads, "Therefore, mountains of Israel, hear the word of the LORD God . . . to the mountains and hills, to channels and valleys, and to the desolate waste places and abandoned cities . . ." Ezekiel 36:6 reads again, "Therefore, prophesy concerning the land of Israel and say to the mountains and hills, to the channels and valleys, thus says the LORD . . ." The final two words in each of these series, "valleys and channels" in 35:8 and "channels and valleys" in 36:4 and 36:6 have been inverted strongly suggesting a link between the two units. Talmon, *Text and Canon*, 53–60. See also Ezek 6:3.

it upon himself in an oath that the rest of the nations would indeed bear (נשא) their own reproach.

Additionally, Ezek 36:7 introduces the repeated use of nominative, independent personal pronouns in the oath formula. This use of the independent personal pronoun marks a material connection to what follows in 36:7b and 36:8. To augment the connection made by נשא, the independent personal pronoun in 36:7ab coordinates the action of God in the lifting of his hand, "I, I lift my hand" with usage of the nominative pronoun in 36:7b in the action of the nations that "they, they would lift their reproach."[55]

The connection between the clauses by means of "lift up" and the nominative independent personal pronoun continues in 36:8. Speaking specifically to them, God says, "and you, mountains of Israel, you will give your branch and your fruit you will lift up for my people."[56] (נשא) The coherence and sense of the composite text appear straightforward. In response to the mountains of Israel "lifting" the reproach of the nations, of which Edom alone is explicit, God "lifts" his hand in oath and will cause the nations to "lift" reproach. Moreover, in Ezek 36:8, the mountains of Israel, in agricultural imagery, will "lift" fruit in due time. In explanation, Ezek 36:9 proceeds by means of dependence upon Leviticus 26 and with agricultural imagery.[57] God will turn to them; they will be cultivated and sown.

Although there is a shift in terminology, the continued verbal association with Leviticus 26 shows that 36:10 elaborates on the כי clause and imagery of cultivation and sowing in 36:9.[58] Ezekiel 36:10 reads "I will multiply upon you *adam*, all the house of Israel, all of it." Significantly, by means of this parallel nominal phrase and adjective plus suffix, "all of it," the connection between "Edom" and "*adam*" becomes apparent. Used only five times in the book of Ezekiel, the aforementioned parallel phrases of 35:15 "Mount Seir and all Edom, all of it," 36:5 "against the rest of the nation, and against Edom, all of it," and 36:10 "*adam*, all the house of Israel, all of it" compel the reader to compare and contrast the phrases.[59] Mount Seir, Edom, all of it, will lift up their reproach while the mountains of Israel will lift up their fruit, *adam*, all the house of Israel, all of it. This coherence within Ezek 35:14—36:10 built through the parallel phrases, the theme of nations, the recurrence of the term "lift up," and the use of indepen-

---

55. See Crane who calls this a "word play"; Crane, *Israel's Restoration*, 48.

56. Although not necessarily pertinent for my main line of argumentation, LXX and Old Latin do not attest "Israel."

57. Lyons, *From Law to Prophecy*.

58. והרביתי.

59. See also Ezek 11:15; 20:40.

dent personal pronouns suggest a deliberate attempt to associate the term "Edom" with the term "*adam*."

Moreover, the cohesion in the passage reinforces the correspondence between God's desolation of "the rest of the nations and Edom, all of it," and God's multiplication of "*adam*, all the house of Israel, all of it." God will make Mount Seir desolate, that is, "Edom, all of it." He will make them lift up their reproach by making the mountains of Israel lift up fruit and branches. He will multiply "*adam*, all the house of Israel, all of it" upon the mountains of Israel. "Edom" is a moniker representing all nations who were in opposition to the God of Israel. The name was syntactically linked with "Mount Seir" and "the rest of the nations" and was, therefore, used intentionally because it sounds like *adam*, a term which denotes mankind, in general, and can connote all humanity upon the earth.

Others have already noted the universal connotation of the term, Edom.[60] Discussing Amos 9, John Sailhamer writes, "Israel's enemies are collectivized here in the form of the nation of Edom, not only because Edom was historically a perennial enemy of Israel, but more importantly because the Hebrew name *Edom* can also be read as "humanity."[61] In his discussion concerning Amos and the theology of the Hebrew Bible, Sailhamer recognizes two issues which concern this analysis. First, "Edom" is used as a moniker indicating all of Israel's enemies. Second, "Edom" is used because the phonemes which make up its name are parallel to "*adam*," a term which denotes humanity. The next section will advance this thesis by examining Genesis 1 language and its usage in this passage.

Genesis 1 Language in Ezekiel 36:10–12

Scholars have often noted a connection between Ezekiel and the book of Leviticus. More specifically, scholars have observed that Ezekiel 36:9–11 has terminological and syntactical connections with the Holiness Code in Leviticus 26.[62] In effect, this "multiplication" oracle of Ezekiel 36 reverses the curses of Leviticus 26 and extends the blessings in an unconditional manner, contra Leviticus 26.[63] The blessings in Leviticus 26 are conditioned upon

---

60. See Stuart, *Hosea–Jonah*, 398, for a similar connection of Edom to "all the nations."

61. Sailhamer, *Introduction to Old Testament Theology*, 251.

62. Lyons, *From Law to Prophecy*, 88–90; Klein, *Schriftauslegung*, 339–40; Ka Leung Wong, *Idea of Retribution*, 116.

63. For a list of the commentaries mentioning the relationship of Ezekiel to Leviticus see Lyons, *From Law to Prophecy*, 5–6. More specifically, Lyon's examines Ezekiel's dependence upon the Holiness Code in Leviticus, contra Zimmerli, *Ezekiel 2*, 230. See

obedience that did not take place and Israel was exiled. Ezekiel 36:8–15 and indeed, throughout the remainder of the book, speaks of an unconditional act of God in which the mountains of Israel would receive multiplication.

Scholars have also noted terminology and syntax in Ezekiel 36:10–11 associated with Genesis 1 and other P texts through the clauses "be fruitful and multiply."[64] In Ezek 36:10, the clause "I will multiply upon you *adam*," while possibly suggestive of Genesis 1, is much more likely strictly associated with previous passages in the book of Ezekiel in which man or beast is cut off and/or dependent upon Lev 26:9 which uses the same "I will multiply" and which also has similar expression as Ezek 36:9.[65] The same could be said for 36:11 initially because of its precise repetition of "I will multiply upon you *adam* . . ." An intentional association with Genesis 1 is made more likely, however, by the pairing of "man and beast." Leviticus never threatens to cut off both "man and beast."[66] The threat in Leviticus was only to בהמה. It appears unlikely then, that the author of Ezekiel was utilizing Leviticus only. A verbatim pairing of "man and beast" does not occur in Genesis 1 although their association with one another is suggested since their fate is often tied to one another in the creation account and early chapters of Genesis.[67] The threat that God would "cut off man and beast" is made earlier in the book of Ezekiel to an unnamed country, to Edom, and to Egypt.[68] The use of "man and beast" is inconclusive in itself to suggest Genesis 1. However, when the phrase is used with the collocation ורבו ופרו, it strongly suggests a contextual awareness of Genesis 1.

Specifically, the use of the terms ורבו ופרו in *qal* perfect, 3rd plural strengthens the intentional association with Genesis 1.[69] In Genesis 1,

---

also Wong, *Idea of Retribution*, 116.

64. One of the complexities is an understanding of how Leviticus 26 and Genesis 1 or other P texts are related in the Pentateuch itself. Although that matter lies outside the parameters of this paper, it is likely, as will be discussed below, that Ezekiel 36 conflates the two passages into a multiplication program. On the association of Ezekiel 36:10–12 with Genesis 1 (or "the blessing formula of P") see Zimmerli, *Ezekiel 2*, 230, 238; Block, *Ezekiel*, 2:334. Both Zimmerli and Block also discuss the relationship to Leviticus 26, Zimmerli, *Ezekiel*, 2:230, 238; Block, *Ezekiel*, 2:333–34. See also Klein, *Schriftauslegung*, 307–9; Crane, *Israel's Restoration*, 50–53; Kutsko, *Between Heaven and Earth*, 130–32.

65. See Lyons, *From Law to Prophecy*, 89, concerning Lev 26:9; see also Ezek 14:13, 17, and 19 when Ezekiel spoke concerning an unnamed country "to cut off from it man and beast." See also Ezek 25:13 and 29:8 when God "will cut off man and beast" from Edom and Egypt.

66. Concerning Lev 26:22, see Lyons, *From Law to Prophecy*, 89–92.

67. Gen 1:24, 25, 26, 2:20, 3:12–14, and 6:7.

68. Ezek 14:13, 17, 19, 21; 25:13, 29:8. See also Jer 32:43, 36:29 and Zeph 1:3.

69. For text-critical issues and lacunae in the LXX, see Crane, *Israel's Restoration*, 53

these same lexemes appear as imperatives but their consonantal spelling is precisely the same as occurs in Ezek 36:11. In Ezek 36:11, they are syntactically joined by *waw* with no intervening material as they also occur in Gen 1:22, 28, 8:17, 9:1, and 7.[70] Although these same verbs appear in Lev 26:9, they occur in the *hiphil* stem, have a different grammatical person, and are syntactically separated by the sign of the accusative with a suffixed pronoun. Additionally, nowhere else in Leviticus nor Ezekiel are these two terms paired together.[71] Furthermore, except for Ezek 36:11, neither Leviticus nor Ezekiel alludes to a multiplication of "man and beast" as occurs in the early chapters of Genesis where the fate of man and beast are tied to one another.[72] Since the collocation "man and beast" does not occur in Leviticus, and since neither Leviticus nor Ezekiel (with the exception of this passage) depict a multiplication and fruitfulness of both man and beast, it appears likely that the passage evinces a contextual awareness of Genesis 1. In a discussion of concepts related to creation, and restoration, John Kutsko discusses this "interpretive gloss" which is not found in some LXX manuscripts. He writes, "Early readers of Ezekiel confirm that this association with creation traditions was conspicuous ... Its absence in the Greek cannot be plainly explained other than by concluding that it is an interpretive gloss, following quite closely, however, the imagery of the text."[73] The multiplication of man and beast appears natural in chapter 36 as a reversal of what was threatened previously in Leviticus and Ezekiel and in connection to the original blessing and intention of Genesis 1.

The verb והטבתי also suggests the well-known adjective in Genesis 1, טוב. God will do "good" more so than in their "beginnings." This verb connected syntactically through the comparative מן to the noun "beginning" likewise demonstrates a contextual awareness of Genesis 1. Here the

---

and *passim*. Although several scholars think the "and they will multiply and be fruitful" is secondary because of the 3rd plural verb, the 3rd plural verbs alone should not dictate that. As Block points out, 36:12 also contains plural references after the accusative noun "*adam*" and commonly understood apposition "my people, Israel." Its absence in the LXX Codex A strongly suggests, however, the likelihood of an addition. If that is the case, the point is made that a scribe also discerned an awareness of Genesis 1 and interpreted this passage in light of that observation. See Jake Stromberg, "Observations on Inner-Scriptural Scribal Expansion in MT Ezekiel" *VT* 58 (2008) 74, 84; and remarks by Kutsko below, *Between Heaven and Earth*, 131.

70. One can account for the different sequence of רבו ופרו in different ways. See Lyons, *From Law to Prophecy*, 89; Crane, *Israel's Restoration*, who quotes Greenberg, 52; Kutsko, *Between Heaven and Earth*, 131.

71. פרה is only used one other time in Ezekiel 19:10 and nowhere else in Leviticus.

72. Gen 1:24–28, 8:17, 9:10.

73. Kutsko, *Between Heaven and Earth*, 130–31.

dubious noun ראשה, translated as "beginnings" leaves little doubt that an association with Genesis 1:1 through the related term ראשית is intended. Only this time, God's multiplication program will be "gooder" [sic] than "in the beginning."[74]

Ezekiel 36:12

The term *adam* is repeated in Ezek 36:12 and indeed, throughout the remainder of the passage, it lies at the center of the multiplication program. God will "cause *adam* to walk upon you." Ezekiel 36:12 links what has come in the previous two verses to what will follow in the subsequent three verses, in part, by the term *adam*.[75] What is the purpose of the dependence upon Genesis 1? The multiplication program involves a return to the garden. It depicts the gathering of God's people from the nations as a multiplication and fruitful time in which God will fill the land again and even do more than he did at their beginnings. The dependence upon Genesis 1 likewise commends a universal connotation of *adam* and accommodates an interpretation of Ezekiel 36 that extends beyond the borders of ethnic Israel. What else can be said about this multiplication of *adam*?

Ezekiel 36:12 develops what came previous in Ezek 36:10–11. God would multiply *adam* (and beast) upon the mountains of Israel. The result was "they will multiply and they will be fruitful." Ezekiel 36:12 repeats the word *adam* as God will cause them to walk upon the mountains of Israel. The difficulty lies in the next clause as the 2nd masculine plural pronoun referring to the mountains switches to singular. A host of text critical problems appear but the sense appears straightforward. "They" would possess the mountains of Israel as an inheritance. Just as the pronoun "they" in "they will multiply . . ." referred to *adam*, now the pronoun "they" in "they will possess" also refers to *adam*. The supplementary material in 36:12a is the commonly understood accusative marker conjoined to "my people, Israel." In other words, the term *adam* is taken to be in apposition with "my people, Israel." Is it possible, however, that the sign of the accusative usually taken to be in apposition to *adam* should be taken as the heteronym "with?" The resulting translation would read "And I will cause to walk upon you *adam*

---

74. For ראשה, see Crane, *Israel's Restoration*, 53; and Stromberg, "Observations," 73–74.

75. An additional connection is the reversal of the bereavement of children theme in 36:13–15 by the "causing *adam* to walk" here in 36:12. Additionally, instead of "cause to walk," LXX 967 has "I will beget." It is difficult not to read John 3 in view of this manuscript.

with my people, Israel, and they will possess you . . ." If this is the case, *adam* and Israel would possess the mountains of Israel as an inheritance.

The use of *adam* could indicate that God's multiplication program would extend beyond the Southern Kingdom to the Northern Kingdom.[76] Indeed, just as Edom is representative of "the rest of the nations," so *adam* represents the inclusion of not only Northern and Southern Israel but also individuals from all mankind. The similarities between Edom and *adam* indicate much more than mere aesthetic tendency and "Bible speak."[77] Indeed as Linda Waugh writes about the poetry and its influence upon meaning, "A parallelism in sound . . . is often taken as a sign of a concomitant parallelism in meaning: equivalence in sound is assumed to signal equivalence in meaning."[78] *Adam* is used with Genesis 1 language because of its universal perspective of the primeval history. *Adam* is also used because it sounds like Edom and like Edom in this passage, similarly connotes a representation of all mankind.

The similarities in these two terms demonstrate a universal perspective in Ezekiel 35 and 36. The contrast between the two terms, moreover, speaks of the judgment upon all nations but the multiplication of all *adam* upon the mountains of Israel. But is there evidence of other interpreters who have understood the accusative marker as the preposition "with?" The next section will briefly consider three texts that indicate similar trajectories of meaning.

In summary, Edom is a moniker for "the rest of the nations" and is used intentionally because it is phonologically related to "*adam*," a term associated with Genesis 1. Ezekiel 36 utilizes terminology from Genesis 1 because God will fill the mountains of Israel with "*adam*" and will do good to them—even better than in the beginning. The use of "*adam*" accommodates an understanding of this multiplication program beyond that of Judah and the Southern Kingdom, even beyond that of the Northern Kingdom, a particular application of this passage in the subsequent chapter, to that of all mankind—Israel and non-Israel. *Adam* with Israel will possess the mountains of Israel. These terms used in conjunction with the verb "possess" reveal a particular reception in the prophets, translation of the LXX, and the New Testament. Israel will "possess" the nations and the nations will "possess" Israel. The next section will briefly address these instances of reception.

---

76. See Ezek 37:15–28.
77. Stromberg, "Observations," 84–85.
78. Waugh, "Poetic Function," 155.

Edom/*Adam* and Ancient Interpreters

Amos 9:12

An exhaustive discussion of these instances of reception is beyond the scope of this paper. Rather, this section will briefly suggest the plausible reception of concepts and terminology related to the thesis of this paper. The famous translational gloss involving Amos 9:12 demonstrates a similar trajectory of interpretation as that suggested above for Ezek 36:12.[79] MT Amos 9:12 reads, "In order that they may possess the remnant of Edom and all the nations which my name is called among them." It appears that the LXX translator read "*adam*," for "Edom," and "seek" for "possess" amid the eschatological nature of Israel's restoration.[80] Amos 9:12 in the LXX reads ὅπως ἐκζητήσωσιν οἱ κατάλοιποι τῶν ἀνθρώπων καὶ . . ."[81] Mike Shepherd suggests one other gloss in the translation of the accusative marker. "Codex Alexandrinus and Acts 15,17 include τὸν κύριον (the Lord) as the direct object of the verb "seek." This is apparently an interpretation of the marker את (the Aleph and the Taw, otherwise known as the Alpha and the Omega, the beginning and the end [Isa 41,4; 44,6; Rev 1:8; 22:13])."[82] Notwithstanding the many text-critical questions this passage raises, it appears at the least, that the LXX demonstrates the manner in which an early community understood the term "Edom" and "possess." It is possible that the translator of the Septuagint even interpreted Amos 9 in light of Ezekiel 35–36. Another likely influence upon the LXX text of Amos 9:12 involves its relationship to another Edom/*adam* passage, its canonical neighbor, Obadiah.

Obadiah

Subsequent to Amos, Obadiah picks up where Amos ended. Edom will be judged for its deeds of arrogance. Moreover, as James Nogalski points out, Edom 1:1 indicates that Edom will be judged among the nations, the same

---

79. For a fuller discussion, see Glenny, *Finding Meaning in the Text*, 216–28.

80. See the phrases "days are coming" and "in that day" in Amos 8:3, 9, 11, 13, 9:11 and 13, both of which have eschatological connotations. Acts 15:15–18 presumably uses the LXX and recognizes the eschatological significance of Gentile inclusion into the people of God.

81. According to the Göttingen LXX, all manuscripts of the LXX have some form of ἐκζητήσωσιν. Some versions have a future plural while others have the subjunctive as seen above. The fact that the LXX manuscripts agree indicates that this was not a later Christian interpolation of an original translation. *Septuaginta VT Graecum Vol XIII*, 98.

82. Shepherd, "Compositional Analysis of the Twelve," 187–88.

terms "Edom" and "nations" as occurring in Amos 9:12.[83] Paul Reddit, in *Introduction to the Prophets*, discerns a problem with Edom's notoriety. He discusses the message of Obadiah as it relates to judgment against Edom on the day of the LORD. The problem "is that Edom was not the real culprit in the sacking of Jerusalem. That culprit was Babylonia. If anyone deserved to be punished severely for what happened to Jerusalem, it was Babylon. To predict the destruction of Edom for whatever minor role it had in the fall of Jerusalem was to ascribe to that role far more guilt than the circumstances might seem to us to warrant."[84] If Edom was not ultimately culpable in Jerusalem's demise, why single out that nation for destruction in the eschaton?

The answer lies in the entire composite text of Obadiah.[85] Edom will indeed be judged for its deeds. Interestingly, one reason for Edom's judgment in Obadiah bears similarity to the reason mentioned in Ezekiel 35 and 36. It will be judged because it "rejoiced over" the ruin of God's people.[86] Indeed, not against Edom only but the "day of the LORD draws near over all nations" in Obadiah 15.[87] Moreover, this oft-mentioned judgment day, occurring repeatedly in Obadiah and Amos 8–9, has been noted as a mark of unity in The Twelve.[88] The short book of Edom transitions from judgment against Edom and the nations to a message of salvation in Obadiah 17. Significantly, the transition involves the lexeme "possess" (ירש). It reads, "[T]he house of Jacob will possess the ones possessing them."[89] The remainder of the book balances the judgment against Edom in the first 16 verses with a message of salvation.

Obadiah 18 closes with the house of Esau lacking a survivor as the house of Jacob and Joseph consume them with fire. Obadiah 19 opens with "and the Negev will possess the mountain of Esau." Moreover, a second occurrence of "possess" insures that the Negev and the lowland, indeed all Israel will be in on the "possession." Remarkable, however, is Obadiah 20. Although an extremely complex text, its complexity lies as much in what is said rather than complex syntax or textual variants. It rather literally reads

---

83. Nogalski, *Literary Precursors*, 28–29.

84. Redditt, *Introduction to the Prophets*, 254–55.

85. For a critical examination of Obadiah, see Ehud Ben Zvi, *A Historical-Critical Study of the Book of Obadiah*.

86. Obadiah 12.

87. Interestingly, in the same manner as Ezek 36:8 indicated that "they [the fruit] draw near."

88. House, *Unity of the Twelve*. For an eschatological day in Obadiah, see vv. 8 and 15. See also ten other occurrences of יום in Obadiah 11–14.

89. For the dubious nature of "the ones possessing them," see *HALOT*, *BDB*, versions, and Ben Zvi, *Obadiah*, 187–89.

"and the captives of this fortress to (?) the sons of Israel who are Canaanites unto Zarepheth and the exiles of Jerusalem who are in Sepharad will possess the cities of the Negev." In other words, the Negev will possess the land of the Canaanites and the captives who are Canaanites will possess the cities of the Negev.

Marvin Sweeney, in his commentary on the Twelve, perceives the difficulty in what is written. After a lengthy discussion concerning the sense of the passage, he writes, "It seems best then to read verse 20 as a statement that 'the exile of this territory of the people of Israel who are Canaanites as far as Zarephath,' i.e. those people of the Northern Israel who lived in the Phoenician/Canaanite territories as far as Zarephath would join the exiles of Judah who are in Sepharad in regaining possession of the Negev."[90] While this understanding would seemingly make sense, it is not what it says. It is interesting to note, however, that Sweeney does understand that "captives . . . who are Canaanites" would take part with the captives of Jerusalem "in regaining possession of the Negev."[91] The difference concerns that which is meant by "captives . . . who are Canaanites." Although ethnically and theologically incredible, the text is not, however, nonsensical. Exiles, who are Canaanites, appear to participate in the possession of the Negev. That is, the Negev and Israel will possess the land of the Canaanites and the captives who are Canaanites will possess the cities of the Negev. Obadiah 21 concludes by saying that the kingdom will then belong to the LORD. John Sailhamer writes in *Introduction to Old Testament Theology*,

> Though the translation of this brief narrative is difficult, the gist of it is clear: Israel's *possession* of Edom is taken as a sign of Edom's (humanity's) membership in God's kingdom. The "survivors" of Edom will be no more (Ob 18b) because the "exiles" of their armies, who are Canaanites(!), will belong to Israel and God's kingdom (Ob 20). The messianic Savior will rule over Edom from Mount Zion in Jerusalem (Ob 21). In the final composition of the book of Obadiah, the writer envisions the inclusion of Edom into God's messianic kingdom as an image of the universal reign of the messianic king. The picture of Edom in the book of Obadiah, then, portrays the inclusion of the gentile nations into God's blessing.[92]

Sailhamer is attempting to describe the importance of the order of books in discerning a theology from a canon.

---

90. Sweeney, *The Twelve Prophets*, vol. 1, 297.
91. Ibid.
92. Sailhamer, *Introduction to OT Theology*, 251.

Shepherd is helpful again as he considers the seam between Amos and Obadiah, "The following 'book' of Obadiah begins with the judgment of Edom, but its conclusion has to do with the messianic kingdom and the possession of Gentile nations like Edom. The five occurrences in Ob 17–21 of words related to the root ירשׁ ("to possess") make the connection with Am 9,12 very strong."[93] Later, as he considers the move from Obadiah to Jonah, Shepherd notes the same theme in Jonah of Gentile inclusion in God's purposes. He concludes, "Jonah 1–4 is a defense of God's right to have compassion on the Gentiles (Jonah 4,11), of whom Nineveh is the representative. Thus, the great city of Nineveh is to Jonah what Edom is to Amos and Obadiah."[94] The book of Jonah describes the salvation of pagan sailors and Israel's enemy, Nineveh, even as their own prophet seemingly fails to grasp the truth of "Salvation belongs to the Lord" and the depth of God's compassion.[95]

The intersection between Amos and Obadiah does not exhaust this treatment of the term "Edom" as it relates to "*adam.*" A significant messianic poem in Numbers 24 likewise comments on Edom's relationship to "Jacob."[96] Numbers 24:18 says of Edom, "Edom will be a possession and Seir, his enemies, will be a possession." The eschatological and messianic context suggests that the passages of Ezekiel, Amos, and Obadiah share a similar communication goal. Sailhamer writes concerning the Balaam oracles, "In Num 24:5, Balaam begins his oracle with a vision of the restoration of the garden planted by Yahweh (24:5–7a) and the rise of a future king in Israel (24:7b–9). The poems continue in 24:17–20 to speak of Israel's future defeat of their historical enemies. Balaam's oracles conclude by casting a broad vision of the future in which the later prophetic events of Daniel and Ezekiel are portrayed."[97] In this poem, the reader again discerns similar terminology and a concept of the eschatological kingdom in which Israel possesses Edom and the nations of the earth.

John 10

Immediately prior to book's prophecy of Edom's desolation in Ezekiel 35, Ezekiel 34 prophesies a Davidic shepherd who will pasture God's flock with

---

93. Shepherd, "Compositional Analysis," 187–88.

94. Ibid., 188.

95. Indeed, Joel, Nahum, Habakkuk, and other 'books' within the Twelve have their own unique emphasis on God's treatment of "all flesh." See Joel 3:1 (EVV 2:28).

96. Sailhamer has demonstrated the eschatological introduction of three major poems in the Pentateuch ("in the last days"), which concerns a messianic king ultimately coming from Jacob/Judah. See his book, *The Pentateuch as Narrative*, 35–37.

97. Sailhamer, "Hosea 11:1 and Matthew 2:15," 94.

justice. Ezekiel states that God will establish over his sheep one shepherd, his servant David, who will feed them and shepherd them. At the end of the chapter, Ezek 34:29c, utilizing the same terminology as in Ezek 36:6–7, says of the new sheep, "they will not lift up again the reproach of the nations." Instead, these sheep know that God is in their presence and because of his presence, they are safe and are the house of Israel. In the final verse of the chapter, Ezek 34:31 says "and you are my sheep, the sheep of my pasture. You are *adam*. And I, I am your God." The Gospel of John, as a first or second century interpretation of Ezekiel and the events surrounding Jesus' life, understands the shepherd imagery of Ezekiel 34 in light of Jesus' own words about being the good shepherd. In an obvious allusion to Ezekiel, Jesus says, "I am the Good Shepherd . . . I have other sheep which are not from this fold and I must also bring them and they will hear my voice and they will become one flock, one shepherd."[98] It seems likely that the author understands the *adam* of Ezek 34:31 to refer to an inclusion of individuals in Jesus' flock beyond that of Jesus' own people, Israel.

Conclusion

Ezekiel 35 and 36:1–15 occur at an important point within the book of Ezekiel. Structurally, these two subunits occur in the oracles of salvation clustered in the second half of the book of Ezekiel.[99] Furthermore, the two subunits follow a messianic oracle and precede two important oracles concerning a future gathering and constitution of God's people to the land. Ezek 36:1–15 with its concern for a future multiplication of God's people on the mountains of Israel has important implications upon the following oracles. These factors suggest that the two subunits play an important role about the constitution of the land and its population in the future. For these reasons, the paper has shown the intentionality behind the use of "Edom." It is intentionally punned with *adam* in Ezek 35:1–16:15 in order to articulate that God's desolation of his enemies from all nations corresponds to his multiplication of his people from all mankind. It has done so by analyzing parallelisms in Ezek 35:1–15 and 36:1–15. The paper analyzed the function of Edom within Ezekiel 35 and its connection to *adam* within Ezekiel 36:1–15. The paper also considered the intentional portrayal of the multiplication of *adam* on the mountains of Israel with the language of Genesis 1 in order to suggest that *adam* was used to indicate an Edenic, universal multiplication of *adam* and not merely a national restoration of Israel. Last, the paper considered the nexus between Amos and Obadiah, as well as Number 24 in

---

98. John 10:14–16.
99. Westermann, *Prophetic Oracles of Salvation in the Old Testament*, 169–77.

order to show other passages with a similar communication strategy. The brief description of the Gospel of John's allusion to Ezekiel 34 was meant to be another example of early interpretation that understood the book's scope to have a universal perspective.

Bibliography

Allen, Leslie C. *Ezekiel 20–48*. WBC 29. Dallas: Word, 1990.
Ben Zvi, Ehud. *A Historical-Critical Study of the Book of Obadiah*. BZAW 242. Berlin: de Gruyter, 1996.
Berlin, Adele. *The Dynamics of Biblical Parallelism*. Rev. and exp. Biblical Resource Series. Grand Rapids: Eerdmans, 2008.
Block, Daniel I. *The Book of Ezekiel*. 2 vols. NICOT. Grand Rapids: Eerdmans, 1998.
Casanowicz, I. M. *Paronomasia in the Old Testament*. Boston: Norwood, 1894.
Cooke, G. A. *The Book of Ezekiel*. International Critical Commentary. Edinburgh: T. & T. Clark, 1931.
Crane, Ashley S. *Israel's Restoration: A Textual-Comparative Exploration of Ezekiel 36–39*. VTSup 122. Leiden: Brill, 2008.
Dahood, Mitchell. "Ugaritic Hebrew Parallel Pairs." In *Ras Shamra Parallels*. Vol. 1. Edited by Loren Fisher, 71–382. Analecta Orientalia 49. Rome: Pontificium Institutum Biblicum, 1972.
Dicou, Bert. *Edom, Israel's Brother and Antagonist: The Role of Edom in Biblical Prophecy and Story*. JSOTSup 169. Sheffield: JSOT Press, 1994.
Eichrodt, Walther. *Ezekiel*. Translated by Cosslett Quin. OTL. Philadelphia: Westminster, 1970.
Forher, Georg. *Exegese des Alten Testaments: Einführung in die Methodik*. Heidelberg: Quelle & Meyer, 1993.
Glenny, W. Edward. *Finding Meaning in the Text: Translation Technique and Theology in the Septuagint of Amos*. VTSup 126. Leiden: Brill, 2009.
Greenberg, Moshe. *Ezekiel 1–20*. AB 22. New York: Doubleday, 1983.
———. *Ezekiel 21–37*. AB 22A. New York: Doubleday, 1997.
Hals, Ronald M. *Ezekiel*. Forms of the Old Testament Literature 19. Grand Rapids: Eerdmans, 1989.
House, Paul. *The Unity of the Twelve*. JSOTSup 97. Sheffield: Almond, 1990.
Howard, David. "Recent Trends in Psalms Study." In *The Face of Old Testament Studies*, edited by David W. Baker and Bill T. Arnold, 329–68. Grand Rapids: Baker, 1999.
Hummel, Horace D. *Ezekiel 21–48*. Concordia Commentary. St Louis: Concordia, 2007.
Jakobson, Roman. "Linguistics and Poetics." In *Style in Language*, edited by Thomas A. Sebeok, 350–77. New York: Wiley, 1960.
Klein, Anja. *Schriftauslegung im Ezechielbuch: Redaktionsgeschichtliche Untersuchungen zu Ez 34–39*. BZAW 391. Berlin: de Gruyter, 2008.
Knauf, E. A. "Mount Seir." In *Anchor Bible Dictionary*, ed. David Noel Freedman, 1072–73. New York: Doubleday, 1992.
Kugel, James L. *The Idea of Biblical Poetry: Parallelism and Its History*. New Haven: Yale University Press, 1981.
Kutsko, John F. *Between Heaven and Earth: Divine Presence and Absence in the Book of Ezekiel*. Winona Lake, IN: Eisenbrauns, 2000.

Lundbom, Jack. *Jeremiah: A Study in Ancient Hebrew Rhetoric.* SBLDS 18. Missoula: Scholars, 1975.
Lust, Johann. "Edom—Adam in Ezekiel, in the MT and LXX." In *Studies in the Hebrew Bible, Qumran, and the Septuagint: Presented to Eugene Ulrich,* 387–401. VTSup 101. Leiden: Brill, 2006.
Lyons, Michael A. *From Law to Prophecy: Ezekiel's Use of the Holiness Code.* LHBOTS 507. London: T. & T. Clark, 2009.
McKane, William. *Hebrew Bible/Old Testament: The History of Its Interpretation.* Edited by Magne Saebo. Göttingen: Vandenhoeck & Ruprecht, 2008.
McKenzie, Tracy J. *Idolatry in the Pentateuch.* Eugene, OR: Pickwick Publications, 2010.
Muilenburg, James. "A Study in Hebrew Rhetoric: Repetition and Style." In *Congress Volume: Copenhagen, 1953,* 97–111. VTSup 1. Leiden: Brill, 1953.
Nogalski, James D. *Literary Precursors to the Book of the Twelve.* BZAW. Berlin: de Gruyter, 1993.
Parunak, Henry Van Dyke. "Structural Studies in Ezekiel." Ph.D. diss., Harvard University Press, 1978.
Pohlmann, Karl-Friedrich. *Ezechiel: Der Stand der theologischen Diskussion.* Darmstadt: WBG, 2008.
Redditt, Paul L. *Introduction to the Prophets.* Grand Rapids: Eerdmans, 2008.
Sailhamer, John. "Hosea 11:1 and Matthew 2:15." *WTJ* 63 (2001) 87–105.
———. *Introduction to Old Testament Theology: A Canonical Approach.* Grand Rapids: Zondervan, 1995.
———. *The Pentateuch as Narrative.* Grand Rapids: Zondervan, 1992.
Shepherd, Michael B. "Compositional Analysis of the Twelve." *ZAW* 120 (2008) 184–93.
Stromberg, Jake. "Observations on Inner-Scriptural Scribal Expansion in MT Ezekiel." *VT* 58 (2008) 68–86.
Stuart, Douglas. *Hosea–Jonah.* WBC 31. Waco, TX: Word, 1987.
Sweeney, Marvin A. *The Twelve Prophets.* Vol. 1. Berit Olam. Collegeville, MN: Liturgical, 2000.
Talmon, Shemaryahu. *Text and Canon of the Hebrew Bible.* Winona Lake, IN: Eisenbrauns, 2010.
Watson, Wilfred G. E. *Classical Hebrew Poetry: A Guide to Its Techniques.* JSOTSup 26. Sheffield: JSOT Press, 1984.
Waugh, Linda R. "The Poetic Function and the Nature of Language." In Roman Jakobson, *Verbal Art, Verbal Sign, Verbal Time,* edited by Krystyna Pomorska and Stephen Rudy, 143–68. Minneapolis: University of Minnesota Press, 1985.
Westermann, Claus. *Prophetic Oracles of Salvation in the Old Testament.* Translated by Keith Crim. Louisville: Westminster John Knox, 1991.
Wong, Ka Leung. *The Idea of Retribution in the Book of Ezekiel.* VTSup 87. Leiden: Brill, 2001.
Woudstra, M. H. "Edom and Israel in Ezekiel." *Calvin Theological Journal* 3 (1968) 21–35.
Ziegler, Joseph, ed. *Septuaginta VT Graecum.* Vol 13. 2nd ed. Göttingen: Vandenhoeck & Ruprecht, 1967.
Zimmerli, Walther. *Ezekiel.* Translated by James D. Martin. 2 vols. Hermeneia. Philadelphia: Fortress Press, 1983.

7

The New Exodus in the Composition of the Twelve

MICHAEL B. SHEPHERD

Cedarville University

THE COMPOSITIONAL UNITY OF the Twelve Prophets (Hosea–Malachi) has become well established over the course of the past twenty-five years on the basis of internal and external evidence.[1] Many scholars continue to treat the Twelve Prophets as twelve separate books, but there are now many widespread attempts to explain the compositional activity within the Twelve as a whole.[2] One of the benefits of reading the Twelve together is the insight gained into the meaning of individual passages from the context of the overall framework of the book. That is, composition at the highest level informs interpretation at lower levels. The final prophetic author/composer has taken the recorded words and events of various prophets from different times and places of the past and recast them as messages and images of the future work of God. This is not unlike the explicit use of sources elsewhere in the Hebrew Bible.[3]

---

1. See Nogalski, *Literary Precursors*; Nogalski, *Redactional Processes*; Shepherd, "Compositional Analysis of the Twelve," 184–93. See also Sir 49:10; 4QXIIa–c, e; 8HevXIIgr; Acts 7:42; 13:40; 15:15; *b. B. Bat.* 14b, 15a; Mic 3:12 (MT).

2. See the debate in Ben Zvi and Nogalski, *Two Sides of a Coin*.

3. For example, the book of Chronicles cites its sources (1 Chr 29:29; 2 Chr 9:29; 12:15; 13:22; 16:11; 20:34; 24:27; 25:26; 26:22; 27:7; 28:26; 32:32; 33:18–19; 35:26–27; 36:8), but the book is not a mere repetition of material from Samuel and Kings. The author of Chronicles is an exegete and a composer who has his own theological representation of the texts before him.

The present essay seeks to trace the exodus/new exodus theme within the compositional seams of the Twelve. Thus, it will be necessary to demonstrate what sets the peculiar endings and beginnings of the books of the Twelve apart from the texts that surround them. From there the compositional strategy of the author will begin to emerge. It will be evident that the final composer was a careful student of the earlier edition of the book of Jeremiah (LXX and 4QJer[b, d]) whose words consistently influence the seam work most clearly attributable to the author. It will also be evident that the author intends to reintroduce any historical hope of a return (new exodus) from Assyria or Babylon in terms of an eschatological new exodus.[4]

The Program of the Twelve

The book of the Twelve is extant in two editions: (1) the arrangement represented by the Masoretic Text (MT), the Greek Minor Prophets Scroll from Nahal Hever (8HevXIIgr), and MurXII (parts of Joel–Zech), which appears in English translations and (2) the arrangement represented by the Septuagint (LXX), which differs in the order of the first six books (Hosea, Amos, Micah, Joel, Obadiah, and Jonah).[5] Apart from the fact that the LXX is a fairly obvious rough rearrangement according to length (and to some extent date) of what is on the surface an unusual arrangement in the MT, it is also evident that the Greek translation itself presupposes the MT order (see Amos 9:12; Obad 16–21; Acts 15:17).[6] The simple fact is that the LXX arrangement disrupts the seam work of the final composer and does not show equally clear signs of composition in comparison with the MT.

The program of Hosea and the Twelve is set forth in Hos 3:4–5: "For the sons of Israel will dwell for many days without a king and without a prince and without sacrifice and without pillar and without ephod and teraphim. Afterwards the sons of Israel will return and seek the Lord their God and David their king and fear to the Lord and to his goodness at the end of the days." These two themes of judgment and messianic restoration in the

---

4. This is comparable to the role of Third Isaiah within the book of Isaiah. Third Isaiah (Isaiah 56–66) shows that the new exodus of Second Isaiah (Isaiah 40–55) did not take place in the post-exilic period, even though there was a return from Babylon. The text thus points the reader to the hope of an eschatological new exodus.

5. Barry Alan Jones argues for the priority of the Septuagint arrangement but places Jonah at the end of the Twelve in accordance with 4QXIIa (*The Formation*).

6. Shepherd, *The Twelve Prophets*, 12, 74–76. The order of the 8HevXIIgr thus has priority over that of the LXX codices even though the translation itself is later than that of the LXX (see Tov, *Textual Criticism*, 145).

last days run through each of the compositional seams of the Twelve.⁷ Verse 4 is based on Hos 3:3. Verse 5, however, likely does not owe its placement here to the eighth-century prophet Hosea but to the final prophetic composer of the Twelve. Hosea was a prophet to the northern kingdom of Israel (Hos 1:1), but the interest of this text is the Davidic king (Hos 1:7; 2:2 [1:11]; 4:15; 5:5, 10, 12–14; 6:4, 11; 8:14; 10:11; 12:1, 3 [12:2, 4]). The source for this post-exilic composer's work was most probably the book of Jeremiah: "In that day . . . they will serve the LORD their God and David their king whom I will raise up for them" (Jer 30:8–9 [see *Tg. Jon.*]; Jer 23:5–6; cf. 2 Sam 7:12).

This text from Jeremiah comes at the beginning of the so-called Book of Comfort (Jer 30–33). It follows the chapter devoted to Jeremiah's letter to the exiles (Jer 29) in which Jeremiah gives his prophecy of the seventy years (Jer 29:10–14). This prophecy also appears in Jer 25:11, but it reads very differently depending upon which of the two editions of the book is followed. In the shorter (and differently arranged), earlier edition of the book represented by the LXX and 4QJer$^{b,\ d}$, the enemy from the north is unidentified (Jer 25:9, 11, 12), leaving the enemy and the number seventy open to an eschatological interpretation in which the enemy would be a future and final enemy. The number would then represent an indefinite, complete period of time. This is the way Jeremiah's prophecy is interpreted in Ezek 38:14–17 and Dan 9:2, 24–27.⁸ The MT, however, consistently identifies the enemy from the north as Nebuchadnezzar (Jer 25:1, 9, 11, 12; but see 50:3) so that the prophecy remains a historical prophecy of a new exodus from Babylon. The earlier edition of the book is open to an eschatological new exodus. With this in mind, it is significant that the context of Jer 30:8–9 includes a reference to the judgment of the enemies of the people of God "at the end of the days" (Jer 30:23–24). Chapter 31 then begins with the phrase "At that time." At that time the LORD will lead his people in a new exodus just like he did in the original (Jer 31:2–6). They will come forth with tambourines and dancing just as they did after the first exodus (Jer 31:4; cf. Exod 15:20). They will set their hearts to the highway of their return, a "new thing" (Jer 31:21, 22, 31–34; cf. Isa 11:16; 42:9; 43:18, 19; 48:3, 6).

---

7. The phrase "at the end of the days" does not mean merely "days to come" or "in the future" (contra Ernst Jenni, "אחר"). It occurs sparingly and strategically at critical junctures in the composition of the Hebrew Bible with reference to the eschatological work of God (Gen 49:1; Num 24:14; Deut 4:30; 31:29; Isa 2:2; Jer 23:20; 48:47; 49:39; 30:24; Hos 3:5; Mic 4:1; Dan 2:28; 10:14; see Staerk, "Der Begrauch der Wendung בְּאַחֲרִית הַיָּמִים im alttestamentliche Kanon," 247–53; see also Sailhamer, *The Pentateuch as Narrative*, 35–37). See Hos 3:5 in *Tg. Jon.* for a "messianic" interpretation.

8. See Shepherd, *Daniel*, 95–99.

Given the connection to Jer 30:8–9, it is clear that Hos 3:4–5 assumes a new exodus through a new wilderness. This is also evident from Hos 2:16–17 [2:14–15]: "Therefore, look, I am about to entice her, and I will walk her through the wilderness and speak to her heart. And I will give to her her vineyards from there and the valleys of Achor for an opening of hope; and she will answer (or, "sing" [Exod 15:21]) to there as in the days of her youth and as when she came up from the land of Egypt." The time without a king (Hos 3:4) meshes with the wilderness imagery (Hos 2:5, 16 [2:3, 14]), and the time of messianic salvation (Hos 3:5) with the exodus (Hos 2:17 [2:15]). The theme of the lack of a good king or any king at all surfaces several times in Hosea (Hos 7:3–7; 8:4; 10:3, 7, 15; 13:10, 11). Parallel to this is the "return to Egypt/Assyria" metaphor (Hos 8:13; 9:3; 11:5 [cf. Deut 28:68]).[9] From this judgment there will be a new exodus (Hos 11:1b, 11; cf. Num 23:22; 24:8) led by a new prophet like Moses (Hos 2:2 [1:11; see *Tg. Jon.*]; 12:14 [12:13]; 13:4; Deut 18:15, 18; 34:10; Mic 2:13).

John Sailhamer on Hosea 11:1b and Matthew 2:15[10]

According to John Sailhamer, Hos 3:5 provides an eschatological context for the reader's understanding of Hosea 4–14. This text has direct implications for the reading of Hos 11:1b ("And out of Egypt I called my son"), which Hos 11:5 (and 11:11) seems to understand in terms of a metaphor that speaks of the future (see Hos 12:11b [12:10b]: "And by means of the prophets, I make comparison").[11] That is, there will be a new Egypt and a new exodus. Sailhamer argues that the message of the book of Hosea as a whole has its basis in careful exegesis of the Pentateuch. The text of Hos 4:2 appears to be an exegesis of the Decalogue in Exod 20:1–17. Likewise, Hos 12:4–5 is a careful reading of the words of Gen 32:23–33, the story of Jacob's wrestling.[12] Furthermore, the exodus event itself occurs as a messianic metaphor in the compositional strategy of the Pentateuch. Here Sailhamer refers to his own work on the poetic seams of the Pentateuch (Genesis 49;

---

9. The context suggests that these are not merely references to refuge in Egypt/Assyria or political alliance with Egypt/Assyria as in Hos 5:13; 7:11 (contra Mays, *Hosea*, 123, 126, 127, 155). Rather, the servitude in Egypt has become a metaphor for judgment from which restoration for the people of God will come in the last days (cf. Stuart, *Hosea-Jonah*, 137).

10. Sailhamer, "Hosea 11:1 and Matthew 2:15," 87–96.

11. See the references to Egypt in Hos 12:10a, 14 (12:9a, 13).

12. See also Hos 9:10 (Num 25) and Hos 11:9 (Num 23:19).

Numbers 24; Deuteronomy 32), which interpret the narratives that precede them eschatologically. In particular, he notes the relationship between Num 23:22a ("God brings them out of Egypt") and Num 24:8a ("God brings him out of Egypt"). The reference to the historical exodus in Num 23:22a has become in Num 24:8a a figure for the new exodus led by the messianic king of Num 24:7-9 (cf. Num 24:9 and Gen 49:8-12; see Num 24:7 LXX). Thus, in Sailhamer's view Hosea had grounds to draw a messianic meaning from the Pentateuch itself. Matthew then did not have to resort to typological interpretation in his quote of Hosea.[13] The text of Matt 2:13-15 anticipates the new work of God envisioned by the Pentateuch and Hosea.

Compositional Seams

Hosea 14:10 (14:9) and Joel 1:2-3

The conclusion to Hosea (Hos 14:10 [14:9]) and the opening of Joel (Joel 1:2-3) stand apart from the prophetic material before and after them. The composer of the Twelve has drawn upon the distinctive language of the wisdom literature for the first compositional seam of the book: the contrast of the righteous and the wicked (Hos 14:10 [14:9]; Prov 10:1-22:16) and the passing of instruction from the older generation to the younger (Joel 1:2-3; Prov 1-9). It is a call for the reader to seek wisdom in the prophecy of the book.[14]

The last verse of Hosea likely does not come from the eighth-century prophet. Rather, the prophetic author of the Twelve has once again borrowed from the book of Jeremiah. The closest parallel to Hos 14:10a (14:9a) in the Hebrew Bible is Jer 9:11a (9:12a) (see also Ps 107:43; Eccl 8:1; Jas 3:13):

---

13. Sailhamer also notes some indications that Matthew was reading Hosea in light of the Balaam oracles in Numbers 23 and 24 (e.g., Num 24:17 [see *Tg. Onk.*] and Matt 2:1-11). The response to Sailhamer's article by Dan McCartney and Peter Enns ("Matthew and Hosea: A Response to John Sailhamer," 97-105) is unfortunately little more than a misunderstanding and caricature of Sailhamer's work. For a full review of the response see Shepherd, *The Twelve Prophets*, 19-22.

14. According Brevard Childs (*Introduction to the Old Testament as Scripture*, 382), the wisdom influence in other prophetic books such as Amos and Isaiah usually belongs to the primary prophetic proclamation, but the final verse of Hosea is on the level of the final redaction: "The verse functions as an explicit directive to the reader to instruct him in the proper understanding of the collection [of Hosea]."

מי חכם ויבן אלה נבון וידעם
Who is wise? (or, Whoever is wise,) Let him understand these things.
[Who] has understanding? (or, [Whoever] has understanding,)
Let him know them.
(Hos 14:10a [14:9a])

מי האיש החכם ויבן את זאת ואשר דבר פי יהוה אליו ויגדה
Who is the wise man? Let him understand this.
And to whom has the mouth of the LORD spoken? Let him declare it.
(Jer 9:11a [9:12a])

What is it that the wise man is supposed to understand in the Jeremiah text? He is to understand that because the people have abandoned the LORD's instruction the LORD will scatter the people among the nations (Jer 9:12–15 [9:13–16]). This is the cause of a sound of wailing (Jer 9:18 [9:19]; cf. 31:15). Furthermore, the wise man is not to boast in his wisdom but in his knowledge of the LORD (Jer 9:22, 23 [9:23, 24]). The LORD will judge those who are uncircumcised of heart (Jer 9:24, 25 [9:25, 26]; cf. Jer 4:4). This directs the faithful reader to the hope of the circumcised heart in the new covenant beyond exile (Deut 30:6; Jer 31:31–34).

The LXX of Jeremiah in general represents an earlier edition of the book than the MT, but in some cases the text of the LXX (and its *Vorlage*) requires restoration. The MT of Jer 9:23 (9:24) reads: "But in this let the one who boasts boast: understanding and knowing me (אותי), that I am the LORD who performs (עֹשֶׂה) covenant loyalty, justice, and righteousness in the land, for in these things I delight, says the LORD." The LXX according to the Göttingen edition (J. Ziegler) does not have the object "me" in the expression "understanding and knowing me." But Isac Seeligmann suggested that the version of this text preserved in the LXX of 1 Sam 2:10 is preferable: "understanding and knowing the LORD (את יהוה) and performing (וַעֲשֵׂה or וְעָשֹׂה) justice and righteousness in the midst of the land."[15]

Not only does this latter text fit better with the wording of Jer 22:15–16, but also it is easy to explain how the Hebrew text behind the present Greek version of Jer 9:23 (9:24) originated from the Hebrew text behind the Greek text of 1 Sam 2:10. The reading את יהוה was abbreviated to אתי (cf. Jer 6:11 MT: חמת יהוה; LXX = חמתי), but the misunderstanding of this as an object marker with a pronominal suffix (אותי) led to the re-vocalization of וְעָשֹׂה (or וְעָשֹׂה) to עֹשֶׂה, making what follows into something the LORD does rather than something that the one who knows the LORD does. This

---

15. Seeligmann, *Gesammelte Studien zur Hebräischen Bibel*, 454–55. This is an exegetical plus in the LXX of 1 Sam 2:10 and its *Vorlage* (cf. 4QSam^a).

then led to the expansion: כי אני יהוה עשה חסד ("that I am the Lord who performs covenant loyalty"). It is evident that the scribe responsible for the LXX *Vorlage* of 1 Sam 2:10 borrowed from the text of Jer 9:23 (9:24). It is also likely that the composer of the Twelve was aware of this intertextual connection between Jeremiah and Samuel when he included the language from Jer 9:11a (9:12a). The author of Samuel uses the reference to the king at the conclusion of Hannah's prayer in 1 Sam 2:10 to introduce the central theme of the book. This king according to the Davidic covenant will build the temple and reign over an everlasting kingdom (2 Sam 7:13). The book of the Twelve does not see this fulfilled in Solomon but in a future messianic figure (Zech 6:12-13; cf. Jer 23:5-6), a leader of a new exodus (Mic 2:12-13; 5:1-4a [5:2-5a]; 7:14-15).

Joel–Amos–Obadiah–Jonah

The well-known quote of Joel 4:16a (3:16a) in Amos 1:2a (cf. Jer 25:30) and the shared view of the Day of the Lord in Joel 2:1-2 (cf. Jer 4:5; 6:1; Hos 5:8) and Amos 5:18-20 are two of the more obvious connections between Joel and Amos. The reference to Edom in Joel 4:19a (3:19a) anticipates the central role of Edom in Amos (Amos 1:6, 9, 11; 2:1; 9:12). The quote of Joel 4:18aa (3:18a1) in Amos 9:13b makes clear the intended connection between Joel 4:19a and Amos 9:12. It is significant then that Edom is also the link between Amos and Obadiah. Amos 9:11-15 is a piece of text employed by the final composer of the Twelve to connect Amos and Obadiah. It stands apart from Amos 1:1-9:10 in that its interest lies in the restoration of the fallen booth of David (Amos 9:11; cf. Hos 3:5). Apart from Amos 2:4-5, the Davidic kingdom does not figure prominently elsewhere in Amos. The prophecy of Amos lacks any real hope of restoration with the exception of the glimmer in Amos 9:8b. The purpose of the restoration in Amos 9:11-15 is "that they may possess (יירשו) the remnant of Edom (אדום) and all the nations upon whom my name is called" (Amos 9:12a). Edom represents the nations to be possessed in the future kingdom. This is the way Codex Alexandrinus interprets this verse: "that the remnant of mankind (אדם) may seek (ידרשו) the Lord" (cf. Acts 15:17). Such an interpretation finds warrant from the conclusion to Obadiah where it says that the southern territory of the Lord's kingdom will possess the mountain or hill country of Esau (i.e., Edom; Obad 19, 21).

The book of Obadiah, like Joel and Amos, has an interest in Edom (Obad 1-14) and an expectation of judgment in the Day of the Lord (Obad 15). The text of Obad 1-5 shares material with Jer 49:9, 14-16. What is the direction of dependence here? Does Obadiah quote Jeremiah? Does Jeremiah quote Obadiah? Was there a third, common source?[16] Of course, there is also the possibility that Obad 1–5 owes its placement to the final composer of the Twelve who has been reading the book of Jeremiah in its first edition. Given the dependence upon Jeremiah elsewhere in the compositional seams of the Twelve, this latter option is particularly attractive. But it will nevertheless be necessary to analyze the two texts together:

<u>Jeremiah 49:9, 14–16; Obadiah 1–5</u>

אם בצרים באו לך לא ישארו עוללות אם גנבים בלילה השחיתו דים
If gatherers were to come to you, would they not leave gleanings?
If thieves were to come at night, they would destroy their fill.
(Jer 49:9)[17]

אם גנבים באו לך . . . הלוא יגנבו דים אם בצרים באו לך לא ישארו עוללות
If thieves were to come to you . . . ,[18] would they not steal their fill?
If gatherers were to come to you, would they not leave gleanings? (Obad 5)

שמועה שמעתי מאת יהוה וציר בגוים שלוח התקבצו ובאו עליה וקומו למלחמה
I heard a report from the Lord, and a messenger was sent among the nations;[19]
"Gather together and come against her, and rise for battle." (Jer 49:14)

שמועה שמענו מאת יהוה וציר בגוים שלח קומו ונקומה עליה למלחמה
We heard a report from the Lord,[20] and a messenger was sent among the nations.

---

16. See Wolff, *Obadja und Jona*, 12, 20.

17. LXX: "They would set their hand on" = ישיתו ידם.

18. An authorial comment appears here to explain the clause: אם שודדי לילה איך נדמיתה ("If nighttime despoilers, [O how could you are ruined!]"). This text has the word לילה from Jer 49:9b.

19. The LXX has the imperative "send" (= שלח). The MT of Obad 1 has the same consonantal text as the *Vorlage* of the LXX of Jer 49:14, but it has vocalized it as a *pual qatal*.

20. The LXX of Obad 1 has a first person singular verb like the MT of Jer 49:14.

"Arise, and let us rise against her for battle." (Obad 1)

כי הנה קטן נתתיך בגוים בזוי באדם
For look, I have made you small among the nations, despised by mankind. (Jer 49:15)

הנה קטן נתתיך בגוים בזוי אתה מאד
Look, I have made you small among the nations; you are very despised. (Obad 2)

תפלצתך השיא אתך זדון לבך שכני בחגוי הסלע תפשי מרום גבעה כי תגביה כנשר קנך משם אורידך נאם יהוה
Your horror has deceived you, the presumption of your heart, dwelling in the crevices of the cleft, grasping height of hill. If you make your nest high like the eagle, from there I will bring you down, the prophetic utterance of the Lord. (Jer 49:16)

זדון לבך השיאך שכני בחגוי הסלע מרום שבתו אם תגביה כנשר קנך משם אורידך נאם יהוה
The presumption of your heart has deceived you, dwelling in crevices of a cleft, the height of his dwelling . . .[21] If you make your nest high like the eagle . . . [22] from there I will bring you down, the prophetic utterance of the Lord. (Obad 3a, 4)

A theory based on a hypothetical common source should be a last resort. Here it is unnecessary. With a few minor exceptions (Obad 1b2, 3a), the Obadiah text is consistently longer than the Jeremiah version (see the additions in Obad 3b, 4a, 5a1), and it is commonly recognized that the tendency of ancient composers and scribes was to preserve and add to their sources rather than delete from them. Thus, the most plausible conclusion is that Obadiah or the composer of the Twelve borrowed from Jeremiah (see also Jer 38:22b; Obad 7a).

What would be the significance of the Jeremiah passage for the eschatological program of the Twelve? In the MT edition of Jeremiah, there would be little significance, since the text in that edition is little more than an oracle against a foreign nation from the past. The MT has arranged the nations corpus of Jeremiah to fit with the order of the nations in Jer

---

21. The text of Obad 3b adds: אמר בלבו מי יורדני ארץ ("Saying in his heart, 'Who will bring me down to the ground?'").

22. The text of Obad 4a has an added comment ("And if among the stars it is set"). Cf. Num 24:21b.

25:19–26 so that the Egypt oracle in chapter 46 follows the narrative about Egypt in chapters 42–44 and so that the book ends with the oracles about the downfall of Babylon (Jer 50–51), which, according to the MT, is the culmination of Jeremiah's prophecy of seventy years. The first edition of Jeremiah, however, arranges the nations corpus after Jer 25:13 (cf. Isaiah and Ezekiel) in the following order: Jer 49:34–39; 46:2–28; 50–51; 47; 49:7–22, 1–6, 28–33, 23–27; 48. In this arrangement, the first (Jer 49:34–39) and last oracles (Jer 48) end with the statement, "At the end of the days I will restore the fortunes of Elam/Moab" (Jer 49:39; 48:47), framing the oracles in such a way that they become images of judgment and restoration in the last days.[23] Joel 4:19a (3:19a) puts this restoration in terms of a defeat of Israel's historical enemies, Egypt and Edom. God will lead his people in a new exodus similar to the original one from Egypt (Amos 2:10; 3:1; 9:7).

The book of Jonah then continues the focus on the nations, making Nineveh/Assyria play the representative role that Edom plays in Joel, Amos, and Obadiah. In Jonah, Nineveh is "the great city" (Jon 1:2; 3:2) from the table of nations in Genesis 10 (Gen 10:11–12) to whom the Lord has the right to show compassion (Jon 4:11; cf. Nah 3:19). That is, the city is of central importance in the Gentile world.

Jonah–Micah–Nahum–Habakkuk

The final chapter of the book of Jonah reveals the reason for the prophet's flight narrated in Jon 1:3: "For I knew that you were a gracious (חנון) and compassionate (רחום) God, slow to anger (ארך אפים) and abundant in covenant loyalty (חסד) and relenting concerning calamity" (Jon 4:2b; cf. Joel 2:13–14). This language comes from God's revelation of himself to Moses at Sinai in Exod 34:6–7 and creates a link to the compositional seam between the following book of Micah and the book of Nahum:

> Who is a God like you, forgiving iniquity,[24]
> And passing over transgression for the remnant of his inheritance?
> (He does not hold on forever to his anger,
> For delighting in covenant loyalty [חסד] is he.
> He will have compassion [from רחם] on us again,
> He will subdue our iniquities;)

---

23. The LXX does not have Jer 48:45–47. A scribe or the translator skipped from "thus says the Lord" at the end of Jer 48:44b to "thus says the Lord" at the end of Jer 48:47a, accidentally omitting the intervening text (homoioteleuton). The text of Jer 48:47b is an editorial addition in the MT (cf. Jer 51:64b).

24. See Exod 34:7a.

> And you will cast into sea's depths all their sins.
> You will give faithfulness to Jacob,
> Covenant loyalty (חסד) to Abraham,
> Which you swore to our fathers long ago.
> (Mic 7:18–20)

> The LORD takes vengeance against his foes,
> And he keeps wrath for his enemies.
> The LORD is slow to anger (ארך אפים) and great of strength,
> But the LORD will by no means leave the guilty unpunished.[25]
> (Nah 1:2b–3a)

The hymn-like text of Mic 7:18–20 follows a prayer for God to lead his people in a new exodus (Mic 7:14–17). This conclusion to the book of Micah builds on the hope of the last days expressed in Mic 4:1–5 when all the nations will come to Zion and enjoy justice and peace, the hallmarks of the messianic kingdom in the Prophets (cf. Isa 2:1–5).

Immediately preceding Micah 4 is the middle verse of the book of the Twelve according to the *Masora parva*: "Therefore, because of you Zion will be plowed like a field, and Jerusalem will be ruins, and the temple mount will become high places of a forest" (Mic 3:12). This text also appears in Jer 26:18 as part of the advice from the elders to the people not to execute Jeremiah for the harshness of his temple gate speech (Jer 7:1–15). Hezekiah did not kill Micah; therefore, the people should not kill Jeremiah. Obviously, this prophecy of Micah preceded the lifetime of Jeremiah, but that does not mean it occupied its current place in the book of Micah before the completion of Jeremiah's book. The clue in the text of Mic 3:12 is the Aramaic plural spelling of "ruins" (עיין) in contrast to the usual Hebrew plural spelling in Jer 26:18 (עיים). The Aramaic masculine plural ending is a feature of later Hebrew texts in the Bible (e.g., הימין Dan 12:13b). Once again, the final composer of the Twelve has taken a text from the book of Jeremiah. This time he has made his quote the central verse of the Twelve.

The Nahum portion of the seam between Micah and Nahum interrupts the beginning of a partial alphabetic acrostic poem (Nah 1:2–9).[26] What was quoted above has been inserted between the *aleph* and *beth* lines. This poem, like Hab 3:3–15, describes God's worldwide judgment of his enemies (the wicked) and his protection of those who take refuge in him (the righteous). The theophanies in Nah 1:2–9 and Hab 3:3–15 form bookends around the words of judgment directed at foreign enemies in Nahum and

---

25. See Exod 34:7b.
26. See Shepherd, "Hebrew Acrostic Poems and Their Vocabulary Stock," 95–98.

Habakkuk, casting those historical judgments as images of things to come in the future and final worldwide judgment. Both passages draw from the exodus story in order to depict future deliverance in terms of a new exodus: "He rebukes the sea and dries it up, and lays waste all the rivers" (Nah 1:4a; cf. Exod 14:21–22). In Habakkuk, the Lord is coming from the south (Hab 3:3) and appears to be angry with the sea (Hab 3:8). He goes forth for the deliverance of his people and his anointed one (Hab 3:13a; cf. Num 23:22; 24:8). The book of Habakkuk also includes what appears to be a quote from Jer 51:58b (Hab 2:13b). It is coupled with a quote from Isa 11:9 (Hab 2:14), which anticipates a new exodus (Isa 11:11–16). These do not seem to be part of the original "woe" oracles in Hab 2:5–20 and could very well come from the final composer of the book of the Twelve.

Habakkuk-Zephaniah-Haggai

One of the verbal links between Nah 1:2–9 and Hab 3:3–15 is the reference in both texts to the "day of distress" (Nah 1:7a; Hab 3:16b). The following work of Zephaniah picks up this term and identifies it with the Day of the Lord (Zeph 1:15; cf. Joel 2:2; Amos 5:18–20; Obad 15). Zephaniah also uses the relatively rare expression "Hush" (הס) from Hab 2:20b (Zeph 1:7a) to indicate that there must be silence before the Lord, "for the Day of the Lord is near." For Zephaniah, this day is first of all a day of judgment (Zeph 1:1–3:8), but his book is also clear that there will be a new exodus for the people of God in days to come (Zeph 3:9, 13, 18–20).

Zephaniah the prophet was a contemporary of Jeremiah (Jer 1:1–3; Zeph 1:1). The first and last words of the book that bears Zephaniah's name contain material very close to that of the book of Jeremiah. In a reversal of Gen 1:1–2:3, the opening words announce that the Lord will make an end of everything on the surface of "the earth" (האדמה) including "people" (אדם), "animals" (בהמה), "birds" (עוף השמים), and "fish" (דגי הים) (Zeph 1:2–3; cf. Ezek 38:20; Hos 4:3). Very similar terminology appears in Jer 7:20; 8:13; 15:3. The last words of Zephaniah include the statement in Zeph 3:17b, "He will rejoice over you" (ישיש עליך). This is similar to Deut 28:63; 30:9; Isa 62:5b; 65:19a. But it is also close to Jer 32:41: "And I will rejoice over them" (וששתי עליהם).

The following book of Haggai builds on the restoration section of Zeph 3:9–20. Just as the description of the new temple in Ezekiel 40–48 is a picture of the restoration prophesied in Ezekiel 33–39, so the call to build the temple in Haggai serves to portray the future restoration revealed in Zeph 3:9–20, giving the book new life and ongoing relevance beyond the historical ministry of the prophet Haggai. A key part of this is the depiction of a new exodus in Hag 2:1–9. The bringing in of silver and gold from the nations in order to build the temple (Hag 2:6–9) recalls the plundering of the Egyptians before the original exodus (Exod 12:35–36), which provided the materials for the construction of the tabernacle.

Haggai-Zechariah-Malachi

The prophets Haggai and Zechariah are associated by the date of their prophetic ministries (Hag 1:1; 2:1, 10, 20; Zech 1:1, 7; 7:1; Ezra 5:1–2). There is also a question raised by the final unit of Haggai (Hag 2:20–23), which is answered only by the following visions of Zechariah 1–8. The Lord refers to Zerubbabel in Hag 2:23 as "my servant" and says, "I will set you like a seal/signet-ring, for I have chosen you." This language is reminiscent of the servant songs of Isa 42:1–7; 49:1–9; 50:4–11; 52:13–53:12. Is Zerubbabel the servant of the Lord, the long-awaited fulfillment of the Davidic covenant, or does he simply prefigure one who is to come? The fourth vision of Zechariah is clear that the chosen servant is someone other than a contemporary of Joshua the high priest, for the servant's coming is imminent, whereas Zerubbabel is already a leader in the midst of the people (Zech 3:8b). This servant bears the title "Branch." According to Zech 6:12–13, this Branch will fulfill the Davidic covenant and build the temple. The image of Joshua with a crown (Zech 6:11) serves to illustrate how this ruler will occupy the positions of king and priest at the same time (cf. Ps 110).

These texts draw directly from the book of Jeremiah.[27] The text of Hag 2:23 is a reversal of Jer 22:24. The Lord announced in Jer 22:24 that he would tear Jehoiachin off his right hand as a seal/signet-ring. But now in Hag 2:23 Zerubbabel, a descendant of Jehoiachin (1 Chr 3:17–19), is the chosen seal/signet-ring. Furthermore, the title "Branch" (Zech 3:8b; 6:12) comes from Jer 23:5–6 (Jer 33:14–26 > LXX). The text of Isa 4:2 also uses this title, but the explicit reference to a descendant of David occurs in Jer 23:5. This Jeremiah passage is part of a complex web of intertextual connections designed to identify the seed of Abraham (Gen 12:3; 27:29; 49:8–9; Num 24:9; Jer 4:2; Ps 72:17; Gal 3:16).

The last two sections of Zechariah share the same heading: משא דבר יהוה ("The oracle of the word of the Lord"). This heading occurs only one other time in the Hebrew Bible, Mal 1:1, thus linking the second half of Zechariah with Malachi. Both Zechariah and Malachi look forward to a new exodus: "I will return them from the land of Egypt, and from Assyria I

---

27 See also the link between the opening of Zechariah (Zech 1:3) and Jer 31:18.

will gather them" (Zech 10:10a). Egypt and Assyria here stand as figures for the present post-exilic situation from which the prophet looks forward to future deliverance. The Lord's "messenger" (מלאך) in Mal 3:1 will prepare the way much like the "angel" (מלאך) in the original exodus (Exod 14:19; 23:20; Mark 1:2–3).

Matthew's quote from the second half of Zechariah is introduced as a quote from the prophet Jeremiah (Zech 11:13; Matt 27:9–10). Of course, some textual witnesses have the variant "Zechariah," but the reading "Jeremiah" is clearly the one that gave rise to the other. Attempts to find this text somewhere in the book of Jeremiah have not been successful (Jer 18:1–6; 19; 32:6–9). Jeremiah was considered the head of the prophets in some circles (b. B. Bat. 14b), but the use of his name to cite another prophet is not attested elsewhere in the New Testament. Did Matthew understand Jeremiah to be the author of Zechariah 9–14? Did Zechariah or Second Zechariah borrow material that came from Jeremiah, material that never found its way into the book of Jeremiah? In any case, yet another compositional seam in the Twelve bears a relationship of some sort to the prophet Jeremiah or the book that bears his name.[28]

Malachi 3:22–24 (Eng., 4:4–6) and Psalm 1:2

The "canonical" seams (Deut 34:10; Josh 1:8; Mal 4:5 [3:23]; Ps 1:2) on the level of the Tanakh as a whole (4QMMT; Luke 24:44) have been noted by Joseph Blenkinsopp and Sailhamer in particular.[29] The expectation at the end of the Pentateuch of a messianic prophet like Moses (Deut 18:15, 18; 34:10) is followed by instruction given to Joshua, the wise man (Num 27:18; Deut 34:9), to murmur in the Torah day and night (Josh 1:8). Likewise, the Prophets conclude with the expectation of a forerunner prophet like Elijah (Mal 3:1; 3:23 [4:5]) followed by a description of a wise and blessed person who murmurs in the Torah day and night (Ps 1:2).[30] Moses and Elijah both led an exodus (Exod 14:21–22; 2 Kgs 2:8; see also Josh 3:13–17), therefore,

---

28. Stead, *The Intertextuality of Zechariah 1–8* argues that Zech 6:9–15 depends upon proto-MT Jer 33:14–26 (> LXX). But Marvin Sweeney's review (*JSS* 56 [2011]: 414–17) notes that the application to Jerusalem in Jer 33:14–26 carries Zechariah's text one step further.

29. Blenkinsopp, *Prophecy and Canon*, 86–95, 120–23; Sailhamer, *Introduction to Old Testament Theology*, 239–49.

30. The last three verses of Malachi have been identified as two appendices (Mal 3:22 [4:4] and Mal 3:23–24 [4:5–6]), which stand apart from the six disputations of the book (Mal 1:2–5; 1:6–2:9; 2:10–16; 2:17–3:5; 3:6–12; 3:13–21 [3:13–4:3]) (see Ralph L. Smith, *Micah–Malachi*, WBC 32 [Nashville: Thomas Nelson, 1984], 340–42).

with the expectation of a new Moses and a new Elijah comes the expectation of a new exodus.

The compositional seam that connects the Prophets to the Writings draws from the image of the blessed person in Jer 17:7–8:

Jeremiah 17:7–8

ברוך הגבר אשר יבטח ביהוה
Blessed is the man who trusts in the Lord (Jer 17:7a)

והיה כעץ שתול על מים
And he will be like a tree planted by water
(Jer 17:8a1)

Psalm 1:1–3

אשרי האיש אשר בתורתו יהגה
Blessed is the man who . . . murmurs in his Torah (Ps 1:1a, 2b)

והיה כעץ שתול על פלגי מים
And he will be like a tree planted by streams of water (Ps 1:3a1)

Psalm 1:1–2 gives concrete expression to the trust the man has in Jer 17:7. The man in Psalm 1 rejects the way of sinners and murmurs in the Torah day and night. This Torah is not the law code that caused fear and trembling at Sinai (Exod 19:16b, 19; 20:18–21; Deut 5:1–5, 22). It is the book of Moses (i.e., the Pentateuch), which is cause for great joy (Neh 8:1–12; Pss 19; 119).[31] Both Jeremiah 17 and Psalm 1 contrast the blessed person with the wicked (Jer 17:5–6; Ps 1:4–6; see also Pss 1:1, 2, 6; 2:1, 12; *b. Ber.* 9b–10a).

Conclusion

The compositional seams of the Twelve present a consistent theological message of judgment and restoration in the last days (Hos 3:4–5). The primary image in which this is cast is that of a new exodus—defeat of the final enemy (like Egypt) and deliverance of the people of God in the messianic kingdom. The final composer of the Twelve has drawn extensively upon material from the first edition of the book of Jeremiah.[32] This is the source material he uses

---

31 Those who argue for the priority of Psalm 1 must explain this later use of *torah*.

32 The text of Ezek 36:23c–38, which does not appear in P. Chester Beatty 967 and La[Wirc], is another type of secondary addition reminiscent of Jeremiah's language (see

to connect the individual books of the Twelve to one another. Appreciation of the intertextual relationship between the Twelve and Jeremiah helps the reader to understand the eschatological outlook of the book.[33]

Bibliography

Ben Zvi, Ehud, and James D. Nogalski. *Two Sides of a Coin: Juxtaposing Views on Interpreting the Book of the Twelve/the Twelve Prophetic Books*. Analecta Gorgiana 201. Piscataway, NJ: Gorgias, 2009.

Blenkinsopp, Joseph. *Prophecy and Canon: A Contribution to the Study of Jewish Origins*. Studies of Judaism and Christianity in Antiquity 3. Notre Dame: Notre Dame University Press, 1977.

Childs, Brevard S. *Introduction to the Old Testament as Scripture*. Philadelphia: Fortress, 1979.

Jenni, Ernst. "אחר." In *Theological Lexicon of the Old Testament*. Edited by Ernst Jenni and Claus Westermann, vol. 1. Translated by Mark E. Biddle. Peabody, MA: Hendrickson, 1997.

Jones, Barry Alan. *The Formation of the Book of the Twelve: A Study in Text and Canon*. SBLDS 149. Atlanta: Scholars, 1995.

Mays, James L. *Hosea: A Commentary*. OTL. Philadelphia: Westminster, 1969.

McCartney, Dan, and Peter Enns. "Matthew and Hosea: A Response to John Sailhamer." *WTJ* 63 (2001) 97–105.

Nogalski, James D. *Literary Precursors to the Book of the Twelve*. BZAW 217. Berlin: de Gruyter, 1993.

———. *Redactional Processes in the Book of the Twelve*. BZAW 218. Berlin: de Gruyter, 1993.

Sailhamer, John H. "Hosea 11:1 and Matthew 2:15." *WTJ* 63 (2001) 87–96.

———. *Introduction to Old Testament Theology: A Canonical Approach*. Grand Rapids: Zondervan, 1995.

———. *The Pentateuch as Narrative: A Biblical-Theological Commentary*. Grand Rapids: Zondervan, 1995.

Seeligmann, Isac Leo. *Gesammelte Studien zur Hebräischen Bibel*. FAT 41. Tübingen: Mohr/Siebeck, 2004.

Shepherd, Michael B. *Commentary on the Minor Prophets*. Kregel Exegetical Library. Grand Rapids: Kregel, forthcoming.

———. "Compositional Analysis of the Twelve." *ZAW* 120 (2008) 184–93.

———. *Daniel in the Context of the Hebrew Bible*. Studies in Biblical Literature 123. New York: Lang, 2009.

———. "Hebrew Acrostic Poems and Their Vocabulary Stock." *Journal of Northwest Semitic Languages* 36/2 (2010) 95–108.

Tov, *The Greek and Hebrew Bible*, 408–410). The difference, however, is that the Ezekiel text is likely part of a later edition of the book. The use of Jeremiah in the Twelve, on the other hand, is an integral part of the seam work in the final composition of the book's first edition.

33 See Shepherd, *Commentary on the Minor Prophets*, forthcoming.

———. *The Twelve Prophets in the New Testament*. Studies in Biblical Literature 140. New York: Lang, 2011.

Smith, Ralph L. *Micah–Malachi*. WBC 32. Waco, TX: Word, 1984.

Staerk, W. "Der Begrauch der Wendung בְּאַחֲרִית הַיָּמִים im alttestamentliche Kanon." *ZAW* 11 (1891) 247–53.

Stead, Michael. *The Intertextuality of Zechariah 1–8*. LHBOTS 506. London: T. & T. Clark, 2009.

Stuart, Douglas. *Hosea–Jonah*. WBC 31. Waco, TX: Word, 1987.

Sweeney, Marvin A. Review of Michael Stead, *The Intertextuality of Zechariah 1–8*. London: T. & T. Clark, 2009. In *JSS* 56 (2011) 414–17.

Tov, Emanuel. *The Greek and Hebrew Bible: Collected Essays on the Septuagint*. VTSup 72. Leiden: Brill, 1999.

———. *Textual Criticism of the Hebrew Bible*. 2nd ed. Minneapolis: Fortress, 2001.

Wolff, Hans Walter. *Obadja und Jona*. Biblischer Kommentar zum Alten Testament 13/4. Neukirchen-Vluyn: Neukirchener, 1977.

8

Psalm 3

Of Whom Does David Speak, of Himself or Another?

Robert L. Cole

It is a pleasure and a privilege to dedicate this article to Prof. Sailhamer, who first introduced me as his student to the concept of reading the Psalter as a unity. He continually kept abreast of recent developments in the field of Old Testament and at the time the idea of an integrated and unified Psalter was comparatively recent. Soon after hearing this from him Wilson's seminal work on the editing of the Psalter appeared.[1] He was of course a student of Childs who had already suggested a few years previously that the book's shape showed signs of deliberate editing.[2]

These developments were actually a return to an idea discussed and debated in antiquity, medieval rabbinic circles, and in the nineteenth century, but with Wilson's publication they took on a new impetus and it continues unabated to the present day. This essay continues in that vein by examining the function and meaning of Ps 3 in its canonical context. The first superscription in the Psalter is found in Ps 3. Psalms 1 and 2 are without heading and function together as a coherent and cohesive introduction to the book.[3] Psalm 3's title takes the reader into the life of David when fleeing from his son Absalom, a story narrated in 2 Samuel 15–18.

1. Wilson, *Editing*.
2. Childs, *Introduction*, 504–25.
3. Cole, *Gateway*.

The relationship between this psalm and the Samuel narrative has been explained in various ways. Sa'adya haGaon (as quoted by Ibn Ezra) noted that the fate of the nations in revolt of Ps 2 was the same as that of Absalom.[4] In the Psalms Midrash a similar comparison is made: "R. Jacob said in the name of R. Aha: why is the Psalm on Gog and Magog (Ps. 2) placed next to the Psalm on Absalom? To tell you that a wicked son works greater cruelty upon his father than will the wars of Gog and Magog."[5] Noteworthy is the attempt both in the medieval period and earlier to explain the position of Ps 3 following Ps 2.

According to Childs the titles in general establish a secondary setting and do not reflect independent historical tradition. Rather they are the result of exegetical activity, which derived its material from within the text itself.[6] He argues that Psalm 3 has no specific linguistic parallels with the Samuel narrative, only conceptual ones similar to those found in many other psalms.[7] Slomovic on the other hand, considers the titles the result of a "midrashic process of placing certain Psalms into specific historical situations because of their linguistic and thematic affinities."[8] However, like Childs, he considers that "virtually every Psalm of individual complaint could be said to allude to this event."[9]

Kraus simply concludes that the application of this psalm to 2 Samuel 15–18 is "erroneous . . . and does not help to elucidate the text. For the singer of our psalm does not flee like David and evinces not a trace of mourning (for Absalom)."[10] Millard responds to Kraus' objection by observing that

---

4. Cohen, *Psalms*, 8.

5. Braude, *Midrash*, 50.

6. Childs, "Psalm Titles," 137–50.

7. Ibid., 143. He notes 2 Sam 15:12 (את אבשלום והעם הולך ורב), which resembles Ps 3:2 in its use of the root רבב, and 2 Sam 18:31 (מיד כל הקמים עליך), which resembles also Ps 3:2 (רבים קמים עלי). He also observes that 2 Sam16:14ff, and 17:22 tell how David arrived weary at the Jordan, spent the night there, and arose just before daybreak to cross the river, which presumably was linked to Ps 3:6. For Childs, "general parallels between the situation described in the Psalm and some incident in the life of David" was the most important factor in the formation of Psalm titles, while "Linguistic parallels, especially word-plays, were of secondary importance" (147–48).

8. Slomovic, "Toward an Understanding," 350–80. He notes 2 Sam 18:32 (קמו עליך), in addition to the previous v. 31 בל הקמים עליך, also uses similar language as Ps 3:2, and suggests that the taunting of Shimei ben Gera in 2 Sam 16:8 was linked to Ps 3:3. He also considers the lifting of the psalmist's head in Ps 3:4 - ומרים ראשי, as compensation for David's degradation while ascending the Mt. of Olives, weeping with his head covered (2 Sam 15:30 - ובוכה וראש לו חוי).

9. Ibid., 365.

10. Kraus, *Psalms 1–59*, 139.

Psalm 3 never denies the flight of David.[11] He sees Psalm 3 as adding a direct address to God not included in the book of Samuel.[12]

Mays attributes the superscription to a "learned sage who made the connection between psalm and story found a number of similarities in them," but that the number of inconsistencies between the psalm and the story "argue against taking the connection between prayer and story as historical."[13] Examples of the latter include the fact that the "tenor of the prayer is not in accord with David's attitude toward Absalom and his allies. Nothing in the story suggests that David believed that there was no help in God for him. Jerusalem was not known as the elect "holy mount" of the Lord in David's time before the temple was built."[14]

According to Craigie, "the parallels between the historical incident (David's flight from Absalom) and the *substance* of the psalm are such as to give some credibility to the value of the superscription . . . the parallels are sufficiently strong to suggest that Ps 3 may have originated in the context of the particular event in the lifetime of David."[15] According to Briggs, "The title mentions an event in the life of David which in many respects suits the experience of the poet."[16]

Hakham links the root ברח in the superscription (בברחו) to the words of David in 2 Sam 15:14: הקומה ונברח ("arise and let us flee").[17] He also considers the possibility that David's worship at the top of the Mt. of Olives (2 Sam 15:32) implies a prayer, which this third psalm cites.[18]

Terrien simply poses the question, "Was the psalm specifically composed to illustrate this traumatic experience, or was it an independent poem—a cry for help *in extremis*—later understood as fitting the Davidic *legenda*?[19] Alexander considers the title to be "in perfect keeping with the

---

11. Millard, *Die Komposition*, 131.

12. Ibid., 131.

13. Mays, *Psalms*, 53.

14. Ibid., 53.

15. Craigie, *Psalms 1–50*, 172–73.

16. Briggs and Briggs, *Psalms*, 25. "His derision as one forsaken by God 2 S.16:7–8, the danger by night 2 S. 17:1 sq., the myriads of people 2 S. 15:18, 17:11, and his high and honourable position."

17. Hakham, *Tehillim*, 10) י).

18. Ibid., שם ישתחוה אשר בא עד הראש דוד ויהי :(12) יב. He links 2 Sam 17:11 (כחול אשר על הים לרב) to Ps 3:2 (רבים קמים עלי), Ps 3:3b to 2 Sam 16:8 where Shimei ben Gera calls on the Lord to bring on David's head the blood of Saul's house, and finally the reference to lying down and sleeping in Ps 3:6 to Hushai's words in 2 Sam 17:16 (אל תלן הלילה) which he sent to David.

19. Terrien, *Psalms*, 90.

psalm itself, as well as with the parallel history," but admits that the terms are very general.²⁰ This is explained as due to the fact that "the psalm, though first suggested by the writer's personal experience, was intended for more general use."²¹

Wilson likewise discusses the reference to David's flight in 2 Sam 15–16 and concludes that there is "no specific reference to that event in the text of the psalm."²²

Delitzsch notes in passing the common references to the "holy hill" in Pss 2 and 3.²³ Hakham sees some similarity in content between Pss 2 and 3, specifically in the submission of the king of Israel's enemies by divine help in addition to the aforementioned noun phrase.²⁴ Kirkpatrick detects a connection between external foes of the kingdom of the LORD's anointed in Ps 2 and those internal in Psalms 3–4.²⁵

The foregoing sampling of studies reveals that scholars have focused on the links between Psalm 3 and the events narrated in 2 Samuel but find them scarce and tenuous. Indeed, the attitude of David in 2 Samuel towards Absalom and that of his words in Psalm 3 towards his enemies are at odds in spite of attempts to the contrary. Psalm 3 represents a dilemma for those who insist that the words of a specific Old Testament text must have direct relevance to its historical situation. In fact, to insist on the interpretation of the psalm according to the historical context of Absalom's uprising is to ignore and even distort authorial intent in the Psalter itself.²⁶

If attempts to relate the events of 2 Sam and content of Psalm 3 are problematic, examination of its location in the Psalter itself yields more positive and definitive results. Its position following the introduction of Psalms 1–2 should not be presumed accidental, notwithstanding Gunkel's statements to the contrary.²⁷ Its content is in fact a perfect complement to

20. Alexander, *Psalms*, 27.
21. Ibid., 27.
22. Wilson, *Psalms*, 128.
23. Delitzsch, *Psalms*, 100.
24. Hakham, *Tehillim*, 13) ג׳).
25. Kirkpatrick, *Psalms*, 14.

26. It is worthy of mention that the Davidic narrative of the book of Samuel itself is deliberately patterned after those of other previous figures such as Samuel himself or others in the Pentateuch and so points ultimately beyond its historical reality. Biblical narrative texts are shaped and composed with prophetic purposes in mind as much as are oracular texts.

27. Gunkel, *Introduction*, 2–3. According to Gunkel, "No *internal ordering principle for the individual psalms has been transmitted for the whole* . . . Thus no certainty exists in questionable cases, whether a psalm should be understood with its neighbor . . . Accordingly, the *particular task of psalm studies should be to rediscover the relationships*

the immediately previous Psalm 2.[28] The words of David in Psalm 3 were considered those of the eschatological messiah in Ps 2, voicing his prayers while enduring the attack against him as described briefly in Ps 2:1–3. He was viewed as a prophet by the one responsible for its present collocation since his prayer uttered in difficult circumstances looked far beyond the particular situation in which he found himself.

Lexical parallels between Psalms 2 and 3 are numerous. Psalm 3 opens with a reference to foes multiplying and rising **against** the speaker (עלי), while the previous Psalm 2 opened with a rebellion against the LORD and **against** his messiah (על משיחו), also using the same preposition.[29] These two instances of this preposition occur at the very end of each psalm's second verse, so that structural affinity accompanies and supports the verbal parallel.

Directly following in verse three of each psalm is a citation of the words of the foe. So, the nations and their rulers conspire with deadly intent and declare rebellion again the divinely established authority of the anointed one. Likewise, the enemies in Psalm 3 attack and then declare God has abandoned him, not saving the life of the speaker. Thus, each psalm opens in similar fashion, and as will be seen, also concludes in an analogous manner. Implied by the juxtaposition of the two psalms and these parallels is that the divinely approved anointed one in Ps 2:2 and the speaker of Psalm 3 are one and the same. He is attacked directly in Ps 2:1–3 as he is in Psalm 3, but the latter cites his words directly and adds further detail regarding the deadly assault against his person. Likewise, the recalcitrant nations and rulers of Ps 2 are to be identified in Ps 3 as the multiplied foes of the speaker.

Psalm 3:2 also includes the exclamatory מה, ("How!"), a form that resonates with the opening interrogative למה of Ps 2:1 ("Why?"). In either case, there is astonishment at the extent of the apparently unchecked plot and attack against him.

Surprise over the assault against the speaker continues in Ps 3:3. He introduces the words of his enemies' confidence that death is inevitable for

---

between the individual songs that did not occur with the transmission, or that occurred only in part . . . But if someone researching the past wants to obtain the true picture of what happened, that researcher first has to disregard the context in which the items came to us more or less accidentally" (emphasis his). Gunkel identified the first three psalms as wisdom (ibid., 17) royal psalm (ibid., 99) and individual lament (ibid., 121). This sequence is presumably "accidental," and without an "ordering principle."

28. Cole, *Gateway*, 142–64.

29. Note עלי in 3:7 in the same hostile sense. The identical preposition in Ps 2:6 functions as a perfect parallel to its counterpart in Ps 1:3, both of which are locative in meaning and both of which also are found in sanctuarial contexts, see Cole, *Gateway*, 110–11.

him with the words, "many are saying concerning my life" (אמרים לנפשי). Their words contrast sharply with YHWH sentiments and declaration in Ps 2:7 where he is called "my son," being introduced by the words, "he said to me" (אמר אלי). They consider him without divine help while in the previous psalm the deity has declared him his son.

In verse four of the third psalm the psalmist continues his direct address to the Lord, but this time adds the second person masculine singular independent pronoun ואתה ("but you"). Here he reacts to the threats against him by expressing trust in the Lord. Then in verse five he calls to the Lord who answers him from מהר קדשו ("from his holy mountain"). In verse six he lies down and sleeps, but deliberately adds pleonastically the first person singular independent pronoun אני ("I") to first person singular verbs (שכבתי ואישנה). In Ps 2 the same two independent pronouns of Psalm 3 also express a dialogue between God and his son and consequently Psalm 3 continues the same divine conversation. Opening Ps 2:6 is a first person singular pronoun ואני ("but I") that is redundant to the first person singular verb immediately following (נסכתי). This pronoun introduces the reaction to the international revolt of the nations, and is introduced by a disjunctive *waw*, just as a disjunctive and contrasting *waw* preceded the pronoun that began the response to the threat of Ps 3:4 (ואתה). The response of Ps 2:6 includes the Lord's establishment of his king on his הר קדשו ("his holy mountain") of Zion, which mount is mentioned in 3:5 between the two pronouns of vv. 4 and 6. So the uprising of Ps 2:1–3 is met with an emphatic first person pronoun and enthronement of the chosen king on the holy mountain, just as the threats against the same anointed one in Ps 3 are met with an emphatic personal pronoun and answer from the holy mountain.

Repeated reference to the holy mountain functions as a bond between the psalms, but the different governing prepositions *on* (2:6–על הר קדש. . .י), and *from* (3:5–מהר קדשו), locate the opening prayer of Pslam 3 between the revolt and threats of Ps 2:1–3 and the enthronement of 2:6.[30] In Psalm 2 the anointed one is esconced on Zion, while Ps 3 takes the reader to the time previous to that exaltation when he calls out to God in distress and receives an answer from the very same place. Zion is clearly the abode or city of God from which this prayer is answered, and so heavenly in location. It is the same celestial city as described in Ps 46:5 of holy abode (קדש) and water channels (פלגיו), which language matches Pss 1:3–פלגי, and 2:6–קדש. In Ps 48:2 the same holy mountain is described as הר קדשו, also called Mt Zion in v. 3 (הר ציון) on "the sides of the north" (ירכתי צפון), identical to descriptions of the heavenly realm in Isa 14:13 (ירכתי צפון).

---

30. Barth, "Concatenation," 30–40,

It becomes evident through verbal parallels that the primary purpose of Psalm 3 in its position is to provide further details about the attack against the messianic king described in Ps 2:2. As will be seen, Psalm 3 also supplies more explicit information about the results of that attack and the divine response. Psalm 2:6 presents the divine reaction to that attack while Ps 3:5–6 reveals further details about its result.

The divine speech of Psalm 2 continues in verse seven, this time in direct address to the son, using the second person singular masculine independent pronoun (אתה בני) as subject of a nominal clause. Immediately following is the independent first person pronoun (אני . . . ילדתיך) used again redundantly and thus emphatically in the presence of a first person perfect. These match the same pronouns found in Ps 3:4 (ואתה), and 6 (אני). Consequently, a parallel sequence exists between the two psalms intended to inform the reader that the conversation between God and his son in Ps 1 continues in Psalm 2. That sequence includes the following elements as seen below. The disjunctive *waw* in either case indicates a contrast between the rebellion and threats in previous verses and the ensuing divine conversation and response.

Psalm 2	Psalm 3
על יהוה ועל משיחו (v. 2)	עלי (v. 2)
ואני (v. 6)	ואתה (v. 4)
על ציון הר קדשי (v. 6)	מהר קדשו (v. 5)
אתה (v. 7)	אני (v. 6)
אני (v. 7)	

Of all these pronouns, only the אתה of 2:7 is fully essential. The remaining pronouns accompany verbal forms that already express inherently the grammatical subject. Their explicit nature in one continues in the other. The "I" and "you" of Ps 2, whose referents are the Lord and his anointed king, correspond to the "you" and "I" of Psalm 3, referring again to the Lord and his chosen king. They signal to the reader of the Psalter that the conversation begun in Psalm 2 continues in Psalm 3 between the same speakers. Both conversations take place in response to attacks against them. Psalm 2 appropriately quotes speech of both the Lord and his anointed in response to the attempt against them. Psalm 3 quotes only the prayer of the anointed one, he being the sole target of attack. The latter is a psalm that adds further details concerning the revolt described initially in Psalm 2, this time focusing on the chosen king.

Psalm 3:8 expresses confidence in the destruction of the wicked by blows to the cheek and the smashing of their teeth. These are the same wicked (רשעים) named explicitly across Psalm 1 and identified as nations and their rulers in Ps 2. While the injuries of the wicked are graphically recounted in Ps 3:8, no offensive weapon is mentioned,[31] presumably because Ps 2:9 has already supplied it. Indeed, the "rod of iron" (בשבט ברזל) there named supplies a cudgel capable of "smashing" (שברת) teeth and cheeks.[32]

Between Psalms 1 and 3 the verbal parallels are essentially two, being the plural noun רשעים - **"wicked"** (Ps 1:1, 4, 5, 6, and Ps 3:8), and the verbal root קום – **"arise"** (Ps 1:5 – לא יקומו, Ps 3:2 – קמים). These two forms are found together as verbal predicate and subject noun of the same clause in Ps 1:5a. Presumably the judgment promised upon the wicked in Ps 1:5a functioned as motivation for the complaint of Ps 3:2 where the wicked have the initial upper hand.[33] However, that initial promise of Ps 1 will be reaffirmed in Psalm 3. The request for the deity to rise in 3:8 (קומה יהוה) functions as a response to the rising of the enemy in 3:2 (קמים) even as does the request for salvation (הושיעני) in 3:8 respond to the assertion by many in v.3 (אין יש ועתה לו) that none exists for him.

Psalm 3 concludes with a blessing pronounced on the LORD's people. Previous to this final verse the psalmist has mentioned only his enemies and his prayer. Leaving references to the faithful until the final verse or verses of the psalm is precisely the pattern of Psalms 1 and 2. The righteous of Psalm 1 appear only in verses five and six, while a blessing pronounced on the faithful in Psalm 2 is given only in the final clause.

Of major importance in the interpretation of Psalm 3 is v. 6. The speaker lies down, sleeps and awakes, because the LORD supports him (ש כבתי ואישנה הקיצותי). Is this normal sleep and awakening, or something more profound? According to Orlinsky, the root שכב appears most often in the Qal, primarily with the meaning "to lie down (in death)" or "to lie down

---

31. Verse four has included the metaphor of "shield" (מגן), used for defensive purposes.

32. The suitability of this weapon for such damage appears to be insinuated by means of consonance as well:

בשבט ברזל – Ps 2:9

שברת – Ps 3:8

Note the identical sequences of *bet resh*, the common use of *shin* and similar dental stops *taw* and *tet*.

33. The question concerning the *uprising* of Ps 2:1–3 was also motivated by the promise of *no rising* for the wicked in Ps 1:5.

(for sexual relations)."[34] Alonso-Schökel notes that sleeping and awakening are customary symbols for death and resurrection.[35]

In Job 14:12 are found the identical verbal roots of Ps 3:6, "lie down," "sleep" and "awake," (שכב ... יקיצו ... משנתם) in an unambiguous reference to death.[36] This is the only other example in the entire Hebrew Bible of the threefold combination of these verbal roots (קיץ – Hiph. both instances, יש‍ן and שכב). David's own death is predicted in 2 Sam 7:12 as a "lying down," (ושכבתי)[37] and throughout Kings and Chronicles the death of monarchs is described using the same verb.[38] Twice more in the Psalter (Pss 41:9; 88:6) "lying down" refers to death.[39]

Psalm 4 following repeats in the first person singular the same two verbal roots (אשכבה ואישן). In no other juxtaposed psalms is this pair repeated, as is the case for the repetition of רבים אמרים in 3:3 and 4:7. Presumably Ps 4:9 also refers to the death of the speaker, and comparison of לבטח of this verse with the same in Ps 16:9 supports the idea of resurrection in Psalm 4 as well. Certainly such examples of *concatenatio* are not merely aesthetic flourish without purpose and meaning, but rather point to a coherence and consistency of message between the two. Examples of this could be multiplied many times over and provide further solid evidence for the deliberate composition of the entire book.[40]

The identical verb "to sleep" in Ps 13:4, (אישן – also in the *yiqtol* first person singular form) explicitly refers to death (האירה עיני פן אישן המות).[41]

34. Hamilton, "שכב."

35. "Dormir y despertar son símbolos acostumbrados de muerte y resurrección." Alonso-Schökel, *Treinta Salmos*, 57.

36. Note as well that the statement "will not arise" (ולא יקום) of Job 14:12 is identical except in number to Ps 1:5b. In six out of twenty-two occurrences of the root קיץ (to awake), it is from the sleep of death: 2 Kgs 4:31; Jer 51:39, 57; Job 14:12; Dan 12:2; Isa 26:9.

37. Note that God will "raise up" (והקימותי) his seed after him and his kingdom will be established, the same verb used in Ps 1:5a.

38. Thirty-eight times in these two books. Note as well Job 7:21, 11:18, 14:12 (mentioned already), 20:11, 21:26, 27:19. Cf. Ezek 31:18, 32:19, 21, 27, 28, 29, 30, 32.

39. Jer. 51:39, 57 uses the same verbs in reference to death as sleeping the eternal sleep and not awakening:

ושנה שנת עולם ולא יקיצו

Similarly Dan. 12:2 – ורבים מישני אדמת עפר יקיצו, where the same root for sleeping and awakening are found in a clear reference to resurrection from the dead.

40. Auwers, *La composition*, 90–92, notes how difficult it is to consider the root כפף in Pss 145:14 and 146:8 to be a fortuitous parallel given the fact that it occurs only one other time in the Psalter (Ps 57:7).

41. Note the parallels between Ps 13:2 (עד אנה תסתיר את פניך ממני) and the aforementioned Ps 88, specifically v. 15: יה יהוה תזנח נפשי תסתיר פניך ממני. Psalm 88 is another psalm describing the death of the same Davidic king.

Psalm 13 is especially pertinent to Ps 3, describing in first person the attack of enemies against the life of the speaker. His enemies are described using the same two terms with first person pronominal suffixes as found in Ps 3 (איבי – Pss 3:8; 13:3, 5; צרי – Pss 3:2; 13:5). The attack "against" him as described in 13:3 (עלי) repeats the same suffixed prepositional form for the attack in 3:2 (עלי). Last, but not least, the salvation which his foes are sure God will not grant him in 3:3 (ישועתה),[42] is that in which he rejoiced of 13:6 (בישועתך). Such parallels between Pss 3 and 13, the latter a psalm referring explicitly to the sleep of death, are significant for the interpretation of the former. The statement of his foes in Ps 3:3b that there is no salvation for him in God reflects certainty that his life is about to end. Identical references to his threatened life are also found in Ps 3:3a (לנפשי) and Ps 13:3 (בנפשי).

Consequently, David's words in Ps 3 speak prophetically beyond the particular situation mentioned in the superscription, a fact the Psalter's composer recognized and so placed it following Pss 1–2. They represent the voice of king messiah portrayed in the Psalter's introduction, adding further details concerning the attack against him in Ps 2:1–2 and the divine dialogue in Ps 2:6–7.[43] That attack ended in his death, but was followed by his resurrection, topics to be discussed again in the Psalter. For example, Ps 31:14b describes an attack against the individual speaker with intent to kill, recalling Ps 2:2 quite explicitly:

Ps 31:14b – בהוסדם יחד עלי לקחת נפשי זממו

Ps 2:2[44] – ורוזנים נוסדו על יהוה ועל משיחו

Thus, a reading of Psalm 3's portrayal of the attack in Ps 2:1–2 as murderous in intent is confirmed by the explicit parallel of Ps 31.[45]

Psalm 3's superscription appears also to play a role in the shape of the Psalter. It serves to set this psalm apart from the introduction, the latter consisting of two psalms without titles enveloped together by an explicit

---

42. In Ps 3:9 the same salvation (הישועה) is ascribed to YHWH.

43. The singular independent pronoun אני opens both Ps 2:6 and 3:6. Ps 3:6 ends with confidence that the LORD "sustains" (יסמכני) the speaker, while 2:6 cites directly the LORD who "establishes" (נסכתי) his own king on Zion. The consonance of *samekh*, *kaph*, and *nun* appears deliberate, and would connect resurrection in Ps 3 to enthronement on heavenly Zion in Ps 2. Consonance is exploited often in the Psalter, not only within bicola or across an individual psalm but also between psalms.

44. Psalm 41:8 expresses in similar language a united attack against the individual speaker:

יחד עלי . . . עלי יחשבו רעה לי

The parallel language to Ps 2:2 (יחד עלי) creates an inclusio across Book I.

45. Note as well that the defamation by "many" (רבים) of the speaker in Ps 31:14a with intent to take his life (לקחת נפשי), is a reprise of the "many" (רבים) in Ps 3:2, 3 who say there is no saving of his life (לנפשי).

example of inclusio and numerous lexical ties. From this point on Book I is dominated by first person "laments," after an opening pair of psalms identified by Gunkel as wisdom and royal respectively.[46] Purported form critical differences were of little consequence to the one giving shape to the Psalter in its canonical form. For the book's author/redactor/composer,[47] the third psalm and those following constituted a perfect sequel to the introduction represented by Psalms 1–2. Focus on the "historical background" of this psalm to the neglect of its context in the Psalter will inevitably eclipse the compositional strategy and meaning. This psalm was born out of a historical context, as the superscription indicates, but the composer recognized its prophetic content and meaning far beyond that setting and positioned it in the Psalter accordingly.

The superscription of Psalm 3 also recalls David's flawed humanity and sin. He is not the ideal priestly and Joshua-like figure of the first psalm, nor is his son Absalom (בנו) the son of God heard and seen in the second psalm (בני). His firstborn offspring resembles more the cabal of unruly nations and rulers of Ps 2. Nonetheless, out of that desperate situation, David uttered words that looked far beyond his own particular circumstances to that of the eschatological king and son of God portrayed in the two previous psalms. Psalm 3's role as a continuation of topics found in the introductory Psalms 1–2 sets a pattern for the rest of the book.

The foregoing reading of Psalm 3 is not innovative by any means and was apparently known in antiquity, as Augustine's opening words of his commentary on Psalm 3 demonstrate: "That this psalm should be understood as spoken in the person of Christ is strongly suggested by the words, *I rested, and fell asleep, and I arose because the* LORD *will uphold me* (Ps 3:6)."[48] Undoubtedly he is the heir of a long held tradition of interpretation in the Christian community. His christological interpretation appears to be based principally on verse 6, also discussed above. Whatever the origin of Augustine's understanding, the surrounding canonical context in the Psalter fully supports it and is fully consistent with the words of Luke 24:44–46: "that it was necessary for all that was written in the law of Moses and the prophets and the Psalms concerning me to be fulfilled . . . thus it is written that the Christ would suffer and rise from the dead . . ."[49]

---

46. Gunkel, *Introduction*, 17, 99, 121.

47. The appropriate term for the one(s) giving the canonical Psalter its final shape is impossible to determine due to the difficulty in identifying different compositional or editorial hands. That the canonical sequence reflects the theology and view of its editor for each psalm from beginning to end is an appropriate reading strategy.

48. Saint Augustine, *Psalms*, 76.

49. My own translation.

Bibliography

Alexander, Joseph A. *Commentary on Psalms.* 1864. Reprint, Grand Rapids: Kregel, 1991.

Alonso-Schökel, Luis. *Treinta Salmos: Poesía y Oración.* Madrid: Ediciones Cristiandad, 1986.

Augustine, Saint. *Expositions of the Psalms.* Vol. 1. Translated by Maria Boulding, introduction by Michael Fiedrowicz, edited by John E. Rotelle. Hyde Park, NY: New City, 2000.

Auwers, Jean-Marie. *La composition littéraire du Psautier: Un État de la question.* Paris: Gabalda, 2000.

Barth, Christoph. "Concatenation im ersten Buch den Psalters." In *Wort und Wirklichkeit: Studien zur Afrikanistik und Orientalistik: Eugen Ludwig Rapp zum 70. Geburtstag,* edited by Brigitta Benzing et al., 30–40. 2 vols. Meisenheim am Glan: Hain, 1976.

Braude, William G., trans. *The Midrash on Psalms.* New Haven: Yale University Press, 1959.

Briggs, Charles A., and Emilie G. Briggs. *A Critical and Exegetical Commentary on The Book of Psalms.* International Critical Commentary. Edinburgh: T & T Clark, 1906–1907.

Childs, Brevard S. *Introduction to the Old Testament as Scripture.* Philadelphia: Fortress, 1979.

———. "Psalm Titles and Midrashic Exegesis." *JSS* 16 (1971) 137–50.

Cohen, Menahem, ed. *Psalms I. Mikra'ot Gedolot 'Haketer.'* Ramat-Gan, Israel: Bar Ilan University, 2003.

Cole, Robert L. *Psalms 1–2: Gateway to the Psalter.* Sheffield: Sheffield Phoenix, 2013.

Craigie, Peter C. *Psalms 1–50.* WBC 19. Waco, TX: Word, 1983.

Delitzsch, Franz. *Psalms.* Commentary on the Old Testament Vol V. Translated by James Martin: Grand Rapids: Eerdmans, 1982.

Gunkel, Hermann. *An Introduction to Psalms: The Genres of the Religious Lyric of Israel.* Completed by Joachim Begrich. Translated by James D. Nogalski. Mercer Library of Biblical Studies. Macon GA: Mercer University Press, 1998.

Hakham, Amos. *Sefer Tehillim.* Jerusalem: Rav Kook, 1979.

Hamilton, Victor P. "שכב." In *Theological Wordbook of the Old Testament,* edited by R. Laird Harris et al., 2:921–22. Chicago: Moddy, 1980.

Kirkpatrick, A. F. *The Book of Psalms.* Cambridge: Cambridge Univeristy Press, 1910.

Mays, James Luther. *Psalms.* Interpretation. Louisville: John Knox Press, 1994.

Millard, Matthias. *Die Komposition des Psalter.* FAT 9. Tübingen: Mohr/Siebeck, 1994.

Slomovic, Elieser. "Toward an Understanding of the Formation of Historical Titles in the Book of Psalms." *ZAW* 91 (1979) 350–80.

Terrien, Samuel. *The Psalms: Strophic Structure and Theological Commentary.* Grand Rapids: Eerdmans, 2003.

Wilson, Gerald H. *The Editing of the Hebrew Psalter.* SBLDS 76. Chico, CA: Scholars, 1985.

———. *Psalms.* Vol. 1. NIV Application Commentary. Grand Rapids: Zondervan, 2002.

9

Canonical Approaches, New Trajectories, and the Book of Daniel[1]

Jordan M. Scheetz

Canonical Origins

CANONICAL APPROACHES TO THE Bible have their roots in the writings of two key authors from the 1970s. James Sanders was the first on the scene with his book *Torah and Canon*, in which he makes it very clear that he is proposing an entirely new discipline: "The following is an essay in the origin and function of canon; it is, in effect, an invitation to formulate a sub-discipline of Bible study I think should be called canonical criticism."[2] This exact title was used in the *Anchor Bible Dictionary* for an over five-page article by Gerald T. Sheppard.[3] Sanders was not looking to overturn the standard historical-critical paradigm, but was looking to add a new discipline to the broader field, a discipline that focuses on the whole of the Bible for the purpose of describing "its shape and function."[4]

The other key voice from the 1970s was Brevard Childs through his *Introduction to the Old Testament as Scripture*. Childs in distinction to Sanders was in no way looking to add a new methodology but to reorient the whole of the field: "I am now convinced that the relation between the historical critical study of the Bible and its theological use as religious literature within a community of faith needs to be completely rethought. Minor adjustments

---

1. In honor of John H. Sailhamer with whom I had the privilege of studying for five formative years.
2. Sanders, *Torah and Canon*, ix.
3. Sheppard, "Canonical Criticism," 861–866.
4. Sanders, *Torah and Canon*, ix.

are not only inadequate, but also conceal the extent of the dry rot."[5] For Childs it is obvious that the problem was not so much the methodology used in historical critical study but the overall goal to which these tools were used, namely the establishing and separating of the various sources for analyzing their individual message. Childs's own work, to the bewilderment of other scholars like John Barton and James Barr, did clearly use the same historical critical methodology but for the purpose of examining how these texts now functioned together within the canonical text. Barton wants to label Childs's approach as a literary approach to the Bible[6] and Barr thought Childs added nothing new other than an "infinite repetition on the word *canon*."[7] However, both Barton and Barr wanted Childs to be doing something, pre-critical reading of the Bible, but were unable to recognize that he was truly offering a new approach by combining historical critical methodology for a theologically unified reading of the Hebrew Bible.

Although it was Gerhard von Rad's work that appears to have led the way for both of these previous perspectives,[8] it is not until the 1980s that Rolf Rendtorff, both von Rad's student and successor at Heidelberg,[9] begins to publish in a similar direction to that of Childs.[10] What maybe was not as pronounced as Barton and Barr would have liked in Childs's work is unavoidable in Rendtorff's case; Rendtorff is functioning fully within the historical critical paradigm but arguing for canonical interpretation. In contrast to Childs's own work, when it came to writing a theology of the Old Testament, Rendtorff in his first volume simply followed the Old Testament books in a Hebrew order[11] while Childs followed a topical outline.[12] Rendtorff took seriously von Rad's statement, "Die legitimste Form theologischen Redens vom Alten Testament ist deshalb immer noch die Nacherzählung."[13] It should be noted that the second volume of Rendtorff's theology did take up a thematic treatment of the Old Testament,[14] but only after a canonical foundation had been established.

5. Childs, *Introduction to the Old Testament as Scripture*, 15.
6. Barton, *Reading the Old Testament*, 89–103.
7. Barr, *The Concept of Biblical Theology*, 379.
8. Von Rad, *Theologie des Alten Testaments* Vol. 1, 128–35.
9. Rendtorff, *Kontinuität im Widerspruch*, 51–63 and 77–99.
10. Rendtorff, *Das Alte Testament*, 137–306.
11. Rendtorff, *Theologie des Alten Testaments*, Vol. 1, 2.
12. Childs, *Biblical Theology of the Old and New Testaments*.
13. Von Rad, *Theologie des Alten Testaments*, 1:134–35.
14. Rendtorff, *Theologie des Alten Testaments*, vol. 2.

John Sailhamer's Canonical Approach

Beginning in the 1990s another Old Testament scholar began to publish a series of volumes arguing for a canonical approach that follows a similar *Nacherzählung* strategy as recommended by von Rad and was followed by Rendtorff. John Sailhamer clearly based his biblical-theological commentary of the Pentateuch on carefully following the (Masoretic) Hebrew text of the Pentateuch.[15] Two years later he published a volume following the same *Nacherzählung* strategy, except it covered both the Old and the New Testaments.[16] Although it follows a Protestant order and scope and lacks scholarly interaction with secondary literature "it is based on a thorough technical reading of the Bible in both Hebrew and Greek" and "[i]t attempts to show how the Bible fits together and how the parts fit into the whole."[17] One year later he published a scholarly discussion of Old Testament biblical theology outlining key options that can be made in relation to doing Old Testament biblical theology, ending with his own canonical proposal which made clear his own formal methodology.[18] However, it appears that the scholarly companion to his whole Bible *Nacherzählung* came several years later in *The Meaning of the Pentateuch*, where Sailhamer makes his most complete argument not only for the compositional strategy of the Pentateuch, but also the Hebrew Bible and the connection between the Old and New Testaments.[19]

Although there are many points of comparison that could be made between Childs, Rendtorff, and Sailhamer, Sailhamer's proposal represents a fundamentally different canonical approach. To many this may belabor the obvious; Sailhamer clearly frames his argument within a classic evangelical framework while Childs and Rendtorff are working within, albeit challenging, the historical critical paradigm. However, any careful reader of Sailhamer's work notes the overwhelming use of what are primarily considered critical scholars. No, the judicious use of critical scholarship is not the primary difference.

One key contrast is found in Sailhamer's canonical text and that of Childs and Rendtorff. For Childs and Rendtorff the canonical text is the proto-Masoretic text, evidently due to the assumption that the canonical text was brought to its conclusion sometime in the latter half of the first

---

15. Sailhamer, *The Pentateuch as Narrative*.
16. Sailhamer, *NIV Compact Bible Commentary*.
17. Ibid., 7.
18. Sailhamer, *Introduction to Old Testament Theology*.
19. Sailhamer, *The Meaning of the Pentateuch*, 460–612.

century CE.[20] For Sailhamer the canonical text is to be found sometime earlier, presumably in the 3rd or 2nd Century BCE, and is very similar in most cases to the proto-Masoretic text but at times similar to the *Vorlage* of LXX text(s) as now corroborated by (some) texts at Qumran.[21]

What is interesting is that at least two scholars in recent Old Testament scholarship have indicated the same time period as the key canonical moment. Stephen B. Chapman argues in *The Law and the Prophets* that the original two part canon, "Law and Prophets," comes to its conclusion with the book of Daniel in the "mid second century B.C."[22] Karel van der Toorn in *Scribal Culture and the Making of the Hebrew Bible* speaks not of the closing of the canon but the conclusion of the prophetic era and yet the book of Daniel, which is presumed to have come after this era and is "[w]ritten just before the middle of the second century B.C.E.,"[23] marks the last book (diachronically) in the collection.[24]

Another key contrast between Sailhamer and Childs and Rendtorff is Sailhamer's view of the development of the canonical text. All three agree with the use of various sources to create the text and the purposeful and intelligent designing of the text.[25] However, both Childs and Rendtorff still function heavily within the Wellhausen paradigm that argues for a gradual development of this/these text(s) presumably over hundreds of years. Sailhamer's approach varies in that he sees decisive moments in the composition of biblical books and the canonical text. In relation to the Pentateuch he views Moses as having composed the Pentateuch based on various written texts.[26] This large composition is in essence the Pentateuch as it is now

20. Childs, *Introduction to the Old Testament as Scripture*, 100–106; and Rendtorff, *Theologie des Alten Testaments*, 2:304–5.

21. Sailhamer, *The Meaning of the Pentateuch*, 55, states, "In a compositional view, passages such as Deuteronomy 34 are considered important additions to the Mosaic Pentateuch. They provide vital clues to how authors at the end of the biblical period (ca. 300 B.C.) understood the Pentateuch." Later he notes, "A working definition of the 'final shape' of the OT is 'the compositional and canonical state of the HB at the time it became part of an established community.' This occurred for the OT sometime before the first century B.C." (160). Sailhamer's argument answering "which canonical text?" depends heavily on the work of Abraham Geiger (141–48).

22. Chapman, *The Law and the Prophets*, 239.

23. Van der Toorn, *Scribal Culture and the Making of the Hebrew Bible*, 260–61.

24. Ibid., 255–61.

25. Sailhamer, *The Meaning of the Pentateuch*, 207–18; Rendtorff, *Theologie des Alten Testaments*, Vol. 1, 1–6; Childs, *Introduction to the Old Testament as Scripture*, 68–83.

26. Sailhamer, *The Meaning of the Pentateuch*, 207, states, "Moses used written texts that he gathered from various sources and provided them with commentary, much like a modern producer of a documentary film."

known.²⁷ However, the canonical text differs from this text in that there are occasional small additions from a later period within the larger text but in particular additions on the edges, redactional seams that consciously join the text with the other portions of the canon.²⁸ In Sailhamer's view these additions are the work of the canonical composer(s) who presumably lived and worked sometime around 300 BCE.²⁹ The observations about these redactional seams found in Deuteronomy 34, Joshua 1, Malachi 3, and Psalm 1 are well documented within Old Testament scholarship.³⁰

Although Sailhamer is well aware of the physical difficulty of supporting such an argument in the sense that the codex has not yet been invented, he argues for this shape based "not in terms of its physical reality, but as a mental construct."³¹ He goes on, "Regardless of its lack of physical shape, the OT likely was construed in terms that reflected a 'semantic shape' and a theological profile. The OT would have been akin to the unassembled pieces of a jigsaw puzzle still in the box. As with the picture of the puzzle on the box, one could have a mental construct of how the pieces fit together, and that construct would be a way of showing the meaning of the individual pieces within the whole. Given the mental force of such a construct, a physical copy of the OT canon would have been unnecessary."³² On the one hand the physical text would have been separated in physical documents and on the other the redactional seams added by the canonical redactor(s) would have demonstrated how these pieces mentally fit together. It is noteworthy that Sailhamer's semantic shape of the Old Testament (the same can be said for Childs and Rendtorff) looks strikingly similar to the text of *BHS* even with its differences from *Baba Batra* 14b. This is striking in that Sailhamer's approach lends itself to exploring LXX texts, including their different early orderings exactly because of their early pre-Masoretic origins.

New Trajectories in Canonical Approaches

It is this last observation that I would like to suggest will render very interesting areas of further research for canonical approaches. Barton noted

27. Ibid., 51.

28. Ibid., 52, notes Gen 36:31 as an example within the larger composition and Deuteronomy 33–34 as an example on the edge (48).

29. Ibid., 55.

30. Koorevaar, "The Torah Model," 64–80, offers a helpful survey and critique of these observations.

31. Sailhamer, *The Meaning of the Pentateuch*, 211.

32. Ibid.

in 1984 the problem of "which canon" in his critique of Childs's canonical approach,[33] a question that far from discounting the whole canonical enterprise as anything other than a literary approach, as it appears was Barton's intention,[34] could open to legitimate critique and actual refinement of canonical approaches. If one were to remain with Sailhamer's argument in relation to which canonical text, continuing text critical considerations from early witnesses could play an important role as well as the consideration of possible variant semantic shapes of the biblical canon. Broader considerations that move beyond the "chronological" canon of Septuagint, Vulgate, and Protestant Bibles, and the "thematic" canon of the Hebrew Bible, may very well reveal similar thematic issues but in a different form. But for this to happen, the assumption that *BHS* or even *Baba Batra* 14b represents the (earliest) canonical form should be critically reconsidered. Contrary to what many think about canonical approaches, they are deeply historical in their foundations, even if the end result leads to reading biblical texts as a part of a larger whole.

As a way of helping methodologically in this endeavor, I would suggest that both internal and external considerations play a role in these further studies. Externally the different witnesses to canon, a group of authoritative texts for the various Jewish and Christian communities, need to be critically engaged and evaluated.[35] It should be noted that complete codices and lists of books only begin to appear in the 2nd century CE, whether Jewish or Christian. Before this time period we must depend on the mention of numbers of books and inferential and partial evidence whether represented through names or identifiable quotations and allusions.[36]

For internal evidence, we are of course dependent on the actual texts themselves in their various forms and languages. Scrolls and codices are of particular importance, but even the smallest of fragments may give hints at various semantic shapes or at the very least a corroboration of a known

---

33. Barton, *Reading the Old Testament*, 91.

34. Ibid., 100–103.

35. Two helpful books in gathering this type of information in relation to the Old Testament are McDonald's *The Bible Canon* and Beckwith's *The Old Testament Canon of the New Testament Church*. However, it must be noted that these are no substitute for examining the primary sources themselves.

36. Houtman and Sysling, *Alternative Targum Traditions*, 236, adopt Julie Hughes's helpful definitions of a quotation and allusion for their work on Targum Jonathan: "we define the term quotation as 'a phrase which is marked, explicitly or implicitly, as referring to the words of a speaker who is not the implied speaker of the composition.' For the term allusion we have adopted her working definition describing it as 'a reference which is recognized by a reader as referring to a textual source, knowledge of which contributes to the meaning for the reader.'"

semantic shape. On the text-critical level this evaluation should have a view to the details as well as the big picture, as the contents of books may at times differ in their overall arrangement, not just the wording of individual verses. The well-known differences between the Masoretic texts of Jeremiah and Ezekiel and LXX texts underscore this point. The placement among other texts becomes the final phase of examination, paying particular attention to what (if anything) happens on the edges of these documents.

The expected outcome of this canonical approach is that there is a significant consensus on the semantic shape of Genesis through Kings with the notable exception of the placement of Ruth. Beyond this the varying semantic shapes represent multiple thematic possibilities that in the end are not really that different from one another. Further, the overall placement of a book may not really change much in its interpretation other than the surrounding contents may help to highlight a component within the book that may go overlooked without this broader context.

Daniel as an Example

The book of Daniel poses an interesting test case for the purpose of illustration in the senses that it has multiple placements in the various canons, has a complicated textual tradition, and has been the key example for all sorts of diametrical arguments with regard to the development of the canon. In the LXX versions Daniel is consistently placed in the prophets while the Hebrew transmission has consistently placed Daniel in the Ketuvim. The text of Daniel is bilingual in the Hebrew transmission with the book basically evenly split between Hebrew and Aramaic while there are two key versions represented in Greek with Theodotion and the LXX both with significant textual pluses in comparison to the Hebrew transmission. Because of the placement in the two different sections in the various canons, arguments for and against the original placement have led to significant theological and canonical conclusions.

My own presupposition when I began my scholarly work in relation to Daniel was that Daniel was rightly placed within the Ketuvim. I assumed this to be the case not based on a three-stage theory of canonization where Daniel was in the Ketuvim because of its late date of composition and therefore was put into the Ketuvim because the Nevi'im were already closed. Instead, my assumption was that the text was thematically placed there for compositional reasons. However, I did assume that the order roughly represented in *BHS* was the older Jewish tradition without critically considering the origin of LXX, Vulgate, Protestant orders, and further early testimony in relation to the book of Daniel.

After having written significantly on the intertextual relationships within the Masoretic text of Daniel, I began to explore further intertextual relationships within the Old Testament and the New Testament.[37] During my research I stumbled upon the article, "Is Daniel Also Among the Prophets?" by Klaus Koch.[38] Although I had considered much of the material discussed in the article, the historical implications had not really sunk in. Was it really possible that at an earlier point in time Daniel was actually in the Nevi'im?[39]

External Evidence

Many assumptions are tied to the text from *Baba Batra* 14b that lists the order of both the Nevi'im and the Ketuvim. This text in practical terms gives the broad framework within which later medieval manuscripts and printed versions of the Hebrew Bible operate, although most do not follow the exact order for the Latter Prophets or the Ketuvim.[40] The text in relation to the Ketuvim states:

סידרן של כתובים רות וספר תהלים ואיוב ומשלי קהלת שיר השירים
וקינות דניאל ומגילת אסתר עזרא ודברי הימים

> Our order of the Writings: Ruth, and the book of Psalms, and Job, and Proverbs, Qohelet, Song of Songs, Lamentations, Daniel, the scroll of Esther, Ezra, and Chronicles.

This statement represents the first clear list within antiquity that actually gives the books and order of the Ketuvim, or at least a version of the Ketuvim. Taken at face value there seems to be no real argument until the realities of the information contained within this text are considered. The codification of the Babylonian Talmud is traditionally dated in the fifth to the sixth century CE.[41] However, the text itself attributes this particular statement in context to oral tradition from the "Tannai Teachers" (תנו רבנן),

---

37. Scheetz, *The Concept of Canonical Intertextuality and the Book of Daniel*.

38. Koch, "Is Daniel also among the Prophets?"

39. Some of the following material is taken from my article, "Daniel's Position in the Tanach, the LXX-Vulgate, and the Protestant Canon," but I have added much new material.

40. For an in depth discussion in relation to the various orders of the Ketuvim see Steinberg's *Die Ketuvim*.

41. Stemberger, *Einleitung in Talmud und Midrasch*, 193–95.

who are understood to have taught from circa 70 CE into the early third century CE.[42] If a generous dating of this statement is granted it places this proposed order and structure against another different tripartite division from the same time period. From a pure literary standpoint this represents a list to be dated somewhere between the fifth and eighth century CE.

Another text that can be dated with a greater level of certainty in the late first century CE is Josephus's *Contra Apionem* 1.38–41:

> οὐ μυριάδες βιβλίων εἰσὶ παρ' ἡμῖν ἀσυμφώνων καὶ μαχομένων, δύο δὲ μόνα πρὸς τοῖς εἴκοσι βιβλία τοῦ παντὸς ἔχοντα χρόνου τὴν ἀναγραφήν, τὰ δικαίως πεπιστευμένα. καὶ τούτων πέντε μέν ἐστι τὰ Μωυσέως, ἃ τούς τε νόμους περιέχει καὶ τὴν ἀπ' ἀνθρωπογονίας παράδοσιν μέχρι τῆς αὐτοῦ τελευτῆς· οὗτος ὁ χρόνος ἀπολείπει τρισχιλίων ὀλίγον ἐτῶν. ἀπὸ δὲ τῆς Μωυσέως τελευτῆς μέχρις Ἀρταξέρξου τοῦ μετὰ Ξέρξην Περσῶν βασιλέως οἱ μετὰ Μωυσῆν προφῆται τὰ κατ' αὐτοὺς πραχθέντα συνέγραψαν ἐν τρισὶ καὶ δέκα βιβλίοις. αἱ δὲ λοιπαὶ τέσσαρες ὕμνους εἰς τὸν θεὸν καὶ τοῖς ἀνθρώποις ὑποθήκας τοῦ βίου περιέχουσιν. ἀπὸ δὲ Ἀρταξέρξου μέχρι τοῦ καθ'ἡμᾶς χρόνου γέγραπται μὲν ἕκαστα, πίστεως δ'οὐχ ὁμοίας ἠξίωται τοῖς πρὸ αὐτῶν διὰ τὸ μὴ γενέσθαι τὴν τῶν προφητῶν ἀκριβῆ διαδοχήν.[43]

> There are not myriads of discordant and opposing books to us, but only twenty-two from the books having of all time the registering, the ones justly having been believed. And of these are the five ones of Moses, which encompass both the laws and the tradition from the origin of man until his last. This time leaves off a little of three thousand years. And from the last of Moses until Artexerxes, the king, after Xerxes of the Persians, the prophets after Moses composed in writing the things having been done, according to them, in three and ten books. And the remaining four encompass hymns to God and suggestions for human things of life. And from Artexerxes until our time all things have been written, they are not thought worthy in a state of assurance equal in force to the ones before them because there is not the exact succession of the prophets.

Josephus's list has a clear structure with the five books of Moses first (καὶ τούτων πέντε μέν ἐστι τὰ Μωυσέως), thirteen books of Prophets *after* the books of Moses (οἱ μετὰ Μωυσῆν προφῆται τὰ κατ'αὐτοὺς πραχθέντα συνέγραψαν ἐν τρισὶ καὶ δέκα βιβλίοις), and four other books of hymns and

---

42. Ibid., 17.
43. Thackeray, *Josephus, The Life and Against Apion* Vol. 1, 178.

of a practical character (αἱ δὲ λοιπαὶ τέσσαρες ὕμνους εἰς τὸν θεὸν καὶ τοῖς ἀνθρώποις ὑποθήκας τοῦ βίου περιέχοισιν). Even without the actual names of the books from Josephus's list, the discrepancy between the two lists is obvious; Josephus has only four books in the third category while *Baba Batra* 14b has eleven.

Two later descriptions that clearly base their lists on the number 22 and in all probability Josephus, Origen, and Athanasius, list four books consistently together although in the middle of the Prophets that fit well with the description given by Josephus. Origin lists these books as Psalms, Proverbs, Ecclesiastes, and Song of Songs with the Hebrew names transliterated into Greek, demonstrating that his argument is based in some way on Hebrew texts (βίβλος Ψαλμῶν, Σφαρθελλειμ· Σολομῶνος παροιμίαι, Μελωθ· Ἐκκλησιαστής, Κωελθ· Ἆισμα ἀσμάτων . . . Σιρασσιρειμ).[44] Athanasius also lists these books in the same order of Psalms, Proverbs, Ecclesiastes, and Song of Songs (μετὰ δὲ ταῦτα βίβλος ψαλμῶν, καὶ ἑξῆς παροιμίαι. εἶτα ἐκκλησιαστὴς, καὶ ἄσμα ἀσμάτων), but it is also clear by the use of μετα before this short list that these books come as a part of a larger structure.[45] These lists also reveal Daniel's various placements within the larger structure. Origen lists Daniel between the Jeremiah corpus that includes Jeremiah, Lamentations, and *The Epistle of Jeremiah*, and Ezekiel, again with their transliterated names from Hebrew into Greek (Ιερεμίας σὺν Θρήνοις καὶ τῇ Ἐπιστολῇ ἐν ἑνί, Ιερεμια· Δανιήλ, Δανιηλ· Ἰεζεκιήλ, Ιεζεκιηλ).[46] Athanasius lists Daniel after both the Jeremiah corpus, this time including *Baruch* as well, and Ezekiel, at the close of the Old Testament (Ιερεμίας, καὶ σὺν αὐτῷ Βαροὺχ, θρῆνοι καὶ ἐπιστολὴ, καὶ μετ' αὐτὸν Ἐζεκιὴλ καὶ Δανιὴλ).[47] Although it could be tempting to discount these two witnesses because of their Christian and later nature, both are clearly in agreement with Josephus's description and predate at the very least from a literary standpoint *Baba Batra* 14b (Origen lived 185–253/254 CE[48] and Athanasius wrote his letter in 367 CE[49]).

Returning to the first century CE, two further witnesses identify Daniel as among the Prophets. Matthew 24:15 yields two interesting pieces of information:

---

44. Eusebius, *Ecclesiastical History*, 2.72.
45. Athanasius, "Ἐκτη τῆς λθ ἑορταστικῆς ἐπιστολῆς," 8.
46. Eusebius, *Ecclesiastical History* 2.72.
47. Athanasius, "Ἐκτη τῆς λθ ἑορταστικῆς ἐπιστολῆς," 8.
48. Stiewe, "Eusebios," 927.
49. Brakke, "Canon Formation and Social Conflict in Fourth-Century Egypt," 395.

Ὅταν οὖν ἴδητε τὸ βδέλυγμα τῆς ἐρημώσεως τὸ ῥηθὲν διὰ Δανιὴλ τοῦ προφήτου ἑστὸς ἐν τόπῳ ἁγίῳ, ὁ ἀναγινώσκων νοείτω.

Therefore when you behold the abomination of devastation, the word through Daniel the prophet, standing in the holy place, let the one reading consider.

Daniel is clearly identified as a prophet (Δανιὴλ τοῦ προφήτου) and further this identification is made in connection with a text that can be read. Both the quote "the abomination of devastation" (τὸ βδέλυγμα τῆς ἐρημώσεως) from Dan 9:27; 11:31; and 12:11, which is understood as "the word through Daniel the prophet" (τὸ ῥηθὲν διὰ Δανιὴλ τοῦ προφήτου), and the admonition, "Let the one reading understand" (ὁ ἀναγινώσκων νοείτω), point to a prophetic text and not just a prophetic person. In this same regard one text from Qumran, 4Q174 Frag. 1 II,3, states, "being written in the book of Daniel, the prophet" (כתוב בספר דניאל הנביא).⁵⁰ Again, this identification is used in reference to what has been written.

Although my own argument is nuanced from Koch's, it is appropriate to return to his article and his conclusion after he examined similar external evidence:

> If one looks for the conclusions to be drawn from this survey of the sources, one is forced to note that there is not a single witness for the exclusion of Daniel from the prophetic corpus in the first half of the first millennium A.D. In all the sources of the first century A.D.—Matthew, Josephus, Qumran—Daniel is reckoned among the prophets. In fact the earliest literary evidence of Daniel's inclusion among the *Ketubim* is to be placed somewhere between the fifth and eighth centuries A.D.⁵¹

This statement needs to be nuanced in that Jerome (340/350–420 CE) wrote clearly about Daniel's placement in the Ketuvim among the "Hebrews": "I remind⁵² that the Hebrews do not have Daniel among the Prophets, but among those which are enrolled 'Holy Writings'" (illud admoneo non haberi Danihelem apud Hebraeos inter Prophetas, sed inter eos qui Agiografa

---

50. Martinez and Tigchelaar, *The Dead Sea Scrolls Study Edition*, 1:354.

51. Koch, "Is Daniel also among the Prophets?," 123. Finley, "The Book of Daniel in the Canon of Scripture," 208, also notes in his conclusion based on Koch's earlier work, "Evidence from the first century and earlier favors the view that the Book of Daniel was originally a part of the Prophets, and only later was moved to the Writings."

52. I have translated *admoneo* with "remind" as opposed to "warn" because Jerome has already given the sections and order of the Hebrew Bible, albeit somewhat different than the numbers mentioned in this passage, in his introduction to Kings in Hieronymus, "Incipit prologus sancti Hieronymi in libro Regum," 364–65.

conscripserunt).[53] However, even if a generous date is given to the source of the *Baba Batra* 14b text, this would only mean that there were possibly two early competing *Jewish* placements for the book of Daniel in a tripartite canon based on the external evidence.

Internal Evidence

The Hebrew text of Daniel is actually a hybrid text with 1:1—2:4a in Hebrew, 2:4b—7:28 in Aramaic, and 8:1—12:13 in Hebrew. In its transmission, it has never received a complete translation into Aramaic, an Aramaic Targum (translation). However, there are two significant translations into Greek, LXX texts and Theodotion. Although Theodotion comes from a period of time after the first century CE, it is helpful in the sense that it also contains similar additions as are found in LXX texts. These additions include *Susanna*, placed variously before and after Daniel proper, and *Bel and the Dragon*, placed after Daniel, and Daniel 3:24–90.[54] Each of these additions serve essentially to enhance the exemplary character of the main Jewish characters, even the prayer of Azariah in 3:24–90 serves this purpose by putting praise on the lips of Azariah while in the midst of the furnace.

Hebrew Orders

Sailhamer in following the Hebrew text tradition has argued that Daniel is placed in close proximity to Ezra-Nehemiah and Chronicles because of a key textual connection in relation to the rebuilding of Jerusalem.[55] Daniel 9 unfolds the difficult reality based on the writings of Jeremiah the Prophet (בספרים . . . ירמיה הנביא) that Jerusalem would be in ruins for seventy years (9:2; cf. Jer 25 and 29). After a lengthy prayer that is semantically similar to Solomon's prayer in 1 Kings 8 which in turn is similar to Leviticus 26 and Deuteronomy 28 (9:3–19), an answer comes to Daniel from "the man Gabriel" (9:21; האיש גבריאל). In this text, there is the reality that after these sev-

---

53. Hieronymus, "Incipit prologus Hieronymi in Danihele propheta," 1342.

54. Niehr, "Das Buch Daniel," 514, states in relation to the placement of *Susanna*, "Im Theodotion-Text wird die Susanna-Erzählung an den Anfang des Danielbuches gerückt oder z.T. auch als eigenes Buch gewerdet. Dies tun auch LXX und S. Die Vg setzt die Susanna-Erzählung als Abschluss an das Ende des Danielbuches." In relation to *Bel and the Dragan* Niehr states, "Dan 14 enthält zwei Erzählungen (14,1–22; 14,23–42). Die Erzählungen liegen wie die Susanna-Erzählung in der LXX und Theodotion vor" (515).

55. Sailhamer, "Biblical Theology and the Composition of the Hebrew Bible," 25–37, and Sailhamer, *The Meaning of the Pentateuch*, 171–75 and 212–15.

enty years there will be seventy weeks, presumably of years (שבעים שבעים; 9:24). However, key to these seventy weeks is that the countdown begins with the "going out of a word to cause to return and to rebuild Jerusalem" (מצא דבר להשיב ולבנות ירושלם, 9:25). What this countdown is leading to is made clear from 9:24:

> [24] שבעים שבעים נחתך על עמך ועל עיר קדשך לכלא הפשע ולחתם
> חטאות ולכפר עון ולהביא צדק עלמים ולחתם חזון ונביא ולמשח קדש
> קדשים:

> [24] Seventy weeks are determined upon your people and upon the city of your holiness, to bring to an end the transgression and to seal up sin and to atone for iniquity, and to cause righteousness to go in forever and to seal up vision and prophet and to anoint the Holy of Holies.

For obvious reasons the decree that starts this whole expectation in motion is of extreme importance.

The opening of Ezra picks up exactly at the intersection between Jeremiah's seventy years and Daniel's expectation that the seventy weeks begin with the decree to rebuild Jerusalem, demonstrating that the decree of Cyrus brings both Jeremiah's seventy years to a conclusion (לכלות דבר יהוה מפי ירמיה; 1:1) and begins Daniel's seventy sevens (יעל לירושלם אשר ביהודה ויבן את בית יהוה; 1:3). This exact connection is where the book of Chronicles ends, both with the conclusion of the seventy years from Jeremiah (לכלות דבר יהוה בפי ירמיהו; 2 Chr 36:22) and the beginning of Daniel's seventy sevens (ויעל; 2 Chr 36:23). Through the placement of these texts in close proximity to one another there is an expectation that moves toward the fulfillment of the seventy weeks. The argument is that the semantic shape is indicated through concrete textual connections. It is notable that the decree of Cyrus is on the edges of both Ezra, at the very beginning, and Chronicles, at the very end. Both may be indications of a semantic shape from a time that predates codices.

Josephus Tradition Orders

When considering the Josephus tradition reflected in the earlier mentioned lists from Origen and Athanasius, the books that are in close proximity to Daniel change from the (later?) Hebrew orders. In Origen's list Daniel is preceded by the Jeremiah corpus, Jeremiah, Lamentations, and *The Epistle of Jeremiah*, and followed by Ezekiel. Jeremiah, even in LXX texts with their significant textual and structural differences from the Hebrew text, closes with a similar text to 2 Kgs 24:18—25:30, which chronicles the fall of Judah and Jerusalem. Lamentations is a text that deals in its entirety with fallen Judah and Jerusalem while *The Epistle of Jeremiah* is a letter to those deported to Babylon. Both Lamentations and *The Epistle of Jeremiah* in LXX texts are clearly attributed to Jeremiah in their respective opening verses, whereas the Hebrew text does not attribute Lamentations to Jeremiah. Even without asking the canonical question in relation to *The Epistle of Jeremiah*, it is obvious that each addition to the end of Jeremiah is focused on the reality of the fall of Judah and Jerusalem and the attribution of these texts to Jeremiah. In this regard, the Hebrew Text makes clear the editorial nature of Jeremiah 52, with the preceding comment in 51:64b, "until here are the words of Jeremiah" (עד הנה דברי ירמיהו), while LXX texts lack this editorial comment.

The connection to Daniel can be seen in two different ways. If *Susanna* is a textual addition to the beginning of Daniel, it serves as a mirror image to *The Epistle of Jeremiah*, demonstrating how upstanding Jews, Susanna and Daniel, live in Babylonian captivity, similar to Daniel 1–6. But the opening of Daniel returns to the fall of Judah and Jerusalem. However, this is the earlier fall of Jerusalem to Nebuchadnezzar for three years during the reign of Jehoiakim (ἀνέβη Ναβουχοδονοσορ βασιλεὺς Βαβυλῶνος, καὶ ἐγενήθη αὐτῷ Ιωακιμ δοῦλος τρία ἔτη; 2 Kgs 24:1) and not the later fall under Jehoiachin. Further, Daniel 1:1–2 brings not only a focus on the (initial) fall of Judah and Jerusalem (καὶ παρέδωκεν αὐτὴν κύριος εἰς χεῖρας αὐτοῦ; 1:2) but also a focus on the consequences this had for the temple in Jerusalem, with not only Jehoiakim being taken to Babylon but also some of the articles from the temple (καὶ παρέδωκεν . . . μέρος τι τῶν ἱερῶν σκευῶν τοῦ κυρίου; 1:2). This theme in relation to the articles that Nebuchadnezzar took from the temple occurs again in Daniel 5 when Belshazzar brings out these exact articles that Nebuchadnezzar had taken (ἃ ἤνεγκε Ναβουχοδονοσορ ὁ πατὴρ αὐτοῦ ἀπὸ Ιερουσαλημ; 5:2).

The connection between Dan 9:2 and Jeremiah demonstrates, as has already been discussed in the Hebrew orders, an obvious internal relationship between Daniel and Jeremiah. However, this internal connection makes a necessary chronological progression, where Daniel is actually reading the text of Jeremiah to come to his conclusion about the seventy years of ruin for Jerusalem. This creates an obvious semantic shape, where Jeremiah needs to come before Daniel.

Even with the differences in shape between LXX texts and the Hebrew text of Ezekiel, there is a purposeful placement of the vision of restoration of the land of Israel (ἐν ὁράσει θεοῦ εἰς τὴν γῆν τοῦ Ισραηλ; Ezek 40:2) at the end of the book. This purposeful structure is demonstrated in that this vision is dated "in the twenty-fifth year of the deportation" (ἐν τῷ πέμπτῳ καὶ εἰκοστῷ ἔτει τῆς αἰχμαλωσίας; Ezek 40:1) whereas the last dated "word of the LORD" (λόγος κυρίου) chronologically in Ezekiel is dated "in the twenty-seventh year" (ἐν τῷ ἑβδόμῳ καὶ εἰκοστῷ ἔτει) in Ezekiel 29:17. The book has been shaped to conclude with this particular vision of hope concerning the land of Israel. In pointing to future hope for Israel, a further connection with Dan 9:24–27 is made transparent, where the rebuilding of Jerusalem points to the future described in 9:24, "eternal righteousness to be given and the vision to be accomplished and to rejoice[56] the Holy of Holies" (δοθῆναι δικαιοσύνην αἰώνιον καὶ συντελεσθῆναι τὸ ὅραμα καὶ εὐφρᾶναι ἅγιον ἁγίων).

Beyond this structural note, Ezekiel uses the name Daniel three times. In 14:14 and 14:20 the same three people, "Noah and Daniel and Job" (Νωε καὶ Δανιηλ καὶ Ιωβ), are used as the example of the righteous three of those alone who would escape judgment in a land that sins against the LORD (14:12). Ezekiel 28:3 connects the name Daniel with wisdom in a rhetorical question: "Are you not wiser than Daniel?" (μὴ σοφώτερος εἶ σὺ τοῦ Δανιηλ). Righteousness and wisdom permeate the character of Daniel in the book of Daniel and a list of such qualities would entail a *Nacherzählung* of the whole book, including the additions of *Susanna* and *Bel and the Dragon*.

One more issue that uniquely connects Ezekiel and Daniel is life after death. Ezekiel 37:1–14 and Dan 12:1–4 speak of a future hope of people rising from the dead. Notably this statement begins the final section of Daniel, with *Susanna* and *Bel and the Dragon* understood as layered additions to the book.

In passing I will only mention that Athanasius's list continues to keep the Jeremiah corpus, Daniel, and Ezekiel in close proximity to one another. However, Athanasius's list adds Baruch to the Jeremiah corpus, and reverses the order of Daniel and Ezekiel, with the order being the Jeremiah corpus, Ezekiel, and Daniel closing the Old Testament (Ιερεμίας, καὶ σὺν αὐτῷ Βαρούχ, θρῆνοι καὶ ἐπιστολή, καὶ μετ' αὐτὸν Ἐζεκιὴλ καὶ Δανιήλ). The choice to place this grouping at the end of the Old Testament emphasizes an eschatological semantic shape to the conclusion of the Old Testament.

What should be obvious is that considering the Josephus tradition complicates canonical considerations not only because of the different order, but also because of the varying textual traditions. In considering Jeremiah, the layers of textual additions are certainly tied to issues of authorial attribution, but there is also a clear thematic connection tied to the destruction of Judah and Jerusalem and the related deportation to Babylon, an

---

56. Lust, Eynikel, and Hauspie, *A Greek-English Lexicon of the Septuagint*, 1:190, note in relation to the LXX's peculiar translation, "לשמח *to rejoice* for MT למשח *to anoint.*"

element that is already present in the edited conclusion of the actual book of Jeremiah. This issue is also seen in the possible inclusion of *Susanna* at the beginning of Daniel, where the story served to demonstrate the exemplary characters of Susanna and Daniel in Babylon, just as the opening scene of Daniel emphasizes Daniel's exemplary character.

As thematically placed additions, the various layers of canonical shaping in the large textual pluses can be removed to reveal various stages of shaping. Clearly the Greek only texts represent a later layer of canonical shaping unless further discoveries reveal an underlying Hebrew tradition. The completely moveable unit of Lamentations appears to be the next layer of canonical shaping, especially since it receives an inscription in the LXX versions which is absent in Hebrew texts. The earliest layer of canonical shaping is at the compositional level, with Jeremiah 52 quoting (?) from 2 Kgs 24:18—25:30, Daniel 1 framing the following Aramaic text with a Hebrew introduction, and Ezekiel 40–48 closing with an eschatological focus, similar to Daniel, on the restoration of the people and land of Israel.

Conclusion

Rather than concluding on the rather historically dubious position that *the* placement of Daniel is to be here or there, I would like to point to a few synthesizing points. First, Daniel is placed in close proximity to two main groupings of books, Ezra-Nehemiah and Chronicles in the Hebrew tradition, and Jeremiah and Ezekiel in the Josephus tradition. At first glance these may appear to be diametrically opposed placements to one another, one in the Ketuvim and one in the Prophets. However, both placements reflect a decided eschatological emphasis, looking to the future restoration of God's people and the land of Israel (e.g., Ezek 40:2; Dan 9:24). In both cases this eschatological expectation is left open, as the decree in Ezra and Chronicles only initiates the seventy weeks, and Jeremiah, Daniel, and Ezekiel only present the eschatological expectation as a future hope. Finally, both clusters present these expectations from the narrative reality that life is presently not what it should be. I would argue that both shapes represent thematic arrangements that in the end are very similar to one another.

However, the most striking aspect of this argument is that *Baba Batra* 14b, contrary to common scholarly assumption, likely gives a later shape of the tripartite canon, with a different distribution of books among the Nevi'im and the Ketuvim. This creates the interesting dynamic that all the books of the two clusters that we have examined in relation to Daniel were among the Prophets, in all likelihood, at an earlier time. Arguments that depend on the fixed boundaries of *Baba Batra* 14b for their assumed time and order of canonization must be reevaluated. Daniel was among the prophets.

Bibliography

Athanasius. "Εϰτη τῆς λθ ἑορταστιϰῆς ἐπιστολῆς." In *Quellensammlung zur Geschichte des Neutestamentlichen Canon bis auf Hieronymus*, edited by Johannes Kirchhofer, 7–9. Zürich: Meyer & Zeller, 1844.

Barr, James. *The Concept of Biblical Theology: An Old Testament Perspective*. Minneapolis: Fortress, 1999.

Barton, John. *Reading the Old Testament: Method in Biblical Study*. Philadelphia: Westminster, 1984.

Beckwith, Roger. *The Old Testament Canon of the New Testament Church*. Grand Rapids: Eerdmans, 1985.

Brakke, David. "Canon Formation and Social Conflict in Fourth-Century Egypt: Athanasius of Alexandria's Thirty-Ninth *Festal Letter*." *Harvard Theological Review* 87 (1994) 395–419.

Chapman, Stephen B. *The Law and the Prophets: A Study in Old Testament Canon Formation*. FAT 27. Tübingen: Mohr/Siebeck, 2000.

Childs, Brevard S. *Biblical Theology of the Old and New Testaments: Theological Reflection on the Christian Bible*. Minneapolis: Fortress, 1993.

———. *Introduction to the Old Testament as Scripture*. Philadelphia: Fortress, 1979.

Eusebius. *Ecclesiastical History*. Vol. 2. Translated by J. E. L. Oulton. Cambridge: Harvard University Press, 1932.

Finley, Thomas J. "The Book of Daniel in the Canon of Scripture." *Bibliotheca sacra* 165 (2008) 195–208.

Houtman, Alberdina and Harry Sysling. *Alternative Targum Traditions: The Use of Variant Readings for the Study in Origin and History of Targum Jonathan*. Studies in the Aramaic interpretation of Scripture 9. Leiden: Brill, 2009.

Ieronymus. "Incipit prologus Hieronymi in Danihele propheta." In *Biblia Sacra: Iuxta Vulgatam Versionem*, edited by Robertus Weber, 1341–42. 4th ed. Stuttgart: Deutsche Bibelgesellschaft, 1994.

———. "Incipit prologus Sancti Hieronymi in libro Regum." In *Biblia Sacra: Iuxta Vulgatam Versionem*, edited by Robertus Weber, 364–66. 4th ed. Stuttgart: Deutsche Bibelgesellschaft, 1994.

Koch, Klaus. "Is Daniel also among the Prophets?" *Interpretation* 39 (1985) 117–30.

Koorevaar, Hendrik. "The Torah Model as Original Macrostructure of the Hebrew Canon: S Critical Evaluation." *ZAW* 122 (2010) 64–80.

Lust, J., E. Eynikel, and K. Hauspie. *A Greek-English Lexicon of the Septuagint* Vol. 1, A-I. Stuttgart: Deutsche Bibelgesellschaft, 1992.

McDonald, Lee Martin. *The Biblical Canon: Its Origin, Transmission, and Authority*. Peabody, MA: Hendrickson, 2007.

Niehr, Herbert. "Das Buch Daniel." In *Einleitung in das Alte Testament*, edited by Erich Zenger, 507–16. 7th ed. Stuttgart: Kohlhammer, 2008.

Rad, Gerhard von. *Theologie des Alten Testaments*. Vol. 1, *Die Theologie der geschichtlichen Überlieferungen Israels*. Kaiser-Taschenbücher. 10th ed. Munich: Kaiser, 1992.

Rendtorff, Rolf. *Das Alte Testament: Eine Einführung*. 6th ed. Neukirchen-Vluyn: Neukirchner, 2001.

———. *The Canonical Hebrew Bible: A Theology of the Old Testament*. Translated by David E. Orton. Tools for Biblical Study Series 7. Leiden: Deo, 2005.

———. *Kontinuität im Widerspruch*. Göttingen: Vandenhoeck & Ruprecht, 2007.

———. *Theologie des Alten Testaments, Ein kanonischer Entwurf*. Vol. 1, *Kanonische Grundlegung*. Neukirchen-Vluyn: Neukirchner, 1999.

———. *Theologie das Alten Testaments, Ein kanonischer Entwurf*. Vol. 2, *Thematische Entfaltung*. Neukirchen-Vluyn: Neukirchner, 2001.

Sailhamer, John H. "Biblical Theology and the Composition of the Hebrew Bible." In *Biblical Theology: Retrospect & Prospect*, edited by Scott J. Hafemann, 25–37. Downers Grove, IL: Intervarsity, 2002.

———. *Introduction to Old Testament Theology: A Canonical Approach*. Grand Rapids: Zondervan, 1995.

———. *The Meaning of the Pentateuch: Revelation, Composition and Interpretation*. Downers Grove, IL: Intervarsity, 2009.

———. *NIV Compact Bible Commentary*. Grand Rapids: Zondervan, 1992.

———. *The Pentateuch as Narrative: A Biblical-Theological Commentary*. Grand Rapids: Zondervan, 1992.

Sanders, James A. *Torah and Canon*. Philadelphia: Fortress, 1972.

Scheetz, Jordan M. "Daniel's Position in the Tanach, the LXX-Vulgate, and the Protestant Canon." *Old Testament Essays* 23 (2010) 178–93.

Scheetz, Jordan M. *The Concept of Canonical Intertextuality and the Book of Daniel*. Eugene, OR: Pickwick Publications, 2011.

Sheppard, Gerald T. "Canonical Criticism." In *Anchor Bible Dictionary*, edited by David Noel Freedman, 1:861–66. New York: Doubleday, 1992.

Steinberg, Julius. *Die Ketuvim—ihr Aufbau und ihre Botschaft*. Hamburg: Philo, 2006.

Stiewe, K. "Eusebios." In *Lexikon der Antiken Welt*, edited by Carl Andresen et al., 1:927–28. Düsseldorf: Patmos, 2001.

Thackeray, H. St. John. *Josephus* Vol. 1, *The Life and Against Apion*. Loeb Classical Library. Cambridge: Harvard University Press, 1926.

Toorn, Karel van der. *Scribal Culture and the Making of the Hebrew Bible*. Cambridge: Harvard University Press, 2007.

10

Ezra, Nehemiah, and Ezra-Nehemiah

When Characters and Characterization Collide

RAY LUBECK

Multnomah University

I FIRST MET JOHN Sailhamer when he came to dinner with a mutual friend during a summer term at Trinity Evangelical Divinity School before he began teaching there full-time. My wife and I lived in an on-campus apartment, decorated primarily with my bookshelves. After expressing surprise that a seminary student should have so many books, he scanned through the titles, zeroing in on Eichrodt's *Theology of the Old Testament*.[1] He asked me if I had read it, and if so, what I thought of it. I replied that I had, and that while I valued many of his insights, I thought that the title was misleading: "It seems to me that it's not really a theology of the *Old Testament* as much as a theology of ancient Israel." He reacted with visible surprise, and asked where I had come across such an idea. In less than ten minutes into our first meeting we were in deep discussion regarding the differences between exegeting a text as opposed to reconstructing the material to which the text refers.

For readers familiar with his writings and for students who have ever had him in class, the discussion of the locus of meaning has been a trademark theme.[2] The "text versus event" distinction which he has care-

---

1. Eichrodt, *Theology of the Old Testament*.

2. See Sailhamer, *Pentateuch as Narrative*, 16–23; Sailhamer, *Introduction to OT Theology*, 36–85; Sailhamer, *Meaning of the Pentateuch*, 68–160; see also Frei, *Eclipse of Biblical Narrative*.

fully maintained throughout his career has left an important imprint upon contemporary biblical scholarship in general, and upon my own teaching and preaching ministry in profound and far-reaching ways. I recognize now how embedded these categories are in my own thinking. I offer the following essay in tribute to him, seeking to demonstrate how this critical distinction can make a significant difference in approaching Ezra and Nehemiah.

Characters and Characterization

Seeking to identify the meaning of biblical narratives is often a challenging task. Rarely does the text state anything like, "and this story teaches us ___." Rather, we are left to infer the authors' implicit truth assertions by tracing characters' actions to their consequences. Put in the most reductionistic form, the way people learn from stories is to avoid the behaviors that get the characters in trouble while adopting whatever works out to their advantage. Thus, we can learn equally from characters' follies and successes. It is important for us to recognize that the (usually subconscious) decisions we make about the characters will be crucial to what we determine is the main point of the story.[3]

Compounding this problem is the often unstated and unquestioned assumption that the primary purpose of the main characters of biblical stories is to provide us with positive role models whose example we are to imitate in our own lives. Yet the reality does not confirm this assumption. Indeed, in most cases the protagonist is a multiplex character, alternating between commendable and contemptible traits and behaviors. We are supposed to become like the protagonist in some ways, but not in others. The same Noah who is described as righteous (צַדִּיק, Gen 6:9) in one passage is drunk and naked in another (9:21–23). The same Moses who is humble (עָנָו עָנָיו, Num 12:3) elsewhere both kills an Egyptian (Exod 2:12) and fails to trust in (לֹא־הֶאֱמַנְתֶּם, Num 20:12) Yahweh. Moreover, most of the main characters in the stories of the Bible are the same blend of both positive and negative: Jacob, Joseph, the judges, David, Peter, John, *inter alia*.

Acknowledging the sins and failures of our heroes, then, not only enables us to learn new lessons from their mistakes, but also to identify with them more closely. We see them less as paragons of virtue who transcend our own lives; instead they become "normal" people who like us are capable of good *and* evil, wisdom *and* idiocy, heroism *and* ignoble self-ism. Once we resist the urge to "clean them up," we may be more receptive to the authorially-intended lessons communicated in the text.

3. I explore these issues in more detail in Lubeck, *Read the Bible*, 101–6.

Biblical stories present patriarchs, matriarchs, and disciples not as perfectly faithful and ethical persons whom we could not hope to emulate but, rather, as persons who are often immoral, unfaithful, and thickheaded. Therefore, in spite of our own failings, we, too, can hope to be disciples.[4]

The larger context of canon often helps us to evaluate biblical protagonists. Hebrews 11 does not commend Abraham's foolish decisions, Jacob's treachery, Moses' anger, Rahab's lie, or David's adultery, but does commend them explicitly for their *faith*. The author helps us to isolate the common, defining feature of their lives which we too are to adopt, namely, their faith, without lending any tacit approval of their many sins and misdeeds. The fact that later biblical authors quote Gen 15:6 multiple times[5] assists us in identifying the bottom line that we are to get from the life of Abraham, "and he trusted in YAHWEH, and he credited it to him as righteousness." His success as a man favored by God is attributable to this single feature. Obviously, we are not to copy the "other lessons" from Abraham, such as how to give away a wife, the treatment of single mothers, abandoning one's child, how to divide property with contentious relatives, and so on.

Ezra, Nehemiah, and Ezra-Nehemiah

The failure to recognize and consider the wrongful actions of biblical characters is particularly commonplace in the stories of Ezra and Nehemiah. From my youth, I remember hearing multiple sermon series on the life of Nehemiah. Frequently these coincided with fund raising campaigns for church building projects. We were all enjoined to follow in the path of Nehemiah, a godly leader with biblical knowledge combined with practical know-how, construction savvy, resolute determination against "opposition from within and without," and social dexterity. Combined with Ezra's passion for moral purity and scrupulous dedication to the Law, they were portrayed as paragons of spiritual leadership, a two-pronged model for spiritual revival (and successful building projects) in our ministries today. Popular-level books and commentaries that reflect this perspective abound.[6] Starting with certain premises, we're predisposed to arrive at the conclusions that follow.

4. Adams, *Prostitute in the Family Tree*, 6.
5. Rom 4:3, 22; Gal 3:6; Jas 2:23.
6. See, for example, Barber, *Nehemiah and the Dynamics of Effective Leadership*; Boice, *Nehemiah*; Campbell, *Nehemiah*; Ponraj & Carlton, *Strategic Coordination in Mission*; Stanley, *Visioneering*; Swindoll, *Hand Me Another Brick*; Tollefson, "Social Transformation in Nehemiah," 3–6; White, *Excellence in Leadership*. Mervin Breneman's

Premise: The book of Ezra is about Ezra.

Premise: The book of Nehemiah is about Nehemiah.

Premise: The main characters of biblical books are role models for today.

Therefore: The purpose of Ezra and Nehemiah is to provide us with positive role models.

Observation: Both Ezra and Nehemiah were leaders in the post-exilic remnant that returned from Babylonian captivity.

Premise: The obstacles faced by the postexilic community are typical, paradigmatic problems faced in churches and ministries.

Therefore: The specific purpose of Ezra and Nehemiah is to provide us with positive role models for *ministry leadership*.

And *therefore*: Ezra and Nehemiah are both intended to teach the church today (1) how to face challenges to successful ministry, and (2) how to follow godly leadership.

It is precisely at this point where the "Text vs. Event" issue comes to bear. In this case, is our goal to interpret the godly character of the *characters* within Ezra-Nehemiah (*E-N*)?[7] If so, the typical focus is on principles from their example of leadership which are instructive for today. In a very real sense, to do so is to look at these biblical character-heroes as an event, i.e. they become referents to which the text points. But to approach *E-N* as a unified text[8] will lead us to ask, how does the author *characterize* them? And what do we do if it turns out that the text of *E-N* stands in conflict with "our" hero-stories of the characters named Ezra and Nehemiah? Do we interpret the characters (event) or the characterization (text)?

---

remark is illustrative: "Just as in Ezra's time, the believing community today often faces crises that demand strong leadership and decisive, united community action" (*Ezra, Nehemiah, Esther*, 165).

7. Hereafter the text of Ezra-Nehemiah will be abbreviated *E-N* to avoid confusion with the characters Ezra and Nehemiah.

8. I will be reading *E-N* as a single, literary, canonical text. See also Eskenazi "Structure of Ezra-Nehemiah," 641–56. For a comprehensive treatment of the arguments, see Boda and Redditt, *Unity and Disunity in Ezra-Nehemiah*.

The purpose of this essay is to call attention to our apparent failure to call to attention to their own failures. I will contend that the text of *E-N* has not "spun" the characters of Ezra and Nehemiah nearly so positively as many contemporary readers do. There are things done by the leaders we encounter in *E-N* which are intended to be instructive to us, some of which are commendable, yet many of which are negative traits intended to warn us.

Upon closer inspection, it turns out that the narrative of *E-N* concerns other, substantive characters besides simply Ezra and Nehemiah. Though the book spans approximately ninety-five years, the lives of Ezra and Nehemiah depicted in the text occupy only the last fourteen years of this story. Ezra is introduced for the first time in Ezra 7:1. First-person narration is found in Ezra 7:28–9:15 (Ezra) and Nehemiah 1:1–7:5 and 12:27–13:31 (Nehemiah). Thus, the first-person words and perspectives of Ezra and Nehemiah occupy only thirty-four percent of the text we have before us. Other significant characters are Cyrus, Zerubbabel, Jeshua, Haggai, and Zechariah.[9] More simply, the text of *E-N* obviously has a scope and purpose which are larger than recounting the ministries of two of its characters, viz. Ezra and Nehemiah. It turns out that the canonical message of *E-N* is both different and much broader than the leadership roles of these two men.

Learning from Their Positive Example

Without a doubt, Ezra and Nehemiah[10] do demonstrate many laudable traits and commendable actions. Here is a listing of many of these positive aspects which we may take as exemplary.

Positive action (*and who is involved*)	Reference
Returned from Babylonian captivity	
family heads of Judah & Benjamin,	Ezra 1:5; 2:1
priests, Levites returned Israelites	Ezra 6:21

---

9. Lesser figures include Darius, Xerxes, Artaxerxes, the Levites, Rehum, Shimshai, Tattenai, Shethar-Bozenai, Shecaniah, Jonathan, Jahzeiah, Meshullam, Shabbethai, Hanani, Sanballat, Tobiah, Geshem, and Eliashib.

10. And to a lesser degree, Jeshua and Zerubbabel, the main characters of the early chapters of Ezra.

Positive action (*and who is involved*)	Reference
Commitment to prayer	
Family heads	Ezra 8:23
Ezra	Ezra 9:6–10:1
Nehemiah	Neh 1:4–11; 2:4; (4:4–5)[11] 4:9 (6:14) 13:14, 22 (29), 31
Levites	Neh. 9:5–37
Praise to Yahweh *Levites*	Ezra 3:10–11
celebrate with joy *People*	Ezra 6:16, 22; Neh 5:13; 8:6, 12; 12:27, 43
Praise to Yahweh *Ezra*	Ezra 7:27–28
Worked within official legal channels; *the elders*	Ezra 5:11–16
Ezra	Ezra 7:6
Nehemiah	Neh. 2:1–9
Skilled in Moses' teaching, commands, decrees; *Ezra* מָהִיר בְּתוֹרַת מֹשֶׁה	Ezra 7:6, 11–12; Neh 8:1–3, 8–9
Devoted to study & carry out torah, & teach the commandments; *Ezra* כִּי עֶזְרָא הֵכִין לְבָבוֹ לִדְרוֹשׁ אֶת־תּוֹרַת יְהוָה וְלַעֲשֹׂת וּלְלַמֵּד בְּיִשְׂרָאֵל חֹק וּמִשְׁפָּט:	Ezra 7:10; Neh 9:7–8
Committed to tasks despite obstacles; *Nehemiah*	Neh. 4:6–6:9
Observed holy days; *People*	Neh. 8:16–18
Remembering past sins & God's faithfulness	Ezra 5:11–16; 9:15; Neh. 1:4–11; 9:5–35

When we combine all these actions which seem unquestionably good, praiseworthy, and appropriate, it is quite understandable that these individuals are usually looked upon as "heroes" of the biblical narrative. So, it is not surprising that we customarily look to them as positive examples, at least as good as Noah, Abraham, Moses, and David. But therein lies the problem, for while we accept each of these other examples as positive role models, we more readily acknowledge that they also did things which we should not imitate.

---

11. Those in parentheses are actually imprecatory prayers.

Telling the Story Backwards

A distinguishing feature of a canonical approach (whether Sailhamer, Childs, or any other) is that interpreters seek to interpret texts as literary wholes rather than isolated units. We cannot really evaluate any particular canonical story, the individual actions that occur within the constituent episodes, or even the characters themselves, until we have reached the end of a narrative. While we may have working theories about certain characters, the author may surprise us with elements that are revealed late in the story. If so, we are forced to revise our earlier evaluations of them.[12]

Even at high school age, I had this vague but strong sense there was something not right about the sermon series I'd heard on Nehemiah. After a strong beginning, the series usually fizzled; the storyline lost its inertia as it moved toward the end of the book. The last chapter of *E-N* is so unremittingly sour and negative that the speaker was left with only two choices. The first I observed is to pretend that it is not there at all, skip the last few chapters, end the sermon series early, and move on to another, more positive biblical book that will sustain its energy better. The other alternative is to say, "Well, not everything ended well, but if we ourselves stay the course, remain faithful and spiritually pure, then we (unlike them) can avoid the same eventual decay." While arguably this message "can preach," it is simply *not* what the ending of the book is actually saying.[13]

The ending in Ezra records the story of Shecaniah coming to Ezra to insist that every Israelite male who had intermarried with a foreign woman should banish that wife and all their children (10:3), and that Ezra was the one to initiate and enforce this policy. Ezra issued a proclamation mandating that every returned exile was to meet in Jerusalem (failure to comply resulted in forfeiture of all their property and expulsion from the community, 10:7–8). When the assembly took place, the people's response included agreement that the separation was a good idea, but that they couldn't do it right away because (1) they were too crowded, (2) it was raining out there, (3) it couldn't be done in just a day or two, (4) it should be done at a later

---

12. For example, our final evaluation of Professor Snape in the Harry Potter series, or Smeagol/Gollum in *The Lord of the Rings* or Darth Vader in *Star Wars VI: Return of the Jedi* is much more sympathetic than our views of these characters earlier in the narrative. And the reverse is also true—a character you initially thought was good turns out to be evil, cowardly, unfaithful, or seriously mistaken. This is a very common plot development in television crime dramas.

13. Wesley Kort's comment is helpful here: "'Story-following' is the process of trying to understand what has already happened by finding out what will happen next. Events . . . reveal the meaning of previous events by revealing their consequences" (*Story, Text, and Scripture*, 79).

time in the individual villages, and (5) some (Jonathan, Hazeiah, Meshullam, and Sabbethai) opposed the idea anyway (10:12–15). So Ezra organized the implementation of the separation (10:16–17), and "they finished dealing with all the men who had married foreign women" (17).[14] Ezra 10 contains simply a list of the offenders with the summation that "all these had married foreign women, and some of them had children by these wives" (10:18–44). At best, this ending is abrupt and dissatisfying.[15] At worst, the reader is struck by its utter heartlessness and its ineffectiveness in getting at the heart of the matter—not the banishment of women and children but the syncretism and failure of the remaining community.[16]

If we take E-N as a single literary unit, then Nehemiah 13, the ending to the entire work, is even more troublesome. It begins with the universal banishment of all foreigners from Israel (13:1–3). It continues with

---

14. The phrasing here is somewhat ambiguous. וַיְכַלּוּ בַכֹּל אֲנָשִׁים could mean either that the divorces were "finished" (i.e. finalized), that all the cases were "finally" heard and individually adjudicated, or perhaps merely that the matter "came to an end."

15. Numerous attempts are made by scholars to soften the severity of the coercive insistence on divorce and expulsion of foreign spouses and their children. The solutions which attempt to minimize the problems caused by divorce include: (1) it was only a relatively small number, (2) they probably would have returned to their original peoples for care, (3) these foreign wives were idolatrous and thus a threat to the religious community as well as national identity of the returnees, (4) perhaps divorce among that community was *already* commonplace, (5) Ezra's day was desperate times calling for singular exceptions to God's normal patterns for marriage, and (6) we don't really know what happened to them anyway. See Allen & Laniak, *Ezra, Nehemiah, Esther*, 81–82; Coggins, *Books of Ezra and Nehemiah*, 65–66; McGonville, *Ezra, Nehemiah & Esther*, 69–72; Throntveit, *Ezra-Nehemiah*, 56–58. On the first claim, Davies maintains that "in spite of all the threats of seizure of property and excommunication the campaign to exclude foreigners only brought about 113 divorces . . . The text is so theologically constructed that we are not expected to worry about the foreign women and children as full characters. We are not meant to ask what their reactions and their fate were" (*Ezra & Nehemiah*, 70). The third claim above, that the wives were guilty of leading the community into sin, is effectively overturned by the arguments of Jensen, *Witch-Hunts, Purity & Social Boundaries*.

16. On the ending of Ezra, Blenkinsopp writes, "the conclusion [is] . . . uncharacteristically abrupt. We might have expected some remarks on the beneficial effects of the reform on the community and something further about Ezra himself. . . . The most likely explanation is that this measure of Ezra's was not successful. The practice of marrying outside the community was still widespread . . . Ezra's solution proved too drastic to win support. The problem remained, and the descendants of those Jews who shivered in the rain in the temple courtyard continued to plot a hazardous course between exclusiveness and assimilation under Persian, Macedonian, and Roman rule" (Blenkinsopp, *Ezra-Nehemiah*, 200–201. Throntveit concurs regarding Ezra's failure: "In Nehemiah's time, the restoration community would soon find themselves perpetuating the same sin [intermarriage] they so vigorously expunged at this juncture [Ezra 10] . . . Sin continues to break out in ever new forms" (Throntveit, *Ezra-Nehemiah*, 58).

Nehemiah returning to Jerusalem and, upon discovering Tobiah living off the largesse of the Temple storehouses, throwing all Tobiah's things outside (13:4–9). Nehemiah then discovers that provision for the Levites had been neglected, and therefore they had each returned to work in his own fields. So Nehemiah organizes the distribution of food to the Levites (13:10–13). He then offers a curiously self-congratulatory prayer for himself, "Remember me for this, O my God . . ." (13:14). Next, he discovers that the Sabbath is disregarded because of work being done, yet his solution is to force Levites to stand guard over the gates (i.e. conscripting them to work) to prevent others from working (13:15–22), and threatening merchants with physical violence (13:21). Following another "remember me for this also, O my God" (13:22), he also discovers "in those days" that there remain many within Judah who have intermarried and had children. He rebukes them, curses them, beats them up, and pulls their hair (13:25), forcing them to take an unspecified oath. He offers a brief, imprecatory "remember them" (13:29). He then purifies (de-contaminates?) the priests and Levites of everything foreign, assigning them duties and providing for them, concluding with a final "remember me with favor, O my God" (13:30–31).[17]

This is certainly not the kind of narrative resolution that convinces us that *E-N* has been a success story. Even if we grant that Ezra and Nehemiah have done certain good things, the net result is that all their efforts to reform the people have been ineffective. Indeed, despite all their combined strategies, sometimes exemplary actions, legislated policies, calls to repentance, and imposed sanctions, the people's hearts remain unchanged.

The Effect of the Ending

If we admit that the end result of the leaders in *E-N* is failure to accomplish any significant positive change in the spiritual climate of their community, then we can entertain the possibility that perhaps not all their endeavors were God-ordained. This sets us up to consider what they did in light of the larger canon. We will begin to see numerous and often serious problems emerging.

If the ultimate goal of *E-N* is to tell us the story of the building of a wall that will keep unwanted people (namely gentiles) away from God's holy city and temple, then Nehemiah was heroically successful. But does a theology of God's plan for gentiles throughout the Tanak support the legitimacy of this goal? Beginning in Genesis, underscored in Deuteronomy, and especially brought out in the Latter Prophets, God's ultimate plan is precisely

---

17. See also Neh 5:19.

the opposite: to *incorporate* the gentile "foreigners" into the worshipping community. In other words, God wants to populate his anticipated people with the very ones the leaders of Ezra-Nehemiah want to exclude. If this is the case, then Nehemiah was "successful"—in doing the wrong thing! [18]

If, on the other hand, the ultimate goal of Ezra-Nehemiah is not with building projects, but with turning the hearts of the people back to internalized love for God and covenant faithfulness, then the ending demonstrates that despite all his efforts, Nehemiah's proposed reforms didn't reform the community at all! They did not experience anything like a real revival—they did not follow through on their earlier promises (Neh 10:29-39). Nehemiah's coercive tactics end up failing anyway. The problems at the end of the book are NOT from the outside (the foreigners), they're from within the people themselves.

Given the negative outcome of the story itself, we now ought to question what it was that contributed to ultimate failure, rethinking the actions that were taken.

1. Should they have refused help in building the temple? (Ezra 4:1-3)

> When the enemies[19] of Judah & Benjamin heard that the exiles were building a temple for YAHWEH, the God of Israel, they came to Zerubbabel and to the heads of the families and said, "Let us help you build because, like you, we seek your God and have been sacrificing to him . . ." But Zerubbabel, Jeshua, and the rest of the heads of the families of Israel answered, "You have no part with us in building a temple to our God. *We alone* will build it for YAHWEH, the God of Israel, *as King Cyrus*, the king of Persia, *commanded us*."

---

18. While a comprehensive theology of the nations merits book-length treatment, a cursory treatment indicates that Yahweh elected certain people through whom he will bless *all* people: Gen 12:2-3; 18:18; 27:29; 35:11; Exod 19:6; Num 24:9; 2 Sam 7:19; Isa 27:13; 42:6; 55:4-5; Jer. 4:1-2; Ezek 36:23; Jonah; Ps 72:11, 17; Dan 7:14; 1 Chr 16:8,24). The attraction of gentiles to a welcoming Jerusalem is seen in Isa 2:2-4; Amos 9:11-12; Mic 4:1-3.

19. There are two interpretive options for the enemies (צָרֵי) here. Either they are *already* enemies in which case this offer of help is simply a ruse, or this is written from a *post facto* perspective, i.e. it is describing those who immediately after this exchange will become entrenched enemies. Given that all gentiles up to this point have been supportive of the temple building effort, the response of Zerubbabel, Jeshua and the other leaders is both surprising and, in terms of the storyline, the very *cause* of the enmity.

This is *not* what Cyrus actually said. In fact, his edict mandates the cooperation of (non-Jewish) supporters in the building of the temple (1:4), narratively indicated in 1:6, "all their *neighbors* assisted them" (סְבִיבֹתֵיהֶם).

| And let each survivor, in whatever place he sojourns, *be assisted by the men of his place* with silver and gold . . . (ESV) | And all the remnant from all the places where he is an alien there *let the men support him* with silver and gold . . . (Formal trans.) | וְכָל־הַנִּשְׁאָר מִכָּל־הַמְּקֹמוֹת אֲשֶׁר הוּא גָר־שָׁם יְנַשְּׂאוּהוּ אַנְשֵׁי מְקֹמוֹ בְּכֶסֶף וּבְזָהָב וּבִרְכוּשׁ וּבִבְהֵמָה עִם־הַנְּדָבָה לְבֵית הָאֱלֹהִים אֲשֶׁר בִּירוּשָׁלָ͏ִם: |

So, Zerubbabel and Jeshua are wrong both theologically (promoting an unscriptural exclusivism) and technically (misquoting Cyrus, their authoritative source). And they are even factually wrong. In their later letter to Darius (Ezra 5:14–16) they state that Cyrus directly commissioned Sheshbazzar—a Babylonian governor—to rebuild the temple, and that it actually was *he*, not they, who had laid the temple foundations.

These two individuals are canonically indicted further by the words of Zechariah, their contemporary:

> Tell him this is what YAHWEH Almighty says: "Here is the man whose name is the Branch, and he will branch out from his place and build the temple of YAHWEH . . . *Those who are far away will come and help to build the temple of* YAHWEH, and you will know that YAHWEH Almighty has sent me to you. (Zech. 6:12–15)

> And *many peoples and powerful nations will come to Jerusalem to seek* YAHWEH Almighty and to entreat him . . . . In those days ten men from all languages and nations will take firm hold of one Jew by the hem of his robe and say, "Let us go with you, because we have heard that God is with you." (Zech 8:22–23)

2. What was the result of the temple-building effort?

Once the foundation had been laid the initial response of the people was mixed (Ezra 3:12–13), mingling joy over finally beginning the restitution of the temple with grief over the loss of the former temple and the comparatively meager nature of this second temple. After spurning the offer of help from other people (Ezra 4:1–3), however, they encountered opposition resulting in a halt to the work (Ezra 4:4–5), leaving it unfinished for many years (Ezra 4:24).[20] Presumably, had they instead welcomed the help, it may have been finished much earlier. Eventually it was finished under the divine prompting through Haggai and Zechariah (Ezra 5:1–2; 6:14–15; Hag. 1–2).

3. Should they have feared the people of the lands surrounding them?

Were Zerubbabel and Jeshua, and later Ezra and Nehemiah and their contemporaries motivated by genuine holiness or xenophobia? Clearly these leaders drew a parallel between themselves and the generation of Israelites coming from Egyptian captivity to enter the land under Joshua. The land back then was occupied by certain people groups whom Yahweh specifically commanded them to destroy, and with whom he had forbidden them to intermarry.

But maintaining these standards against a different people, viz. all non-Israelites and mixed race people, at this now very different historical context amounts to nothing less than racial bigotry, a pro-Israelitism that counters scripture by adding their endogamy to its teachings.[21] Even when they are praising Yahweh, this ethnocentrism emerges (Ezra 3:11):

He is good, his loyal-love *to Israel* endures forever.[22] כִּי טוֹב כִּי־לְעוֹלָם חַסְדּוֹ עַל־יִשְׂרָאֵל

Jeremiah anticipates even their captors being fully incorporated into the worshipping community, provided they themselves (1) call upon Yahweh and (2) learn from his people.

> As for all my *wicked neighbors* (כָּל־שְׁכֵנַי הָרָעִים) who seize the inheritance I gave my people Israel, I will uproot them from their lands . . . But after I uproot them, I will again have compassion and will bring each of them back to his own inheritance and to his own land. And if they learn well the ways of my people and

---

20. "Thus the work on the house of God in Jerusalem came to a standstill until the second year of the reign of Darius king of Persia."

21. These people who are rejected in *E-N* are those who came from other nations during Assyrian occupation and had intermarried with the survivors of Israelites. Even besides the fact that the two kingdoms were to be reunited after captivity (Hos 1:11; 3:4–5; Amos 9:11–12), Zerubbabel and Jeshua hereby finalize a hostility between themselves and these "Samaritans" that continues through New Testament times.

22. Jer 33:11; Pss 106:1; 107:1; 118:1, 29; 136: *passim*; 1 Chr 16:34; 2 Chr 5:13; 7:3. In each of these cases, it simply says, "he is good, his loyal-love endures forever." In the context of 1 Chronicles 16, this phrase is explicitly for all peoples (vv. 23–24, 28). Yet here under Jeshua's direction, that loyal-love is to be restricted *to Israel*.

swear by my name ... then they *will be established among my people* (בְּתוֹךְ עַמִּי). (Jer 12:14–16)

At that time they will call Jerusalem "The Throne of YAHWEH, and all nations will gather in Jerusalem to honor the name of YAHWEH." (Jer 3:17)

4. Did Yahweh forbid intermarriage between Israelites and non-Israelites in Scripture?

The commands regarding intermarriage with non-Israelites are given in Deuteronomy.

> When YAHWEH your God brings you into the land you are entering to possess and drives out before you many nations—the *Hittites, Girgashites, Amorites, Canaanites, Perizzites, Hivites and Jebusites,* seven nations larger and stronger than you—and when YAHWEH your God has delivered them over to you and you have defeated them, then you must destroy them totally. Make no treaty with them, and show them no mercy. *Do not intermarry with them.* Do not give your daughters to their sons or take their daughters for your sons. (7:1–3)

Here we learn that there are seven specific people groups indigenous to the land of Canaan during Joshua's day with whom they are strictly forbidden to intermarry. Beyond these, a further limitation is found in Deut 23:3, 6–8.

> No Ammonite or Moabite may enter the assembly of the LORD. They shall not enter the assembly of the YAHWEH even to ten generations' duration.[23] ... You shall not seek peace or goodness with them for all coming days. You shall not abhor an *Edomite,* for he is your brother. You shall not abhor an *Egyptian,* for you were an alien in his land. Descendents born to them in the *third generation* may enter the assembly of YAHWEH.

However, beyond these four specific groups plus the "dirty seven," there are no racial or ethnic restrictions on any other non-Israelite who seeks to be part of the worshipping community (Num 15:14–16).

> For the generations to come, whenever an alien or anyone else living among you presents a food offering with aroma pleasing

---

23. גַּם דּוֹר עֲשִׂירִי לֹא־יָבֹא לָהֶם בִּקְהַל יְהוָה עַד־עוֹלָם. I take the עַד־עוֹלָם as indicating long duration here rather than forever, since specific ordinals (tenth, third) are employed here.

to Yahweh, he shall do what you do. The assembly shall have the *identical rule for you and for the alien* living among you; this is an enduring rule for future generations. *You and the alien shall be the same before* Yahweh: The same Torah and judgments apply equally *you and to the alien* living among you.²⁴

So, at Sinai the list of restricted peoples is expanded to include Ammonites and Moabites for ten generations, and Edomites and Egyptians for three. Though the statute of limitations had long since passed for these people groups by the lifetimes of Ezra and Nehemiah, we find that they go far beyond what Deuteronomy commands. *Any* neighboring people are now regarded like the restricted peoples of Joshua's day, with a blanket statement forbidding any intermarriage with *anyone ever* in Nehemiah.

> [T]he leaders came to [Ezra] and said, "The people of Israel, including the priests and the Levites, have not kept themselves separate from the neighboring peoples with their detestable practices, *like* those of the Canaanites, Hittites, Perizzites, Jebusites, Ammonites, Moabites, Egyptians and Amorites.²⁵ They have taken some of their daughters as wives for themselves and their sons, and have mingled *the holy race* (זֶרַע הַקֹּדֶשׁ) with the peoples around them. (Ezra 9:1–2)

> On that day the Book of Moses was read aloud in the people's hearing and in it was found written that no Ammonite or Moabite should *ever* be admitted into the assembly of God,²⁶ . . . And as the people heard this Torah, they excluded *all mixed people* (כָּל־עֵרֶב) from Israel. (Neh 13:1, 3)

Just as they misrepresented Cyrus' edict, they now are also misrepresenting the Torah, heightening the proscriptions both in time and scope. There are many clear canonical examples of Israelite leaders who married those of foreign descent without biblical or community censure: Joseph and Asenath (Egyptian), Moses and Zipporah (Midianite), Salmon and Rahab (Canaanite), Boaz and Ruth (Moabite),²⁷ Bathsheba and Uriah (Hittite), Es-

---

24. In Deuteronomy 20, when attacking any foreign city other than the "dirty seven," they were to extend an offer of peace. If it was refused, then it was permissible to take the surviving women (20:10–18).

25. Note that this claim is not an equation but a comparison, i.e. the current neighbors are not literally descended from the "dirty seven," but are *like* them in practice (as are the syncretized Israelites themselves).

26. לֹא־יָבוֹא עַמּוֹנִי וּמוֹאָבִי בִּקְהַל הָאֱלֹהִים עַד־עוֹלָם: Notice that the reference to ten generations has been omitted.

27. Myers sees Ruth as the antidote to the flawed social policies seen here: "The

ther and Xerxes (Persian). Under the endogamous regime of the leaders of *E-N*, however, each of these couples would be required to divorce.

5. Should Nehemiah have built the walls around Jerusalem?

It may come as a surprise to discover that nowhere in the text is Nehemiah commanded by God to rebuild the walls. Most simply assume that what he does is *prima facie* the right thing to do.[28] But it is instructive to look at the canonical intertexts. Nehemiah categorically forbids any participation of non-Israelites within the community of the remnant.

> But when Sanballat the Horonite, Tobiah the Ammonite official and Geshem the Arab heard about it, they ridiculed and despised us. "What is this you are doing?" they said. "Are you rebelling against the king?" I responded to them saying, "The God of heaven will prosper us. We his servants will begin rebuilding, *but as for you, you have no share in Jerusalem* or any claim or historic right to it." (Neh 2:19–20)

Yet Zechariah, who assures the success of the completion of the second temple by Zerubbabel (Zech 4:9) and whose ministry predates Nehemiah, had already revealed God's intent for an Jerusalem as an inclusive community *not needing* walls.

> '*Jerusalem will be inhabited without walls* because of the great number of men and livestock in it. And *I myself will be a wall* of fire around it,' declares YAHWEH, 'and I will be its glory within.' ... *Many nations* will be joined with YAHWEH in that day and *will become my people*." (Zech 2:3–4, 11)

Book of Ruth is regarded by most scholars as a reaction against the demands of Ezra-Nehemiah" (Myers, *Ezra-Nehemiah*, 84).

28. Twice in the text Nehemiah makes the claim that "the gracious hand of my God was upon me" (2:8, 18). Similarly he also says, "I had not told anyone what my God had put in my heart to do for Jerusalem" (Neh 2:12). But given that both Cyrus and Torah have already been misrepresented by leaders within *E-N*, and that it is Nehemiah who is both speaker and narrator here, it would be unwise to accept this claim uncritically, just as today we don't always accept people claiming, "God told me . . . ." Roberts offers this cautionary note: "Sometimes . . . in our zeal for righteousness we misconstrue God's leading no matter how honorable our intentions may be" (Roberts, *Ezra, Nehemiah, Esther*, 155).

Similarly Isaiah sees Jerusalem, the future temple, and the people of Israel as magnetically attracting foreigners to be included into the worshipping community.[29]

> Let no *foreigner* who has bound himself to YAHWEH say, "YAHWEH will surely exclude me from his people." ... And *foreigners* who bind themselves to YAHWEH to serve him, to love the name of YAHWEH, and to worship him, all who keep the Sabbath without desecrating it and who hold fast to my covenant—these I will bring to my holy mountain and give them joy *in my house of prayer*. Their burnt offerings and sacrifices will be accepted on my altar; for my house will be called a house of prayer *for all nations*. The Sovereign YAHWEH declares—he who gathers the exiles of Israel: "I will gather still *others* to them besides those already gathered. (Isa 56:3, 6–8)

> *Foreigners* will rebuild your walls, and their kings will serve you. ... *Your gates will always stand open*, they will never be shut, day or night, so that men may bring you the wealth of the nations (גּוֹיִם). (Isa 60:10–11)

So also Ezekiel envisions the cohabitation of gentile believers among the Israelites.

> "You are to allot [this land] as an inheritance for yourselves and *for the aliens who have settled among you and who have children. You are to consider them as native-born Israelites;* along with you they are to be allotted an inheritance among the tribes of Israel. In whatever tribe the *alien* settles, there you are to give him his inheritance. (Ezek 47:22–23)

Since these passages precede Nehemiah and his ministry, he should have known that Yahweh's plans for the gentiles did not exclude them, but offered them full participation into the worshipping community of faith.[30]

---

29. God is concerned with all of the nations and all creation. Restoration from exile must not be a return to a self-secure, insulated nationalism, yet another attempt at building a home with even higher protective walls. Rather, for Isaiah it is a matter of renewed covenant. Isaiah 42:5–7 does not say that Yahweh will make a covenant *with* Israel, but rather that Yahweh will give Israel to *be* a covenant to the peoples. See Walsh and Middleton, *Truth Is Stranger*, 160.

30. In the Torah, aliens were not only allowed to live in the land with equal rights and responsibilities (Exod 12:48–49; 22:21; 23:9; Num 9:14; 15:14–16, 26, 29; Lev 17:8–16; 24:22; 25:35; Deut 24:14, 17, 19; 27:19), but also were to be loved by the Israelites (Lev 19:33–34; Deut 10:18–19; 26:12–13). Thus this group was *always* to be admitted.

Indeed, walls meant to exclude are the antithesis to the Isaianic vision of Jerusalem following the captivity.[31]

6. Should Ezra and Nehemiah have acceded to the leaders' demands for divorcing foreign wives?

That Ezra and Nehemiah not only allowed these divorces but also commanded and implemented them is the most troublesome aspect of the book. Virtually all who take them to be exemplars of godliness have difficulty explaining away the obvious problems that this creates for readers of the Bible,[32] attributing the actions taken as unfortunate but necessary.[33]

Whose idea was it that the wives of foreign descent and their children should be banished? It was prompted not by direct command of Yahweh, nor a prophetic utterance, but demanded by others. Ezra was pressured by the leaders into mandating the banishment of foreign wives and children (9:1–2; 10:2–5, 10–11) and the compulsory registration of the returnees to verify their racial pedigree (10:7–8) upon pain of forfeiture of their property.

Nowhere else in scripture is divorce encouraged. At best it is tolerated, under limited circumstances, due to hardness of heart (Matt 19:3–9), but it is never presented as a command to reverse any problems associated with intermarriage.[34] Indeed, the text indicates that four individuals did speak out in opposition to divorce policy (Ezra 10:15).

---

31. Davies clearly understands these implications: "By demanding endogamy Ezra is asking Israel to recognize the pragmatic limits of its receptivity to grace. This is the end of Zechariah's vision of Jerusalem 'inhabited as villages without walls' and Second Isaiah's vision of Israel as a 'light to the nations'" (Zech 2:4 [MT = 2:9]; Isa. 49:6; Davies, *Ezra & Nehemiah*, 70).

32. E.g., "Ezra 9–10 is a notoriously difficult Bible passage that upsets our emotional instincts . . . . [T]he events of Ezra 10 seem to contradict our biblical and theological commitment to the sanctity of marriage . . . . [W]as it right for them to divorce these wives? Did two wrongs make a right? . . . A commitment to biblical authority does not compel us to agree with Ezra. Nowhere does God actually speak in Ezra 10, telling us through a prophet whether Ezra and the people correctly understood God's will or not . . . At most Ezra 10 shows us that in an extreme instance God's people believed that divorce was correct. In no way does the passage indicate that God blesses divorce . . . . Was Ezra correct? Honestly, I do not know" (Roberts, *Ezra, Nehemiah, Esther*, 152).

33. Eichhorst summarizes the reasons for questioning Ezra's decision: (1) previous tolerance of intermarriage, (2) its breaking up established families, (3) its failure to eliminate the problem, (4) its unfairness to the wives, and (5) lack of Mosaic sanction. Ultimately, however, he defends the divorces [!] as "what was right" ("Ezra's Ethics," 16–28).

34. "The requirement that [the divorcing] be done 'according to the law' is puzzling at first sight, since Pentateuchal law nowhere requires an Israelite to divorce his foreign

Writing after this time, Malachi exposes the total failure of the community of returnees. Worship in the second temple is corrupt and insincere. The priesthood is abnegating their responsibilities, the people have nothing but contempt for God, and it is widely believed that the wicked and arrogant are those who are blessed and prosper (3:15). The heart of their failure, however, stems from the fact that they have "broken faith" with their covenant relationships, both figuratively with Yahweh (2:11–12) through idolatry as well as literally with their wives through divorce. The very thing that Ezra and the leaders insist upon is what displeases God.

> You flood Yahweh's altar with tears. You weep and wail because he no longer pays attention to your offerings or accepts them with pleasure from your hands. You ask, "Why?" It is because Yahweh is acting as the witness between you and the wife of your youth, because you have broken faith with her, though she is your partner, the wife of your marriage covenant. Has he not made them one? . . . So guard yourself in your spirit, and *do not break faith with the wife of your youth.* "*I hate divorce,*" says Yahweh God of Israel . . . (Mal 2:13–16).

This is borne out later in the canon, when Paul clearly teaches that a believing spouse is *not* to divorce the unbelieving partner (1 Cor 7:12–14).

7. Should the leaders of E-N have used social reforms to effect inward change?

Perhaps one of the most important lessons to be learned from the book of *E-N* is that, however well-intentioned, leaders cannot precipitate inward change by prescribing outward measures. While strong-arming behavioral demands may achieve short term conformity, there is little evidence that doing so causes a change of heart or perspective: "[Laws] do reflect values. But laws cannot generate values, or instill values, or settle the conflict over values."[35] For all of the effort expended by the leaders in *E-N*, the changes are neither profound nor lasting.[36]

---

wife. We must conclude that what is implied here is a particular interpretation of law, and specifically a rigorist interpretation of the Deuteronomic law forbidding marriage with the native population" (Blenkinsopp, *Ezra-Nehemiah*, 189).

35. Hunter, *To Change the World*, 171.

36. The social policies which are backed by force in Nehemiah concern lending practices (5:5ff), guarding of the gates (7:1–3), purging of the temple storehouses (13:8–9), neglect of the house of God (13:10–13), shutting of the doors to prevent Sabbath-day commerce (13:19–22), and forbidding intermarriage with foreign wives (13:23–28).

Conclusion

Before we can evaluate how we are to view Ezra and Nehemiah as narrative characters overall, we should ask several, very basic but important story level questions. What we make of the book of *E-N*, and of these characters especially, hinges precisely upon how we answer these questions.

1. What were their goals?

To build things? If so, then they are successful. To catalyze lasting change in people's lives? Then they failed.

2. Did they do what they were supposed to do?

They did return to the land. The temple was completed. Sacrifice, prayer, worship, scripture reading, and the Levitical order were all re-established, and these we must affirm as positive steps.

However, they also added their own rules and interpretations to their reading of God's word, attempted to evoke spiritual reform through coercion, instituted both polices and a spirit of ethnocentrism that excluded foreigners, and forced the dissolution of families. All of these were far from God's intent, clearly revealed in other scriptures, and should be rejected.

3. Were they successful?

They were successful in some things that were good (see above).

However, they also failed in other, very important things, viz. in leading the people into lasting, constructive change.[37]

---

37. Levering points out: "While the temple sacrifices and festivals resume, the returned exiles appear to make little effort in general to practice holiness in accord with the Torah.... For his part, Ezra the Scribe induces a certain obedience to the Torah, but even this obedience seems a halfhearted and sad affair.... Does it not seem that these leaders' continuous struggles are hopeless, at best a noble exercise in religious nostalgia and at worst an exemplar of nationalistic fanaticism in religious garb?" (Levering, *Ezra & Nehemiah*, 113–14). His solution to the book is seen in this statement: "Salvation history does not stop building upward, toward a greater and greater divine presence.... [The people's] striving and limping are increasingly embodied only in a remnant and indeed (ultimately) can be embodied only truly and fully in one man, Christ Jesus" (114–15).

Further, they were "successful" in doing things that were not good, such as adding to God's word, their legalism, their exclusionary policies, and in forcing people to break their marriage covenants.

So if the book of *E-N* presents us with examples of leaders who are not successful in leading people into spiritual revival and reform, then what value can this book offer us? Why is it in the Bible?

- *E-N* demonstrates to us how easily and how dangerously we can confuse our ministry goals and agenda with God's will. This is an ever-present risk for all those in leadership.
- It exposes how very wrong it is when God's people seek to hoard his grace as if they own it, refusing to share it with "outsiders."[38] Thus it implicitly condemns any forms of classism, racism, nationalism, or legalism.
- *E-N* teaches us that misguided religious fervor and zeal cannot compensate for misusing God's Word.
- By offending our sensitivities toward family abandonment, it teaches us to prioritize family commitment and fidelity.
- It should cause us to have a healthy cautiousness toward those who abuse their roles and power in spiritual leadership.
- *E-N* shows us that morality and spiritual renewal cannot be legislated or precipitated through external policies.

As a sobering reminder of the gravity of these lessons above, we should note that the Pharisees, whom we know so well from our New Testament, consider Ezra to be the founding father of their movement.[39] Did they pray? Read Scripture? Fast? Take their faith seriously? Expect others to conform to their standards? Assiduously work at keeping every command? Exclude all outsiders? Deem themselves as better than others? Add their own rules to God's commands? Were they sincere? The answer to all these questions

---

38. This was the problem that needed to be dealt with in the first church dispute in Acts 15—what to do with God-fearing gentiles who want to have a part of OUR messiah, OUR new covenant, OUR status as the people of God? This is the "mystery" that Paul needs to explicate in Ephesians. In a very real sense, the very "wall of hostility" that Christ demolishes in Eph. 2:14–16 was constructed by Nehemiah "the wall-builder." Similarly many of Jesus' parables of the kingdom communicate that his kingdom extends beyond the boundaries of Israel, and that Israel's response will be to begrudge God's grace being given to anyone else.

39. "In the Pharisaic tradition Ezra was regarded as—after Moses—the real founder of Judaism" (*Universal Jewish Encyclopedia*, 8:474).

is, of course, yes, just like we find in *E-N*. But clearly we ought not to make leaders of *E-Z* heroes any more than we would the Pharisees.[40]

What is the overall, canonical message of *E-N*? Its key function in the storyline of the Tanak is to point out to the readers that the remnant who returned following Cyrus' edict faced frustration and failure. This return from captivity was clearly *not* the prophetically-anticipated return. This return is at best penultimate; at worst a foil to the real thing. Just as canonical Judges points to Samuel for the solution, viz. the need for a king, so *E-N* points ahead to a greater-than-Jeshuah (cf. Zech. 3:8), the messiah who incorporates the very people whom Ezra and Nehemiah reject into his kingdom purposes.

Bibliography

Adams, Douglas. *The Prostitute in the Family Tree: Discovering Humor and Irony in the Bible*. Louisville: Westminster John Knox, 1997.

Allen, Leslie C., and Timothy S. Laniak. *Ezra, Nehemiah, Esther*. New International Biblical Commentary: Old Testament Series. Peabody, MA: Hendrickson, 2003.

Barber, Cyril J. *Nehemiah and the Dynamics of Effective Leadership*. Neptune, NJ: Loizeaux, 1976.

Blenkinsopp, Joseph. *Ezra-Nehemiah: A Commentary*. OTL. Philadelphia: Westminster, 1988.

Boda, Mark J., and Paul L. Redditt, eds. *Unity and Disunity in Ezra-Nehemiah: Redaction, Rhetoric, and Reader*. Hebrew Bible Monographs 17. Sheffield: Sheffield Phoenix, 2008.

Boice, James Montgomery. *Nehemiah: Learning to Lead*. Old Tappan, NJ: Revell, 1990.

Breneman, Mervin. *Ezra, Nehemiah, Esther: An Exegetical & Theological Exposition of Holy Scripture*. Nashville: Broadman & Holman, 1993.

Campbell, Donald K. *Nehemiah: Man in Charge*. Wheaton, IL: Victor, 1979.

Coggins, R. J. *The Books of Ezra and Nehemiah*. Cambridge Bible Commentary. Cambridge: Cambridge University Press, 1976.

Davies, Gordon F. *Ezra & Nehemiah: Studies in Hebrew Narrative and Poetry*. Berit Olam. Collegeville, MN: Liturgical, 1999.

Eichhorst, William R. "Ezra's Ethics on Intermarriage and Divorce." *Grace Theological Journal* 10/3 (1969) 16–28.

Eichrodt, Walter. *Theology of the Old Testament*. 2 vols. Translated by J. A. Baker. OTL. Philadelphia: Westminster, 1961–67.

Eskenazi, Tamara C. "The Structure of Ezra-Nehemiah and the Integrity of the Book." *JBL* 107 (1988) 641–56.

Frei, Hans W. *The Eclipse of Biblical Narrative: A Study in Eighteenth and Nineteenth Century Hermeneutics*. New Haven: Yale University Press, 1974.

Hunter, James Davidson. *To Change the World: The Irony, Tragedy, and Possibility of Christianity in the Late Modern World*. New York: Oxford University Press, 2010.

---

40. The ex-Pharisee Saul/Paul regards all this effort as σκύβαλα (Phil 3:8).

Jensen, David Jensen. *Witch-Hunts, Purity and Social Boundaries: The Explusion of the Foreign Women in Ezra 9–10*. JSOTSup 350. Sheffield: Sheffield Academic, 2002.

Kort, Wesley A. *Story, Text, and Scripture: Literary Interests in Biblical Narrative*. University Park: Pennsylvania State University Press, 1988.

Levering, Matthew. *Ezra & Nehemiah*. Brazos Theological Commentary on the Bible. Grand Rapids: Brazos, 2007.

Lubeck, Ray. *Read the Bible for a Change: Understanding and Responding to God's Word*. 2005. Reprint, Eugene: Wipf & Stock, 2009.

McConville, J. G. *Ezra, Nehemiah, and Esther*. Daily Study Bible–Old Testament. Philadelphia: Westminster, 1985.

Myers, Jacob M. *Ezra-Nehemiah*. AB 14. Garden City: Doubleday, 1965.

"Pharisees." *The Universal Jewish Encyclopedia*, 8:474. New York: Universal Jewish Encyclopedia, 1939. http://www.come-and-hear.com/uje/uje_474.html.

Ponraj, S. Devasagayam, and R. Bruce Carlton. *Strategic Coordination in Mission: Training Manual for Nehemiah Institute for Strategic Coordination*. Chennai, India: Mission Educational Books, 2001.

Roberts, Mark D. *Ezra, Nehemiah, Esther*. Communicator's Commentary Series: Old Testament 11. Dallas: Word, 1993.

Sailhamer, John H. *Introduction to Old Testament Theology: A Canonical Approach*. Grand Rapids: Zondervan, 1995.

———. *The Meaning of the Pentateuch: Revelation, Composition, and Interpretation*. Downers Grove, IL: IVP Academic, 2009.

———. *The Pentateuch as Narrative: A Biblical-Theological Commentary*. Grand Rapids: Zondervan, 1992.

Stanley, Andy. *Visioneering*. Sisters, OR: Multnomah, 1999.

Swindoll, Charles R. *Hand Me Another Brick*. Nashville: Nelson, 1978.

Throntveit, Mark A. *Ezra-Nehemiah*. Interpretation. Louisville: John Knox, 1992.

Tollefson, Kenneth D. "Social Transformation in Nehemiah." *Transformation* 6/1 (1989) 3–6.

Walsh, Brian J., and Richard J. Middleton. *Truth Is Stranger Than It Used to Be: Biblical Faith in a Postmodern Age*. Downers Grove, IL: InterVarsity, 1995.

White, John. *Excellence in Leadership: Reaching Goals with Prayer, Courage, & Determination*. Downers Grove, IL: InterVarsity, 1986.

11

Choosing the Right Words

Kings, Chronicles, and the Canon[1]

JOSHUA WILLIAMS

Southwestern Baptist Theological Seminary

RECENT RESEARCH REGARDING THE book of Chronicles has focused on one of the book's most prominent characteristics: its relationship to other parts of the Hebrew canon. This focus hardly comes as a surprise since about half the material of Chronicles has a parallel elsewhere within the Hebrew canon.[2] Furthermore, it is clear that even texts which do not share a parallel have still played a role in the formation of Chronicles, especially material from the Pentateuch.[3] One may even call it the "most canonical" book of the OT.[4]

In light of this background, this study is an attempt to address the relationship between Chronicles and the canon. Specifically, the scope of this

---

1. An earlier version of this essay was presented at the Evangelical Theological Society National Meeting in Providence, RI, November 21, 2008.

2. The vast majority of parallels stem from Samuel-Kings and a few from Psalms, Pentateuch, Joshua, Ruth, Ezra-Nehemiah; cf. Kalimi, *The Reshaping of Ancient Israelite History in Chronicles*, 1, for a list of resources listing parallels.

3. Cf. Kalimi, *The Reshaping of Ancient Israelite History in Chronicles*, for a thorough analysis of the historiographical techniques of Chr and his connection to other canonical works in the production of his own text.

4. Cf. Steins, *Die Chronik als kanonisches Abschlußphänomen*, 506, where he describes Chronicles as "most canonical" (*kanonischste*) since "no other writing [among the Writings] maintains such intensive contact with the writings of both older parts of the canon [Law and Prophets] as Chronicles ([K]eine andere Schrift steht in einem so intensiven Austausch mit Schriften der älteren beiden Kanonteile wie die Chronik)."

study is the relationship between Kings and Chronicles in the area of word choice. My concern is to examine more-or-less verbatim parallel passages between Kings and Chronicles in which the Chronicler has replaced one word of his *Vorlage* with a different word. Such an investigation is not novel; however, my intent is to speak specifically to those cases where it appears that the Chronicler's word choice might be influenced by other passages in the OT. Verbatim parallel passages provide the clearest and most focused opportunities to study Chr's word choice, for it is in these situations, that is, situations where he is closely following his *Vorlage* and then deviates from it, that the Chronicler has been compelled by some reason to modify his source text and choose a different word.[5]

The aims of the examination are as follows: 1) to evaluate claims regarding specific passages that Chr's word choice has been influenced by another passage in the canon, 2) if such a claim is verified, to describe the circumstances in which the reference occurs, and 3) to synthesize the results and draw out their implications for further study. To accomplish these aims, I will set out criteria for evaluating textual influence, examine some case studies, and synthesize the results.

Criteria

One text may influence the language and style of another text at several levels, ranging from quotation to similar subject matter.[6] In this study, I am attempting to identify influence that arises from Chr's deliberate reference to other canonical texts through a lexical alteration of his *Vorlage*. These alterations may refer to a different scope of material: 1) a specific passage, 2) a group of passages which share similar, but not the same, language, and 3) a distinctively characteristic expression of another book or large section of a book.

The following criteria will help detect if a deliberate reference occurs and to what scope of material. The starting point for drawing up criteria is Schultz's work on prophetic quotation in which he proposes two basic criteria for identifying quotation[7]: 1) "verbal and syntactical correspondence"

---

5. Cases with textual variants are excluded from this study, e.g. 2 Chr 6:37//Jer 46:27; 2 Chr 34:24//Deut 29:19; 2 Chr 34:25//Jer 7:20.

6. See Kittel, *The Hymns of Qumran*, 49, for her delineation of how biblical texts affect the *Hodayot* from Qumran; see also Schultz, *The Search for Quotation*, 20–40, for a historical survey of the question regarding influence with reference to prophetic quotation.

7. Schultz, *The Search for Quotation*, 21, defines quotation as "examples in which an exegetical purpose in reusing earlier material can be demonstrated or where an

and 2) "contextual awareness, including interpretive reuse."[8] Others have elaborated on these criteria;[9] the following list of criteria builds on previous work and considers the unique circumstances of parallel passages shared by Kings and Chronicles in which Chr's alteration may refer to another text.

Verbal Criteria

The criteria are organized into three categories: verbal, syntactical, and contextual. The first verbal criterion is the number and distribution of verbal parallels shared between Chronicles and the reference text. Discovering several verbal parallels in close proximity shared between Chronicles and the reference text increases the likelihood that Chr has intended to refer to the reference text. For instance, a text in which four out of six words occurring together is shared with another text is more likely a connection than a text with four words dispersed throughout a lengthy sentence.[10]

The second criterion requires an examination of the frequency of the words that compose the verbal parallels. If the words composing the verbal parallels are rare, a connection more likely exists.[11] The word's frequency should be examined within the scope of the OT, but also within the three contexts involved: Kings, Chronicles, and the reference text. Within these contexts, the following scenario most likely represents a connection between Chronicles and the reference text: a common word in Kings is rendered into Chronicles using a rare word (either rare in the OT or in Chronicles) and that shared word occurs distinctively in the reference text.

---

understanding of the earlier text and context is helpful, if not essential, for a proper interpretation of the new text."

8. Ibid., 222.

9. Works relating specifically to Old Testament contexts, e.g., Maurer, "The Book of Ecclesiastes as a Derash of Genesis 1–4," 35–66; Leonard, "Identifying Inner-Biblical Allusions," 241–65; Lyons, *From Law to Prophecy*, 67–75; McKenzie, *Idolatry in the Pentateuch*, 54–59.

10. Cf. Leonard, "Identifying Inner-Biblical Allusions," 249–53, offers this same guideline and two other observations important for this task: the existence of non-shared language does not render a reference less likely and shared phrases are more aid more than individual shared terms. See also Lyons, *From Law to Prophecy*, 68–69.

11. Cf. Leonard, "Inner-Biblical Allusions," 251; Lyons, *From Law to Prophecy*, 69. Of course, the use of rare language does not prove a connection. On the other hand, the use of common language does not disprove it, especially if common vocabulary is used in combinations and meanings that are distinctive.

Syntactical Criteria

By syntax, I am referring not only to the specific function of the words, but also the word order and the way in which the clauses are connected. At the syntactical level, just as with the verbal, the more similarity between the syntax of Chronicles and the reference text, the more likely a connection exists. The case is made stronger if the Chronicler has modified the syntax of Kings with the result that it is more like the syntax of the reference text.[12]

Contextual Criteria

Unlike the other criteria in which more is better, contextual criteria require a balance of elements in order for the connection to be more likely. Generally, the more thematic overlap between Chronicles and the reference text, especially if such themes are narrow in scope, the more likely a reference exists. However, there are two important factors that make such overlap less likely an influence on Chr's word choice. The first is genre. If Chronicles and the reference text consist of a genre in which certain formulaic patterns are common, then the repetition of those elements makes influence less likely.[13]

The second factor is lexical options. If the subject matter is such that Biblical Hebrew only offers two or three lexical options for expressing the content, then it is less likely that a reference exists since Chr does not have other options available to him.[14]

These criteria, of course, are used in order to build a cumulative case. There is no single key to determining whether a reference exists, nor does the existence of a reference require meeting all criteria. Determining whether a reference exists is not a scientific procedure that produces the same results regardless of the one who applies it. At the same time, they are intended to provide guidelines for a more consistent evaluation of textual influence on the Chr's word choice.

---

12. The fact that Chr performs such an alteration may meet Lyons's criterion of "interaction with the source" (Lyons, *From Law to Prophecy*, 72–75), that is, Chr must take up the reference in a meaningful way within his own work.

13. Cf. Leonard, "Identifying Inner-Biblical Allusion," 256–57.

14. Lyons, *From Law to Prophecy*, 72. It is difficult to determine the number of lexical options available to Chr because there is only a limited sampling of Biblical Hebrew and since that sampling concerns a limited sphere of religious content.

Case Studies

Having established the criteria for determining if the Chronicler's word choice has been influenced by another passage of the OT, I will now work through several examples which are candidates for this type of influence. These passages are a sampling of passages that appear to be the most likely candidates in which Chronicles shares a parallel with Kings and another canonical text may have influenced Chr's word choice. I do not presume that these case studies are the only possible candidates; however, they should serve to meet the aims of this study.

1 Kings 8:9 // 2 Chronicles 5:10 // Exodus 40:20

While describing the dedication of the temple, 1 Kgs 8:9 and 2 Chr 5:10 record that the Ark of the Covenant contained only the two tablets which the LORD gave Moses. The two passages are nearly verbatim; however, there is a lexical alteration: נוח hi. changes to נתן. The language of Exod 40:20 may have prompted this alteration. C. F. Keil notes this passage as a cross-reference in his commentary,[15] and Georg Steins has argued that this alteration is an intentional attempt to bring Chr's *Vorlage* in line with the language of Exod 40:20.[16]

1 Kgs 8:9	2 Chr 5:10	Exod 40:20
אין בארון רק שני לחות	אין בארון רק שני הלחות	ויקח *ויתן* את־העדת אל־הארן
האבנים אשר *הנח* שם משה	אשר־*נתן* משה בחרב אשר	וישם את־הבדים על־הארן
בחרב אשר כרת יהוה עם־בני	כרת יהוה עם־בני ישראל	ויתן את־הכפרת על־הארן
ישראל בצאתם מארץ מצרים	בצאתם ממצרים	מלמעלה

The connection requires another look. First, in terms of frequency, נתן q. occurs far more frequently than נוח hi., especially in the form closely synonymous with נתן.[17] In fact, נתן is one of the most frequently occurring

---

15. Keil, "1 and 2 Chronicles," 325, mentions the cross-reference because he is concerned to show that Chr did not misrepresent the historical picture since it uses the same language as that found in Exod 40:20.

16. Steins, *Die Chronik als kanonisches Abschlußphänomen*, 453; technically, he argues for textual harmonization to two different passages: replacing האבנים לחות with הלחות is an attempt to harmonize the text with Deut 10:5 and replacing הנח with נתן is an attempt to harmonize with the text of Exod 40:20. I will deal specifically with the latter reference since it involves a lexical change, rather than an addition or omission, although my conclusions concerning the Exod 40:20 will have implications for Deut 10:5.

17. It is clear that the two words may be used in synonymous ways in Chronicles; cf.

verbs in the Old Testament, in Kings and in Chronicles.¹⁸ Since נתן is such a common word, the fact that it occurs in both 2 Chr 5:10 and Exod 40:20 is not positive evidence for the likelihood that Exod 40:20 exerted influence on Chr's word choice here.

Second, looking at the content reveals that the passages are similar. Each concerns the placement of the stone tablets which the Lord gave Moses into the Ark. First Kings uses the word נוח hi., which occurs in some passages of the Pentateuch concerning the Ark: Exod 16:33–34 referring to the placement of the manna before the Ark and Num 17:19 referring to the placement of Aaron's rod before the Ark. On the other hand, 2 Chronicles uses נתן, which occurs in Exod 25:16, 21 as part of a command to put whatever God says to put in the Ark. Exodus 40:20 refers to placing the tablets in the Ark; however, it does not refer to tablets directly. Since the verbs used in both Kings and Chronicles occur in the Pentateuch to refer to the placement of some item either before or in the Ark, the use of the verb נתן is not likely a specific reference to the Pentateuch.

Furthermore, the closest parallel to the passages in Kings and Chronicles is Deut 10:2, 4–5. Verse 2 records the Lord's commanding Moses to write the tablets and place them in the Ark; verses 4–5 record Moses' doing so. These verses overlap considerably with the vocabulary and content of the passages in Kings and Chronicles; however, the verb used for placing the tablets in the Ark is neither נוח nor נתן but שׂים. Therefore, if Chr wanted to choose a word that would bring the text in line with the Pentateuch, the more likely candidate would be שׂים, which he did not choose.

Steins has argued that the alteration of נוח hi. to נתן q. is an example of a "subtle scribal work" as "the Chronicler brings his text in line with reference texts in the Torah."¹⁹ However, another look at the evidence reveals that the alteration is not likely due to an intentional reference to the Pentateuch. In this case, it is more likely that the alteration is the result of some other factor.²⁰

---

2 Chr 4:6–8 and Japhet, "Interchanges of Verbal Roots in Parallel Texts in Chronicles," 33.

18. In OT, נתן occurs 2021 times; in Kings, 173 occurrences; in Chronicles, 154.

19. Steins, *Die Chronik als kanonisches Abschlußphänomen*, 453: "subtiler schriftgelehrter Arbeit . . . gleicht der Chronist seinen Text Bezugstexten in der Tora an."

20. The two verbs, נוח hi. and נתן q., occur synonymously in 2 Chr 4:6–8; therefore, the alteration does not point to a significant semantic variation. This type of alteration where one synonym of approximate frequency replaces another likely results from what Carr calls a "memory variant," a slight variation that occurs when a scribe is working from memory; cf. Carr, "'Empirical' Comparison and the Analysis of the Relationship of the Pentateuch and the Former Prophets," 75.

2 Kings 21:7 // 2 Chronicles 33:7 // Deuteronomy 4:16

Manasseh's action to put an idol within the temple is recorded in 2 Kings 21:7 and 2 Chr 33:7. The passages are nearly verbatim. There is a lexical change: אשרה changes to סמל. Deuteronomy 4:16 may have influenced Chr's word choice here.

2 Kgs 21:7	2 Chr 33:7	Deut 4:16
וישם את־*פסל האשרה*	וישם את־*פסל הסמל*	פן־תשחתון ועשׂיתם
אשר עשׂה בבית אשר	אשר עשׂה בבית	לכם *פסל* תמונת
אמר יהוה אל־דוד ואל־	האלהים אשר אמר	כל־*סמל* תבנית זכר או
שלמה בנו בבית הזה	אלהים אל־דויד ואל־	נקבה
ובירושלם אשר בחרתי	שלמה בנו בבית הזה	
מכל שבטי ישראל	ובירושלם אשר בחרתי	
אשים את־שמי לעולם	מכל שבטי ישראל	
	אשים את־שמי לעילום	

Comparing אשרה and סמל reveals the following. First, the two terms have widely differing frequencies. The word סמל occurs only three other times in the OT including once within the same context of 2 Chr 33:7.[21] The word אשרה occurs forty times, sixteen times in Kings and eleven times in Chronicles. Second, סמל is a common noun whereas אשרה as used in 2 Kgs 21:7 is a proper noun. Third, singular אשרה occurs only once in Chronicles though the plural occurs ten times, including two parallels in which the *Vorlage* is singular but Chronicles is plural.[22] It should be noted that the Pentateuch has four occurrences of אשרה. Only one is singular, and it clearly refers to a cultic pole.[23] This evidence suggests that Chr may have been motivated to distinguish between cultic objects and the goddess since both would occur in the same context (cf. 2 Chr 33:3, 19).[24]

Beyond the lexical comparison, other textual factors suggest a connection between 2 Chr 33:7 and Deut 4:16. First, other verbal parallels exist between 2 Chr 33:7 and Deut 4:16. The words פסל and עשׂה occur in the immediate context of both passages. Even though עשׂה is a very common word, פסל is less frequent, occurring thirty-one times in OT. Second, סמל is closely related to פסל in 2 Chr 33:7 and Deut 4:16. In 2 Chr 33:7 it is clearly in a genitive relation to פסל. In Deut 4:16 סמל occurs at the end of a construct chain תמונת כל following פסל.[25]

---

21. 2 Chr 33:15; Ezek 8:3, 5.

22. 2 Kgs 18:4//2 Chr 31:1; 2 Kgs 21:3//2 Chr 33:3.

23. It occurs in the singular in Deut 16:21 as the object of the verb נטע, clearly marking it as a cultic object.

24. Cf. Japhet, *I & II Chronicles*, 1007.

25. The accents of MT suggest that סמל כל תמונת belong as a unit in apposition to פסל.

Examining the content reveals significant overlap. Deuteronomy 4:16–17 prohibits making an idol; 2 Chr 33:7 recounts Manasseh's setting up an idol which he had made. The immediate context of both passages addresses worshipping כל צבא השמים: Deut 4:19 prohibits it while 2 Chr 33:3 shows that Manasseh violated it in the language of the prohibition.[26]

The evidence cited above would suggest that a connection between 2 Chr 33:7 and Deut 4:19 may exist. Another piece of evidence must also be considered. The only other occurrences of סמל are in Ezek 8:3, 5. These verses begin a description of abominations that Ezekiel observes taking place near or within the temple compound. The first object that Ezekiel sees is a סמל. The content of 2 Chr 33:2–8, outlining the abominations which Manasseh did, overlaps considerably with the content of Ezek 8:3–18.

Japhet has suggested that perhaps Chr changed אשרה in his *Vorlage* to סמל because he "distinguished between these cultic forms [אשרה sg. and אשרה pl.], and under the influence of Ezek 8:3, 5, chose a different term for the present context."[27] The evidence cited above concerning the sole instance of אשרה in the singular, strengthens the first part of Japhet's suggestion. However, looking at the contexts in which סמל occurs weakens the suggestion that Ezek 8:3, 5, influenced his word choice. Deuteronomy 4:16 would be a more likely candidate. However, beyond which text served as a possible influence, the question of lexical options becomes important. It is not clear what lexical options would have been available.[28] Therefore, even though Chr may have been motivated to alter אשרה in order to distinguish between an image of the goddess or the cultic poles, it is not clear that he chose the word סמל because of its occurrence in other texts.

2 Kings 18:4 // 2 Chronicles 31:1 // Deuteronomy 7:5

The parallel passages 2 Kgs 18:4 and 2 Chr 31:1 describe the destruction of certain places of worship under Hezekiah's rule. Although there is a bit more editorial activity than the other examples, the passages are still clearly parallels. There are two lexical changes to be considered: סור hi. parallels נתץ q. and כרת q. parallels גדע q. Deuteronomy 7:5 may have influenced Chr's word choice in this passage.[29]

---

26 כל צבא השמים ונדחת והשתחוית להם ועבדתם// וישתחוו לכל־צבא השמים ויעבד אתם

27. Japhet, *I & II Chronicles*, 1007.

28. Cf. Dohmen, "Heißt סֶמֶל 'Bild, Statue'?," 263–6, in which he argues that סמל is a specialized term within the vocabulary of images.

29. Kalimi argues that Chr's activity in this passage is an example of textual harmonization to Deut 7:5; 12:3; cf. Kalimi, *The Reshaping of Ancient Israelite History in*

CHOOSING THE RIGHT WORDS

Deut 7:5	2 Chr 31:1	2 Kgs 18:4
כי־אם־כה תעשו להם	וככלות כל־זאת יצאו	הוא *הסיר* את־הבמות
מזבחתיהם תתצו	כל־ישראל הנמצאים	*ושבר את־המצבת וכרת*
ומצבתם תשברו	לערי יהודה *וישברו*	*את־האשרה* וכתת נחש
ואשירהם תגדעון	*המצבות ויגדעו האשרים*	הנחשת אשר־עשה
ופסיליהם תשרפון באש	*וינתצו* את־הבמות *ואת־*	משה כי עד־הימים
	המזבחת מכל־יהודה	ההמה היו בני־ישראל
	ובנימן ובאפרים ומנשה	מקטרים לו ויקרא־לו
	עד־לכלה וישובו כל־בני	נחשתן
	ישראל איש לאחזתו	
	לעריהם	

Weighing the criteria discussed above suggests that Deut 7:5 has influenced Chr's word choice. Comparing the vocabulary of סור//נתץ and גדע//כרת reveals that in both cases Chr has selected a word that is far less common than the word found in his *Vorlage*.[30] Examining other vocabulary reveals that 2 Chr 31:1 and Deut 7:5 share no fewer than six words in a cluster of eight. Examining the syntax of that shared vocabulary reveals that the words function similarly.[31] The only significant syntactical difference within this cluster of eight is word order and Chr's inclusion of a word from his *Vorlage*: את־הבמות. Examining the content reveals that the passages share a similar context: Deut 7:5 recounts God's instructions to destroy religious sites when the sons of Israel enter the land while 2 Chr 31:1 recounts how Israel destroyed the religious sites in the land under Hezekiah's reign.

The evidence suggests that Deut 7:5 influenced Chr's choice of נתץ and גדע. However, looking beyond Deut 7:5 shows that Chr is likely not directly referring to this particular passage alone. He is likely referring to the Pentateuch more generally since the language of Deut 7:5 is quite similar to Deut 12:3 and Exod 34:13.

Exod 34:13	Deut 12:3	Deut 7:5
כי את־מזבחתם תתצון	ונתצתם את־מזבחתם	כי־אם־כה תעשו להם
ואת־מצבתם תשברון	ושברתם את־מצבתם	מזבחתיהם תתצו
ואת־אשריו תכרתון	ואשריהם תשרפון באש	ומצבתם תשברו
	ופסילי אלהיהם *תגדעון*	ואשירהם תגדעון
	ואבדתם את־שמם מן־	ופסיליהם תשרפון באש
	המקום ההוא	

Chronicles, 126–27.

30. סור occurs 298 times compared to 42 נתץ times; כרת occurs 289 times compared to 22 גדע times.

31. In 2 Chr 31:1 and Deut 7:5 מזבח functions as the object of נתץ; מצבה functions as the object of שבר; אשרה functions as the object of גדע.

A close look at these parallels shows one significant difference: Exod 34:13 uses כרת while Deut 7:5; 12:3 use גדע. This same distinction is true for 2 Kgs 18:4 and 2 Chr 31:1: the former uses כרת while the latter uses גדע. The numerous parallels in vocabulary, syntax, and content between 2 Kgs 18:4 and these passages reveal that these passages already affected 2 Kgs 18:4. The effect, although not necessarily the intention, of Chr's change from כרת to גדע is that the connection is more prominent since גדע occurs much less frequently.

One final observation regarding the way Chr rendered 2 Kgs 18:4. By inserting את־הבמות as an element of a compound object of וינתצו, Chr was able to preserve the word from his *Vorlage* while also preserving מזבח as an object of שבר, its same function in Deut 7:5.

The examination brings to light the following: 1) for each pair (סור// נתץ, כרת//גדע), Chronicles has a rarer word than its *Vorlage*, 2) Chronicles combines two elements through coordination in order to maintain its connection to the *Vorlage* and to the Pentateuch, and 3) Chr has modified a passage which is already influenced by the Pentateuch with the result that his alteration marks the connection more prominently.

1 Kings 8:38 // 2 Chronicles 6:29 // Exodus 3:7

As Solomon dedicated the temple, he prayed that those who suffer, whether an individual or a nation, and turn to the temple in prayer will have their prayers answered. The prayer occurs in both 1 Kgs 8:38 and 2 Chr 6:29. The two passages are nearly verbatim; however, לבבו changes to ומכאבו. Exodus 3:7 may have influenced Chr's word choice in this case.

1 Kgs 8:37–8	2 Chr 6:28–9	Exod 3:7
רעב כי־יהיה בארץ דבר כי־יהיה שדפון ירקון ארבה חסיל כי יהיה כי יצר־לו איבו בארץ שעריו כל־נגע כל־מחלה ³⁸כל־תפלה כל־תחנה אשר תהיה לכל־האדם לכל עמך ישראל אשר ידעון איש נגע *לבבו* ופרש כפיו אל־הבית הזה	רעב כי־יהיה בארץ דבר כי־יהיה שדפון וירקון ארבה וחסיל כי יהיה כי יצר־לו אויביו בארץ שעריו כל־נגע וכל־מחלה ²⁹כל־תפלה כל־תחנה אשר יהיה לכל־האדם ולכל עמך ישראל אשר ידעו איש נגעו *ומכאבו* ופרש כפיו אל־הבית הזה	ויאמר יהוה ראה ראיתי את־עני עמי אשר במצרים ואת־צעקתם שמעתי מפני נגשיו כי ידעתי את־*מכאביו*

Comparing the word choice of Kings to that of Chronicles reveals that Kings uses a term, לבב, which occurs far more frequently than the term in Chronicles, מכאב.³² The word מכאב only occurs sixteen times in the OT.³³ This passage in Chronicles is the only occurrence of מכאב in Kings or Chronicles, and the word occurs only once in the Pentateuch: Exod 3:7. Since מכאב occurs infrequently in these books, it leaves open the possibility that the language of Exod 3:7 directly influenced the word choice in Chronicles.

Comparing the vocabulary, syntax, and genre of 2 Chr 6:29 and Exod 3:7 provides limited positive evidence towards a claim that Exod 3:7 influenced 2 Chr 6:29. First, the passages share some vocabulary beyond מכאב: The words עם and ידע occur in both passages. These words are quite common so their usefulness in identifying the relationship is limited. Second, the word מכאב functions syntactically the same way in both passages. It is the object of ידע although in 2 Chr 6:29 it is part of a compound object. Third, the words are grammatically different since מכאב is singular in Chronicles and plural in Exodus. Fourth, the passages do not share the same genre. Chronicles records a dedicatory prayer while Exodus records God's call to Moses. Genre does not explain why מכאב occurs in both texts.

Comparing the context of 2 Chr 6:29 and Exod 3:7 reveals several similarities. First, they share a pattern of suffering, crying out, and responding. In 2 Chr 6:29 Solomon prays that whenever a person or nation suffers from any of a variety of disasters and prays to God, God will hear the prayer and act. Exodus 3:7 reports God saying that he knows the affliction of Israel, has heard their outcry, and decided to act.

Second, in 2 Chr 6:28 Solomon begins his prayer with a list of disasters. Even though the list brings together several shorter lists found throughout the OT,³⁴ looking at the list as a whole, there are many words which are reminiscent of the Pentateuch's narrative regarding Israel's life in Egypt. Solomon mentions famine רעב (Genesis 43:1), pestilence דבר (Exodus 5:3; 9:3, 15), locusts ארבה (Exodus 10:4), plague נגע (Exodus 11:1), and sickness מחלה (Exodus 15:26), each corresponding to the larger Exodus narrative. The only terms absent from the Exodus narrative are the collocation שדפון and ירקון and the term חסיל. The presence of שדפון and ירקון are likely due

---

32. לבב occurs 252 times in OT; מכאב occurs 16.

33. Exod 3:7;2 Chr 6:29; Job 33:19; Pss. 32:10; 38:18; 69:27; Eccl 1:18; 2:23; Isa 53:3, 4; Jer 30:15; 45:3; 51:8; Lam 1:12 (2x's), 18.

34. The phrase שדפון וירקון appears in Deut 28:22 as a curse for disobeying the covenant; the words רעב and דבר occur frequently together, especially in Jeremiah (most often also with חרב;2 Sam 24:13;1 Kgs 8:37;1 Chr 21:12; 2 Chr 6:28; 20:9; Jer 14:12; 21:7, 9; 24:10; 27:8, 13; 29:17–18; 32:24, 36; 34:17; 38:2; 42:17, 22; 44:13;Ezek 5:12, 17; 6:11–12; 7:15; 12:16; 14:21); and both types of insect (ארבה and חסיל) are found in Ps 78:46 and Joel 1:4; 2:25.

to the influence of Deuteronomy.³⁵ The word חסיל may help connect this passage to the Exodus. In Ps 78:46 it occurs with ארבה describing what the Lord did to Egypt during the Exodus.³⁶ The list of disasters reveals sufficient overlap in vocabulary with the larger Exodus narrative to make a connection between 2 Chr 6:29 and Exod 3:7 plausible.

One final observation may help determine the nature of the relationship between 2 Chr 6:29 and Exod 3:7. The syntax of the parallel word differs between Kings and Chronicles. In Kings לבבו functions as a genitive following נגע; however, in Chronicles נגע changes to נגעו and מכאבו is connected to it with a *waw* conjunction. This type of syntactical shift may signal a deliberate shift rather than merely a synonymous expression.

In this case, even though the evidence is somewhat ambiguous, it is likely that Exod 3:7 influenced 2 Chr 6:29. Certainly, the rarity of מכאב and other verbal, syntactical, and thematic connections indicate that Exod 3:7 may have played a direct role in the word choice of the Chronicler. If so, then the Chronicler has altered the syntax of his *Vorlage* and chosen a rare word to draw attention to the connection.

1 Kings 9:7 // 2 Chronicles 7:20 // Deuteronomy 29:27

When God appears a second time to Solomon, God warns him that if he or his descendants disobey God's commandments and worship other gods, then God will remove them from the land. The warning occurs in 1 Kgs 9:7 and 2 Chr 7:20. Even though they are nearly identical, there are three lexical changes: כרת hi.//נתש q.; שלח pi.//שלך hi.; and היה q.//נתן q. Deuteronomy 29:27 may account for changes between the two accounts.

1 Kgs 9:7	2 Chr 7:20	Deut 29:27
והכרתי את־ישראל מעל פני האדמה אשר נתתי להם ואת־הבית אשר הקדשתי לשמי *אשלח* מעל פני *והיה* ישראל למשל ולשנינה בכל־העמים	ונתשתים מעל אדמתי אשר נתתי להם ואת־הבית הזה אשר הקדשתי לשמי *אשליך* מעל פני *ואתננו* למשל ולשנינה בכל־העמים	*ויתשם* יהוה *מעל אדמתם* באף ובחמה ובקצף גדול *וישלכם* אל־ארץ אחרת כיום הזה

---

35. This collocation occurs only three times outside of 1 Kgs 8:38 and 2 Chr 6:29: Deut 28:22, Amos 4:9, and Hag 2:17. The reference in Amos 4:9 is the most interesting because the next verse states that God sent a plague דבר against the people in the manner of Egypt. Even though the reference is indirect, Egypt occurs in close proximity.

36. By making this observation, I am not claiming that Kings depended upon Ps 78 or vice versa, only that both ארבה and חסיל are used to summarize some of the plagues on Egypt.

The first pair to examine is שלח//שלך. The reading in 1 Kgs 9:7 is likely the result of textual corruption where the original preserved a reading of שלך hi.; therefore, this pair will not be considered further.[37]

The next pair to examine is היה//נתן. Both are among the most frequently occurring verbs in the OT, so frequency is not an issue. The collocation למשל ולשנינה may point to other passages in the OT. For instance, Jer 24:9 and Deut 28:37 include the collocation as a consequence of God's judgment upon Israel. In fact Deut 28:37 is a close parallel to the last clause of 1 Kgs 9:7//2 Chr 7:20: והיית לשמה למשל ולשנינה בכל העמים. Although Jer 24:9 does use the verb נתן, if a specific passage influenced Chr's word choice for this part of the verse, Deut 28:37 would be the most likely candidate; however, it reads with Kings rather than Chronicles. This evidence demonstrates that the alteration from היה to נתן is not intended to refer to a specific passage; rather, it is likely the result of some other factor.[38]

The final pair to examine is כרת//נתש. This pair involves a rarer word replacing a more common one.[39] Japhet has pointed out that כרת hi. is more common than נתש q.; however, נתש q. occurs with a high density in Jeremiah.[40] She suggests that the language of Jeremiah may have influenced Chr to replace כרת hi. with נתש.[41] However, Kalimi has argued that Chronicles contains a textual harmonization with Deut 29:27.

The evidence supports Kalimi's claim. First, as mentioned, נתש occurs rather infrequently in the OT and only once in the Pentateuch. Second, there are other verbal connections beyond the use of נתש. Chr has omitted the פני in the phrase מעל פני האדמה and added a pronominal suffix so that its reading מעל אדמתי aligns more closely with Deuteronomy's מעל אדמתם. Furthermore, the verb שלך hi. occurs in both texts. Finally, the passages deal

---

37. This emendation is proposed by Jepsen in BHS apparatus; also Japhet argues that the phrase השליך מעל פני is characteristic of Deuteronomistic literature and appropriate to the setting of 1 Kgs 9:7; Japhet, "Interchanges of Verbal Roots in Parallel Texts in Chronicles," 42.

38. Here again the category of a "memory variant" may prove useful both for the relationship between Jeremiah and Deuteronomy and for the relationship between Kings and Chronicles; for "memory variant," cf. Carr, "'Empirical' Comparison and the Analysis of the Relationship of the Pentateuch and the Former Prophets," 75.

39. כרת occurs 289 times, 78 of them in the hiphil stem; נתש occurs 21 times.

40. Jeremiah contains 13 of 21 occurrences.

41. Japhet, "Interchanges of Verbal Roots in Parallel Texts in Chronicles," 20. It should also be noted that Chr uses כרת hi. less frequently than Kings (in Chronicles twice; in Kings 8 times) so that other factors may have influenced Chr to render the word differently. Japhet's point is that the specific word chosen may have been influenced by Jeremiah.

with similar content: they are warnings that God will remove Israel from the land if they disobey his commandments.

In this case, Chr has aligned his text with a passage in Deuteronomy. It should be pointed out that the language of 1 Kgs 9:7 is already heavily influenced by Deuteronomy. The result of Chr's work is that 2 Chr 7:20 sharpens the connection to Deuteronomy. One may also notice that another small change accompanies the lexical change: פני is omitted after מעל and a pronominal suffix is added to אדמה.

Synthesis

Having examined the case studies, a few of observations are in order. First, for most of the cases there is not sufficient evidence to demonstrate that Chr's word choice is the result of a deliberate reference to another canonical text. On the other hand, there is sufficient evidence to demonstrate that at least some of the alterations are references to other texts. This evidence suggests both caution in making too much of minor variations, but also making too little of them.[42]

Second, all of the case studies have possible reference texts in the Pentateuch. Although it is true that there are connections in Chronicles to other parts of the canon, they do not occur within the types of nearly verbatim texts examined in this study.[43] Therefore, in these types of texts in which Chr is nearly verbatim copying his *Vorlage*, minor changes that refer to other passages are the result of his reading the Pentateuch. Such an observation falls in line with the notion that Chronicles is connected to Torah in the recapitulation of the entire history of Israel from its beginning (even before) to the edict of Cyrus.[44]

---

42. This same caution has been voiced on several occasions, for text-critical reasons, see especially Lemke, "The Synoptic Problem in the Chronicler's History," 349–63; for reasons concerning multiformity in textual development, cf.Person, *The Deuteronomic History and the Book of Chronicles*,125–27; for reasons concerning the use of memory in scribal activity, cf. Carr, "'Empirical' Comparison and the Analysis of the Relationship of the Pentateuch and the Former Prophets," 74–78.

43. For a discussion of such connections, cf. Talshir, "Several Canon-Related Concepts Originating in Chronicles," 386–403; several have noted connections to prophetic material (especially in speeches in Chronicles). These connections raise the question of whether the connections reflect literary convention or literary influence, cf. Warhurst, "The Chronicler's Use of the Prophets," 165–81.

44. Steins and Dempster argue that this recapitulation in light of Torah serves as a signal for the closing of the Hebrew canon; Steins, "Torabindung und Kanonabschluß," 250; Dempster, "Canons on the Right and Canons on the Left," 68–77.

Third, the material that appears to affect the specific word choice of Chr is found in contexts in which God speaks, most often in law. Chr renders his *Vorlage* in light of what God said about what he has done (Exod 3:7), what he will do (Deut 29:27), or what he requires the people to do (Deut 7:5). One should not make too much from this slight evidence; however, it is reasonable given the character of Chronicles that Chr would align his retelling of Israel's history with what God has said.[45]

Fourth, a common feature of the Chr's means for noting a connection with another text is to alter the syntax of his *Vorlage*. For instance, he replaces לבבו in 1 Kgs 8:38 with ומכאבו in 2 Chr 6:29, resulting in a lexical and syntactical modification. He also combines features from his *Vorlage* and reference text, such as 2 Chr 31:1 in which he combines both במות from 2 Kgs 18:4 and מזבחת from Deut 7:5. In 2 Chr 7:20 he omits the word פני and adds a pronominal suffix with the result that the syntax of his text reflects that of the reference text more closely. Such syntactical alterations may serve as guides for noticing similar activity in other passages.

Fifth, even though the case studies examine Chr's choice of a single word, the word choice draws references to different passages at different levels of dependence. In 2 Chr 6:29; 7:20, Chr has connected his text with a specific passage in another book. In 2 Chr 31:1, he seems to refer to a group of passages, that is, the shared content of those passages rather than a specific passage. One can see that even though Chr alters his *Vorlage* in the slightest textual detail, his reference is to his larger understanding of the Law, not just a particular passage.[46]

Sixth, when Chr refers to other canonical passages through his word choice, the reference already exists in his *Vorlage*. For instance, God's warning to Solomon and his descendants in 1 Kgs 9:7 already has verbal and syntactical parallels to Deut 29:27 in which it describes God's coming destruction of Israel because it will forsake the covenant. However, Chronicles sharpens these connections with less frequent vocabulary and syntactical modifications, identifying God's warning to Solomon and his descendants not only with the spirit of the warning, but the letter as well.[47]

Finally, these case studies have demonstrated that although referring to other canonical texts, especially the Pentateuch, may not account for Chr's every word choice, these references do occur not only in the material unique to him, nor the material in which he significantly reworks

---

45. Cf. Kalimi, *The Reshaping of Ancient Israelite History in Chronicles*, 159–65.

46. Cf. Ben Zvi, "One Size Does not Fit All," 26–28, where he shows that detailed textual interpretation is made in light of Chr's sense of the whole.

47. Cf. Willi, *Die Chronik als Auslegung*, 148–49.

his *Vorlage*, but also to the minutest of textual alteration. These kinds of references reveal how well Chr knew the content and language of the Law and how he incorporated them into his own work even when he closely followed his *Vorlage*.

Bibliography

Ben Zvi, Ehud. "One Size Does not Fit All: Observations on the Different Ways That Chronicles Dealt with the Authoritative Literature of Its Time." In *What Was Authoritative for Chronicles?*, edited by Ehud Ben Zvi and Diana Edelman, 13–36. Winona Lake, IN: Eisenbrauns, 2011.

Carr, David M. "'Empirical' Comparison and the Analysis of the Relationship of the Pentateuch and the Former Prophets." In *Pentateuch, Hexateuch, or Enneateuch?: Identifying Literary Works in Genesis through Kings*, edited by Thomas B. Dozeman et al., 73–98. AIL 8. Atlanta: Society of Biblical Literature, 2011.

Dempster, Stephen. "Canons on the Right and Canons on the Left: Finding a Resolution in the Canon Debate." *Journal of the Evangelical Theological Society* 52 (2009) 47–77.

Dohmen, Christoph. "Heißt סֶמֶל 'Bild, Statue'?" *ZAW* 96 (1984) 263–66.

Japhet, Sara. *I & II Chronicles: A Commentary*. OTL. Louisville: Westminster John Knox, 1993.

Japhet, Sara. "Interchanges of Verbal Roots in Parallel Texts in Chronicles." *Hebrew Studies* 28 (1987) 9–50.

Kalimi, Isaac. *The Reshaping of Ancient Israelite History in Chronicles*. Winona Lake, IN: Eisenbrauns, 2005.

Kittel, Bonnie. *The Hymns of Qumran: Translation and Commentary*. SBLDS 50. Chico, CA: Scholars, 1981.

Keil, C. F. "1 and 2 Chronicles." In *C. F. Keil and F. Delitzsch Commentary on the Old Testament*. Vol. 3. Peabody: Hendrickson, 1989.

Lemke, Werner E. "The Synoptic Problem in the Chronicler's History." *Harvard Theological Review* 58 (1965) 349–63.

Leonard, Jeffery M. "Identifying Inner-Biblical Allusions: Psalm 78 as a Test Case." *JBL* 127 (2008) 241–65.

Lyons, Michael. *From Law to Prophecy: Ezekiel's Use of the Holiness Code*. LHBOTS 507. New York: T. & T. Clark, 2009.

Maurer, Bernard. "The Book of Ecclesiastes as a Derash of Genesis 1–4." Ph.D. diss., Southeastern Baptist Theological Seminary, 2007.

McKenzie, Tracy J. *Idolatry in the Pentateuch: An Innertextual Strategy*. Eugene, OR: Pickwick, 2010.

Person, Raymond F., Jr. *The Deuteronomic History and the Book of Chronicles: Scribal Works in an Oral World*. AIL 6. Atlanta: Society of Biblical Literature, 2010.

Schultz, Richard. *The Search for Quotation: Verbal Parallels in the Prophets*. JSOTSup 180. Sheffield: Sheffield Academic, 1999.

Steins, Georg. *Die Chronik als kanonisches Abschlußphänomen*. Bonner Biblische Beiträge 93. Weinheim: Belz Athenäum: 1995.

Steins, Georg. "Torabindung und Kanonabschluß." In *Die Torah als Kanon für Juden und Christen*, edited by Erich Zenger, 213–56. Herders biblische Studien 10. Freiburg: Herder, 1996.
Talshir, Zippora. "Several Canon-Related Concepts Originating in Chronicles." *ZAW* 113 (2001) 386–403.
Warhurst, Amber. "The Chronicler's Use of the Prophets." In *What Was Authoritative for Chronicles?*, edited by Ehud Ben Zvi and Diana Edelman, 165–81. Winona Lake, IN: Eisenbrauns, 2011.
Willi, Thomas. *Die Chronik als Auslegung: Untersuchungen zur literarischen Gestaltung der historischen Überlieferung Israels*. Forschungen zur Religion und Literatur des Alten und Neuen Testaments 106. Göttingen: Vandenhoeck & Ruprecht, 1972.

John H. Sailhamer:
A Comprehensive Bibliography

Prepared by

CHED SPELLMAN

Dissertation

Sailhamer, John Herbert. "The Translational Technique of the Greek Septuagint for the Hebrew Verbs and Participles in Psalms 3-41." PhD diss., University of California at Los Angeles, 1981.

Books

———. *Biblical Archeology*. Zondervan Quick Reference Library. Grand Rapids, MI: Zondervan, 1998.
———. *Biblical Prophecy*. Zondervan Quick Reference Library. Grand Rapids, MI: Zondervan, 1998.
———. *Books of the Bible*. Zondervan Quick Reference Library. Grand Rapids, MI: Zondervan, 1998.
———. *Christian Theology*. Zondervan Quick Reference Library. Grand Rapids, MI: Zondervan, 1998.
———. *First & Second Chronicles*. Everyman's Bible Commentary. Chicago, IL: Moody, 1983.
———. "Genesis" in *The Expositor's Bible Commentary: Genesis–Numbers*, edited by Tremper Longman and David E. Garland, Volume 2, 21–333. Revised Edition. Grand Rapids, MI: Zondervan, 2008.
———. *Genesis Unbound: A Provocative New Look at the Creation Account*. Sisters, OR: Multnomah, 1996. Second Edition: Colorado Springs, CO: Dawson Media 2011.
———. *How We Got the Bible*. Zondervan Quick Reference Library. Grand Rapids, MI: Zondervan, 1998.

———. *Introduction to Old Testament Theology: A Canonical Approach*. Grand Rapids, MI: Zondervan, 1995.

———. *The Life of Christ*. Zondervan Quick Reference Library. Grand Rapids, MI: Zondervan, 1998.

———. *The Meaning of the Pentateuch: Revelation, Composition and Interpretation*. Downers Grove, IL: IVP, 2009.

———. *NIV Compact Bible Commentary*. Grand Rapids, MI: Zondervan, 1994. Abridged as *NIV Bible Study Commentary*. Grand Rapids, MI: Zondervan, 2011.

———. *Old Testament History*. Zondervan Quick Reference Library. Grand Rapids, MI: Zondervan, 1998.

———. *The Pentateuch as Narrative: A Biblical-Theological Commentary*. Grand Rapids, MI: Zondervan, 1995.

———. *The Translational Technique of the Greek Septuagint for the Hebrew Verbs and Participles in Psalms 3-41*. Studies in Biblical Greek. Volume 2. New York: Peter Lang, 1991.

Articles and Essays

———. "1 Chronicles 21:1—A Study in Inter-Biblical Interpretation." *Trinity Journal* 10 (Spring 1989) 33–48.

———. "2 Samuel 13:1-4 and a Database Approach to the Analysis of Hebrew Narrative." In *Bible et Informatique: Interprétation, Herméneutique, Compétence Informatique*, 99–122. Paris: Champion, 1992.

———. "Archaeology and the Reliability of the Old Testament." *Contact* (Winter 05/06) 7–10.

———. "Biblical Theology and the Composition of the Hebrew Bible." In *Biblical Theology: Retrospect and Prospect*, edited by Scott J. Hafemann, 25–37. Downers Grove, IL: IVP, 2002.

———. "The Canonical Approach to the OT: Its Effect on Understanding Prophecy." *Journal of the Evangelical Theological Society* 30.3 (September 1987) 307–315.

———. "Compositional Strategies in the Pentateuch." In *Introduction to Old Testament Theology*, 272–89. Grand Rapids, MI: Zondervan, 1995.

———. "Cosmic Maps, Prophecy Charts, and the Hollywood Movie: A Biblical Realist Looks at the Eclipse of Old Testament Narrative." *Criswell Theological Review* 7.2 (1994) 65–81.

———. "Creation, Genesis 1-11, and the Canon." *Bulletin for Biblical Research* 10.1 (2000) 89–106.

———. "A Database Approach to the Analysis of Hebrew Narrative." *MAARAV* 5-6 (Spring 1990) 319–335. Also in *Sopher Mahir: Northwest Semitic Studies Presented to Stanislav Segert*. Santa Monica, CA: Western Academic Press, 1990.

———. "Evidence from Isaiah 2." In *A Case for Premillennialism: A New Consensus*, edited by Donald K. Campbell and Jeffrey L. Townsend, 90–101. Chicago, IL: Moody, 1992.

———. "Exegesis of the Old Testament as a Text." In *Tribute to Gleason Archer*, edited by Walter C. Kaiser and Ronald F. Youngblood, 27–96. Chicago, IL: Moody, 1986.

———. "Exegetical Notes: Genesis 1:1-2:4a." *Trinity Journal* 5 (1984) 73–82.

———. "Genesis." In *A Complete Literary Guide to the Bible*, edited by Leland Ryken and Tremper Longman, 109-20. Grand Rapids, MI: Zondervan, 1993.

———. "The Hermeneutics of Premillennialism." *Faith and Mission* 18.1 (Fall 2000) 96-109.

———. "Hosea 11:1 and Mathew 2:15." *Westminster Theological Journal* 63 (2001) 87-96.

———. "Introduction to a New Concordance of the Old Testament." In *A New Concordance of the Old Testament*, i-xxxii. Grand Rapids, MI: Baker, 1989.

———. "Johann August Ernesti: The Role of History in Biblical Interpretation." *Journal of the Evangelical Theological Society* 44.2 (June 2001) 193-206.

———. "The Messiah and the Hebrew Bible." *Journal of the Evangelical Theological Society* 44.1 (March 2001) 5-23.

———. "The Mosaic Law and the Theology of the Pentateuch." *Westminster Theological Journal* 53 (1991) 24-61.

———. "Preaching from the Prophets." In *Preaching the Old Testament*, edited by Scott M. Gibson, 115-36. Grand Rapids, MI: Baker, 2006.

———. "Walter C. Kaiser, Jr." In *Bible Interpreters of the Twentieth Century: A Selection of Evangelical Voices*, edited by Walter A. Elwell and J. D. Weaver, 375-87. Grand Rapids, MI: Baker, 1999.

———. "What Have They Done to My Genesis?" *Christianity Today*, January 6, 1997, 46-47.

———. "A Wisdom Composition of the Pentateuch?" In *Way of Wisdom: Essays in Honor of Bruce Waltke*, edited by J. I. Packer and Sven K. Soderlund, 15-35. Grand Rapids, MI: Zondervan, 2000.

Book Reviews

———. Review of *The Book of Genesis: Chapters 1-17*, by Victor P. Hamilton. In *Hebrew Studies* 33 (1992) 132-35.

———. Review of *Eschatology in the Greek Psalter*, by Joachim Schaper. In *Journal of the Evangelical Theological Society* 42.4 (December 1999) 739-41.

———. Review of *The Face of Old Testament Studies: A Survey of Contemporary Approaches*, edited by David W. Baker and Bill T. Arnold. In *Faith and Mission* 18.3 (Summer 2001) 110-11.

———. Review of *Genesis 1-15*, by Gordon Wenham. In *Trinity Journal* 9.2 (Fall 1988) 231-36.

———. Review of *Israel's Messiah in the Bible and the Dead Sea Scrolls*, edited by Richard S. Hess and M. Daniel Carroll. In *Journal of the Evangelical Theological Society*. 46.4 (December 2003) 711-12.

———. Review of *Religion in Geschichte und Gegenwart*, edited by Hans Dieter Betz. In *Faith and Mission* 20.1 (Fall 2002) 70-73.

———. Review of *Story as Torah: Reading the Old Testament Ethically*, Gordon Wenham. In *Faith and Mission* 21.1 (Fall 2003) 90-92.

———. Review of *Systematische Theologie im Kontext Biblischer Geschichte und Eschatologie*, by Hans-Joachim Kraus. In *Trinity Journal* 6.1 (Spring 1985) 91-94.

Papers and Presentations

———. "A Compositional Approach and Mosaic Authorship." Presented at the Annual Meeting of the Evangelical Theological Society, San Francisco, CA, November 15, 2007.

———. "Messiah and the Hebrew Bible." Presidential Address presented at the Annual Meeting of the Evangelical Theological Society, Nashville, Tennessee, November 16, 2000.

———. "The Nature, Purpose and Tasks of a Theological Seminary." Presented at Dallas Theological Seminary, July 22, 1993. Unpublished paper available at Turpin Library, Dallas Theological Seminary, Dallas, TX (Call No: BV 4022 .S34). 46 pages.

———. "The Quest for the Biblical Jesus." Presented at the Annual Meeting of the Evangelical Theological Society, Atlanta, Georgia, November 20, 2003.

Interviews

———. "Finding Meaning in the Pentateuch." Interview by Colin Hansen at *Christianity Today* (January 2010). Available at http://www.christianitytoday.com/ct/2010/januaryweb-only/12-11.0.html.

www.ingramcontent.com/pod-product-compliance
Lightning Source LLC
Chambersburg PA
CBHW062024220426
43662CB00010B/1465